Where the Ancestors Walked

Dr Philip Clarke started at the South Australian Museum in 1982, after finishing a Science degree majoring in biology at the University of Adelaide. Based in the ethnographic collections, his early work was on Aboriginal use of plants. This eventually broadened out to Indigenous perception and use of the land, leading to a PhD on the Aboriginal cultural geography of the Lower Murray in South Australia. Since this time, Dr Clarke has worked mainly in Central and Northern Australia, investigating Aboriginal links to land. During 1998–2000 he curated the Australian Aboriginal Cultures Gallery Project. Dr Clarke is presently the Head of Anthropology and Manager of Sciences at the Museum.

Where the Ancestors Walked
Australia as an Aboriginal Landscape

Philip Clarke

ALLEN&UNWIN

First published in 2003
Copyright © Philip Clarke 2003

Allen & Unwin
83 Alexander Street
Crows Nest NSW 2065
Australia
Phone: (61 2) 8425 0100
Fax: (61 2) 9906 2218
Email: info@allenandunwin.com
Web: www.allenandunwin.com

National Library of Australia
Cataloguing-in-Publication entry:

Clarke, Philip A.
Where the ancestors walked : Australia as an
Aboriginal landscape.

Bibliography.
Includes index.
ISBN 1 74114 070 6.

1. Aborigines, Australian. 2. Aborigines, Australian –
Religion. 3. Aborigines, Australian – Antiquities.
I. Title.

306.0899915

Set in 11/14 pt Caslon Regular by Midland Typesetters, Maryborough, Victoria
Printed by South Wind Productions, Singapore

10 9 8 7 6 5 4 3 2 1

To Kyle and Cameron

Contents

Preface

The ancestors of modern Aboriginal people arrived in Australia about 50,000 years ago. Aboriginal people have not remained unchanged since initial human settlement on the continent, but have successfully adapted to a changing Australian environment. More recently they have had to cope with the impact of European colonisation. Many Aboriginal people did not survive this and many of those that did suffered from alienation from their land and the loss of cultural traditions. Europeans in the past harshly judged Aboriginal cultures as 'primitive', primarily on the basis of the apparent simplicity of their hunting and gathering tools. Yet Aboriginal people had—and continue to have—unique ways of life and possess deep spiritual attachments to their country, strong senses of community, and an ability to draw upon their traditions and respond to new situations in creative and innovative ways. This is evident to many people today who interact with Aboriginal people in a multitude of ways. It is also evident through the study of Aboriginal societies and their heritage.

Museums are responsible for the preservation of objects that relate to cultural and natural heritage. They achieve this by researching, publishing and displaying culturally and scientifically based themes or stories through the media of graphics and artefacts. The focus on cultural and natural heritage by museums has made them attractive places to work for people with broad scientific and cultural interests. I arrived at the South Australian Museum in 1982, with a basic degree in the biological sciences. My first task was to help organise the Aboriginal collections, which had been neglected over the previous two decades. Curating the artefact collection gave me an appreciation of Indigenous relationships with the environment and exposed me to the diversity of Aboriginal artefact styles across Australia. The development of my own research interests coincided with a blossoming of awareness in both Australians and international visitors of Australian Indigenous cultures. By the early 1980s, Aboriginal studies as a subject was becoming more common in schools and universities. Australian Indigenous people were also beginning to study their own cultures through schools, universities and museums. There was a critical need for museums to develop new exhibitions to satisfy the demand for knowledge by the public.

My initial research at the South Australian Museum focused on the plants and animals that Aboriginal people used as food, medicines and for making artefacts. This grew into an interest in the wider set of Aboriginal relationships with the land, as reflected in language and mythology, which helped as background information in the recording and interpreting of biological data that I was then collecting across southern and Central Australia. It was this broadening of focus that led me to return to university during the mid-1980s for further study in social anthropology and human geography. I became interested in using cultural geography to explain the relationship that Aboriginal people had with their land and environment.

Cultural geographers have provided a useful way of looking at relationships between people and their surrounding landscapes. They explain the cultural landscape as the product of a culture modifying the land it occupies. The cultural landscape is also an expression of how people engage with their world, how they create explanations for and experiences of their surroundings. Cultural landscapes are not only the outcome of economic activity, material culture and settlement patterns, but of the attitudes and perceptions about that landscape of those living in it.[1] The land and the people who live upon it are deeply entwined, so much so that it would be wrong to simply treat the environment as a stage upon which people live. Rather, those same environments are very much part of the cultural act, for cultures are expressions of how people engage with their worlds.

Every culture has a unique relationship with the land. It is a fundamental assumption by cultural geographers that later waves of colonisers do not encounter lands that were previously occupied as blank canvases. Yet new arrivals nevertheless tend to take it upon themselves to connect with the features of the land according to their own traditions, to give the land their own meanings, and in the process to begin the creation of new cultural landscapes. The anthropologist Veronica Strang has called this tendency for different cultural groups to give different meanings to the same places 'uncommon ground'.[2]

Since the original act of human colonisation in Australia, the continent has undergone massive changes in the physical environment due to global climatic change and as the result of Aboriginal hunting and gathering practices. This book considers the cultural landscapes that Aboriginal people have occupied, developed and responded to during their long history in Australia. It uses the land and material possessions as a doorway through which Aboriginal people and culture can be investigated. Of key interest are the dimensions of the meaningful world that Aboriginal people have created for themselves.

From the beginning of British settlement, the newcomers have exploited Australia's natural resources and wherever possible transformed the land into new cultural landscapes, based largely upon Western European models. Although modern Australians recognise the impact of British settlement on the physical environment, through practices such as vegetation clearing, the introduction of foreign plants and animals, and through the establishment of irrigation schemes, there is little awareness of how pre-existing Aboriginal landscapes have shaped Australian history and culture. All Australians, regardless of their cultural backgrounds, are part of the story of the human engagement—the human occupation and transformation—of this continent.

In 1998 I became Principal Curator for the development of the Australian Aboriginal Cultures Gallery, launched at the South Australian Museum, Adelaide in March 2000.[3] This book develops the main themes of this permanent national exhibition. The Museum's involvement in Australian and Pacific Indigenous cultural displays for over a hundred years reflects the institution's longstanding academic interest in anthropology and the environment. The material presented here draws upon the extensive collections at the Museum, the published literature, and from my personal research and fieldwork, which now stretch back twenty years.

The scope of Aboriginal cultures is vast, far too large for adequate treatment of all cultural groups in a single volume. In this book, therefore,

I attempt to offer an overview to help interpret the wealth of literature written about Aboriginal Australia. The primary focus is Australia as it was when first settled by Europeans, with particular regard to Indigenous relationships with their surroundings. This does not ignore the importance of dealing with contemporary social issues. Rather it aims at a better historical understanding and appreciation of the diversity of Aboriginal cultures and the complexity of Aboriginal relationships to the land. That should indirectly contribute to ongoing social and political processes.

Indigenous words used here are standardised when there is an accepted spelling system for the source language; in the absence of this they are spelt in the form as originally recorded. There are excellent published dictionaries of Australian Indigenous languages available, such as for Pitjantjatjara and some of the Arrernte language varieties of Central Australia. For south-eastern Australia, however, there is only a smattering of words recorded from most of the languages spoken by the groups who live or lived there. Aboriginal English and Australian English are regional varieties of speaking, the former containing a vocabulary of some Indigenous words. Aboriginal English and Kriol (northern Australian Creole) terms are used in this book in situations where it can add to the reader's understanding of a situation. These contact forms of speech are rapidly becoming *lingua franca* among the Indigenous peoples of Australia.[4] Scientific names, such as those for plants and long extinct fauna, are given only when it is important to distinguish one particular genus or species from another.

The term 'European colonists' when used in relation to Australia during the eighteenth and nineteenth centuries refers to people who would have generally considered themselves to be English, Irish, Welsh, Cornish, Prussian, French or Scottish. In the twentieth and twenty-first centuries, this term chiefly refers to 'White Australians', in other words people of European extraction who live in Australia and who do not link their identity to Indigenous Australians. As much as possible, the particular Indigenous maker and artist of any artefact and artwork figured here is properly acknowledged. Sadly, it was not the practice of many early European collectors to record the names of the Aboriginal people from whom they obtained artefacts. Similarly, the names of Indigenous people who appear in early photographs and paintings were not always recorded. In the case of quotations from early writers, these include some phrases or descriptions of Indigenous people that can cause offence. Unless otherwise referenced, the information on Aboriginal artefacts comes from documentation held at the South Australian Museum.

Through highly publicised issues, such as the return of the Strehlow collection of ceremonial Aboriginal men's objects to Central Australia during the 1990s, there is a general appreciation by non-Indigenous people that Aboriginal cultures have categories of information that are limited to particular recognised custodians. In the case of such restricted topics this book follows the practice of the Australian Aboriginal Cultures Gallery at the South Australian Museum in avoiding the discussion or display of information and objects that will cause serious grief to Indigenous people due to cultural sensitivities. Although this avoidance of discussing aspects of secret sacred life results in a restricted description of Aboriginal culture, it is in keeping with how Indigenous people in Australia deal with such matters in public.

Acknowledgments

The following people provided helpful comments to various drafts of this book: Kim Akerman, Ron Brunton, Judith Clarke, Bruno David, Tim Flannery, Robert Foster, David Jones and Jane Simpson. Ray Marchant provided the map and charts, and Lea Gardam assisted with finding archival images. The South Australian Museum has given the author interesting opportunities to explore Aboriginal culture over two decades of employment.

Unless otherwise specified, all illustrations in this book are from the South Australian Museum Archives. All artefacts featured in photographs are from the ethnographic collections at the South Australian Museum.

Part I

ORIGINS *of* ABORIGINAL AUSTRALIA

One

First Human Colonisation

The ancestors of Australian Aboriginal people probably came to the southern continent on rafts, when the climate and sea level fluctuations created portals that allowed human movement from west to east across the Indonesian Archipelago. In Australia the first human settlers found a unique flora and fauna. Over many millions of years, the tectonic plate upon which the Australian continent rides has drifted in comparative isolation from the processes of biological evolution occurring in the rest of the world. The human migration from Asia across the Timor Sea to Australia must have involved a number of sea crossings and represents a remarkable feat of endeavour.

Bridging the Gap

For about the last two million years the world has been subjected to cycles of climate change, including cold periods called 'ice ages', each lasting about 100,000 years. In between the ice ages were 'interglacials', brief periods of warmth that lasted a few thousand years. The last ice age ended about 10,000 years ago and we are now in an interglacial. As the world became colder at the beginning of an ice age, the growing polar icecaps

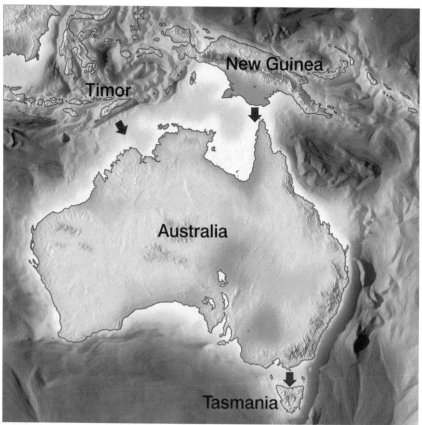

The probable early migration routes that the ancestors of the Australian Aboriginal people took when reaching the Australian mainland and Tasmania. The shaded areas show relative seawater depth, with the white area being land during low sea levels.

absorbed more of the ocean's water, lowering global sea levels. With the weight of water upon the earth's crust reduced, seabeds also rose, further lowering sea levels. At the height of each ice age the continent of Australia was generally a much cooler, drier and windier place than it is now. Weather patterns and the shapes of landmasses vary considerably through the ice-age cycles. The lowering of the present sea level by 30 metres would reveal the landmass connecting Australia and New Guinea. From about 80,000 to 6500 years ago, sea levels were consistently low, revealing a combined landmass scientists have called Greater Australia.[1] When sea levels were 65 metres below present levels, Tasmania and mainland Australia were also joined. This occurred during several long periods of lower seas between 60,000 and 10,000 years ago. At times when sea levels were extremely low, say 160 metres below present, the combined landmass of Australia and New Guinea was up to a quarter more than its present size, including much land now covered by the Arafura Sea. At those times when New Guinea and Australia were connected, the Asian landmass was also much larger. At present, world sea levels are higher than they have been for over 100,000 years.

The movement of hominids eastwards from South East Asia towards Greater Australia possibly began hundreds of thousands of years ago, with *Homo erectus* or another hominid species reaching as far as Flores in Indonesia using some kind of seafaring watercraft. It is generally thought that humans first encountered the shores of Greater Australia some time about 50,000 years ago, during a period of low sea level.[2] This continent was then, cultural geographers would agree, a complete wilderness—a natural place waiting to be made into a cultural landscape. The first people to arrive here were neither Papuans nor Australian Aboriginal people as we recognise them today, although they would have been the biological and cultural ancestors of both these groups.

Taking into account the expansion and contraction of the seas, there are two likely routes to Australia from Asia: through Timor across to the north-western shelf of Western Australia; and by island hopping from Sulawesi to New Guinea and then onto Australia across the plain now submerged under the Arafura Sea. There were several periods, totalling about half of the time during the last 50,000 years, when it would have been physically possible for a person to walk from northeast New Guinea to the southern-most beach in Tasmania. We can discount a pathway from the east, as the nearest landmass that is capable of supporting a human population in that direction is New Zealand, which was first colonised as recently as about a thousand years ago by Austronesians. The isolation of the rest of the Australian coast apart from the north removes all other possibilities for early migration routes. The spread of humans from Indonesia into New Guinea involved crossing sea channels that have persisted throughout the last 50 million years. Even when seas were approaching a low level, at 53,000 years ago, a voyage of 90 kilometres over water was still required to cross from Timor to Australia. It was at some time near these low sea levels, probably about 50,000 years ago, that the ancestors of the Australian Aboriginal people first entered Australia. It is likely that at various times both the Timor and Sulawesi routes were used, producing several phases of early human occupation.

The travelling distances between landmasses that were required for the first settlement of Australia and New Guinea were significant when considering the type of watercraft probably available about 50,000 years ago. There is no direct evidence of what South East Asian watercraft were like back then, although the migrants to Australia would already have been capable raft mariners. It is tempting to infer what the craft would have been like from those being used by Aboriginal people when the British arrived in Australia two hundred years ago. However, we must disregard the dugout canoes and outriggers that Torres Strait Islanders and Macassans introduced over the last three thousand and one thousand years respectively, which originated with later migrations of Austronesians across the Pacific. In fact, the first vessels were probably rafts made from lengths of bamboo lashed together with rattan. These are common South East Asian materials which are easily cut without edge-ground stone tools, such as axes and adzes. During favourable weather, bamboo rafts in skilled hands could traverse the 15–50 kilometre stretches of open water between the Indonesian islands, and possibly traverse the 90 kilometre-wide sea that separated Timor from the continental shelf of Australia during the period

Aboriginal women and their dogs on a raft along the Kimberley coast. The first of their ancestors to arrive in Australia may have used similar watercraft. PHOTO: E.J. STUART, SUNDAY ISLAND, WESTERN AUSTRALIA, 1917.

of lowest sea levels. The summer monsoon and use of tides would also have assisted in the easterly movement of people from South East Asia towards Australia and Papua New Guinea. With the distance and watercraft involved, however, the journey may well have resulted in many seafarers drowning before one group happened to make the crossing.

Although many scholars favour a theory of an accidental discovery of Australia by the ancestors of Aboriginal people, I prefer to believe there was a more deliberate process of them advancing eastwards across the Indonesian Archipelago. In an age of maps and satellites it is difficult to imagine anyone setting off into uncharted waters in relatively flimsy watercraft even with a definite destination in mind. Nonetheless, seafarers 50,000 years ago were not operating without any data. There were physical signs available to give them clues to what lay over the horizon. For example, many of the northern islands in the tropics, such as in Indonesia, have high mountains that are visible from a long way out to sea. There are also 'land clouds' that form above such mountains soon after dawn, as the result of moist air chilling as it rises over a peak. These atmospheric phenomena remain stationary during the day while other clouds pass them by and they are visible from a long way off, providing a definite indication of land. This would have kept people moving east along the Indonesian Archipelago towards New Guinea. About 50,000 years ago in Timor there would also have been strong indications that there was land somewhere to the southeast. Although from this vantage point Australia was below the horizon, there would have been times when smoke and red glare would have been visible from wild fires started by lightning strikes in north-western Australia on land that is now under the sea. Where there is smoke there is fire, and by extension, land. From the coastal mountains of Timor, people could see well out to sea. Bird migrations and floating debris would also have provided clues that there was a significant piece of country lying somewhere beyond the sea to the east.

Occupying the 'New' Land

The number of initial settlers to Australia may have been extremely small. From a single family group who made a successful crossing, a whole continent could have been colonised in a matter of a few thousand years.

The settlement of Greater Australia was probably a response to economic pressures in South East Asia, which may have included conflict and a growing scarcity of resources. The first sparse settlements of newcomers will probably never be found, as they must have existed on a coastline that is now largely a seabed.[3] Further inland, due to the negligible impact that small family groups would initially have had on the Australian environment, it is unlikely that archaeologists will find much evidence of human existence before at least several hundred years after the first group had arrived and their descendants had spread out to eventually populate the whole landscape. Once on the coastline of Australia, a shortage of raft materials, such as bamboo, probably discouraged people from attempting a return. Furthermore, with a vacant continent to conquer, the newcomers had little reason to return to Asia.

In 1954, Norman B. Tindale and Harold A. Lindsay produced a book about the first Aboriginal colonists for schoolchildren. Their fictional account, *The First Walkabout*, enabled Tindale to popularise his theories of three waves of people who arrived in Australia to become the modern Aboriginal people. In their book, Tindale and Lindsay describe a family group of Negritos—short dark people—who lived a sedentary life in tropical Asia alongside *Meganthropus* (literally the 'large people', who were early Hominids known from only a few fossils found in South East Asia). The Negritos were forced out of their ancestral home by a physically larger group of newcomers who frequently burned the landscape, who Tindale called Murrayians. After island-hopping through Borneo and New Guinea, the Negritos succeeded in colonising Australia, but due to the extremes of the seasons were forced to adopt a nomadic way of life. To Tindale and Lindsay, the Tasmanians were genetically derived from the Negritos, with some mixture of Murrayian people.[4] The Carpentarians were believed to be a later-arriving race restricted to northern Australia.

Modern anthropologists and archaeologists have now entirely rejected the once-popular concepts of 'Negritos', 'Murrayians' and 'Carpentarians', due to more recent research that shows a more complex settlement process. Nevertheless, it is likely that people left their ancient homelands to the northwest of Australia as a result of social pressures of increasing populations on the resources of Timor and its surrounding islands. Whether these population increases involved incoming migrants, naturally rising local populations, or even increasing population densities as sea levels began to rise and land areas decrease, remains a mystery. Some of the Indonesian islands may have had their ecology disrupted enough by human occupation to cause changes in vegetation structure and therefore food shortages. The potential for conflict, due to population pressure, could further have provided a reason for some family groups to leave their island homes. These basic factors may well account for many of the world's human migrations. If the settlement of Australia was the result of an economic/political push and the pull of a landmass whose existence was inferred by various physical means, it was not an accidental settlement.

The first people to reach the combined landmass of Australia and New Guinea would have been hunters and gatherers who specialised in making a living on the coast, concentrating on fish, shellfish and small animals from the adjacent inland areas. In spite of the faunal differences between Greater Australia and Indonesia after such a long period of isolation, there was some similarity in the climate and vegetation. Much of lowland New Guinea would have supported similar tropical-adapted flora as Indonesia, with some foods, such as tropical yams, in common. Between New Guinea and northern Australia, the land now submerged under the Arafura Sea probably also had a monsoonal climate similar to Indonesia. The first people arriving in northern Australia would still have found in pockets of coastal rainforest many plants that were familiar to them from back home.[5] This overlap, as small as it was, could have sustained them until they had more experience with the Australian landscape, with the interior dominated by desert. There was also the potential for the spread of plants and animals brought by the migrating people.

For 80 per cent of the time that humans are thought to have occupied the Australian continent, it has been joined to New Guinea. Therefore, during the first 40,000 years or so of human occupation here, the Indigenous people of Australia and New Guinea had a common history. Once people had arrived and established themselves in the coastal regions of Greater Australia, it is likely that the rest of the coastal and riverine areas of the continent were occupied fairly quickly. The first colonizers, probably in small bands of less than a dozen people, would have reached the vast unoccupied expanses of the interior by moving along the larger rivers. The northern Australian landscape had a different climate to the Indonesian Archipelago and New Guinea due to it being further south and it being part of a larger and drier land mass. This movement to the interior may have started relatively early as population increased. The economics of spreading into a 'new' land for inland-moving groups would have meant the loss of some island-based technologies, such as watercraft building, while gaining new knowledge about living in the interior. At present there are insufficient archaeological dates determined from sites across Australia to enable us to develop a broad picture of the settlement process. The first Aboriginal occupation of the south-western corner of Tasmania has been put at 35,000 years ago, at a time when the interior landscape had glaciers.[6]

In a world context, the colonising achievements of the ancestors of the Australian Aboriginal people are remarkable. About the time that they were first settling Australia approximately 50,000 years ago, the Neanderthals were losing their hold on Europe to the Cro-Magnons.[7] Modern-looking people expanded into northern Eurasia about 20,000 years ago. North America was settled about 13,000 years ago, with people reaching the southern end of South America less than a thousand years later. Agriculture commenced in the Middle East around 10,000 years ago, spreading to nearby regions of Europe and North Africa. In the highlands of Papua New Guinea agriculture began either around 9000 or 6000 years ago—depending on whether or not the earliest archaeological evidence is reliable—and about 8000 years ago along the lower Yangtze River in China. The Austronesians, who were a Mongoloid people originally from mainland China, began their conquest of the Pacific Ocean long after Australia was first settled. Austronesians settled Taiwan about 5500 years ago, then the Philippines about 5000 years ago. Borneo and Timor were settled by Austronesians some 500 years later. By approximately 3200 years ago they had reached Samoa; by 1500 years ago the Austronesians had spread to Hawaii and Easter Island in the eastern end of the Pacific Ocean and to Madagascar in the Indian Ocean near Africa. About 1000 years ago Austronesian ancestors of the Maori people settled in New Zealand.

The period in which Aboriginal people have lived in Australia is immense, providing ample time for biological and cultural adaptations to this landscape. The number of generations that have lived here during the estimated 50,000 years is staggering. If we assume conservatively that the average age of a parent is 25 years, then there are four generations per century. This rate equates to 2000 generations of Indigenous people living in Australia during a 50,000 year period. Put in other terms, the number of people who had lived in Australia before the arrival of European invaders in 1788 must number in the hundreds of millions.

Within human populations, any prolonged restriction in the inter-mingling of genes—as would occur when landforms such as river basins or mountain ranges isolate a population—increases the likelihood of biological variations particular to that group occurring. Variation may also be explained by migration. Modern Australian Aboriginal people have variable physical features. Whether they were descendants of a single wave or of a number of waves of migrants arriving in Australia still remains to be determined by archaeologists, human biologists and geneticists of the future.[8] Two things are certain: people arrived here from South East Asia some time before about 45,000 years ago, and people came again some time between between 4000 and 3500 years ago, this time bringing the dingo with them. Nevertheless, it is most likely that small groups of people arrived on Australian shores more or less continuously during Australia's long human history. If so, this would have contributed to the diversity of present day Indigenous people in Australia.

Human Impact

Past scientists often regarded the collective impacts of hunter and gatherers upon the environment as minor. This was because groups such as the Australian Aborigines were regarded as 'primitive' and therefore more subject to the 'laws of nature', particularly in comparison with horticul-turalists who engaged in active landscape development through vegetation clearance and irrigation.[9] While hunting and gathering activities have less direct impact than those of agriculture, more recent scientific opinion has it that the actions of hunters and gatherers over many millennia will even-tually also permanently alter the ecological balance of an ecosystem. For instance, the prolonged harvesting of economically important plants may favour the distribution and abundance of some species. Regular burning by humans would also have caused some environmental change. Nevertheless, it is often difficult to distinguish between ancient environmental changes primarily caused by changes in world climate and those brought on by human activity. For instance, during dry-climate periods when wild fires are more frequent, plants that are fire-adapted, such as eucalypts and banksias, become common at the expense of other plant species that are not. Long-term burning has tended to produce more open savannah environments to the detriment of denser tropical forests, and it is difficult for the researcher

Arrernte men sawing a spearthrower across a softwood shield to make a fire.
Aboriginal burning practices had a significant impact on the Australian ecology.
PHOTO: F.J. GILLEN & W.B. SPENCER, MACDONNELL RANGES, NORTHERN TERRITORY, 1896.

to distinguish between naturally occurring fires of the past and those caused by human activity. If Aboriginal people later contributed to the overall increase in burning, this could have helped accelerate a change in vegetation that was primarily due to a shift in the climate.

From the evidence left behind by Aboriginal people, there is little doubt that they shared the landscape for a considerable period with at least some animal species that became extinct before Europeans arrived. It has been suggested that there is rock art in western South Australia that features tracks of *Genyornis*, a large goose-like bird,[10] which is estimated to have died out by about 40,000 years ago. Similarly, in Western Arnhem Land there is a rock painting of a mother thylacine (or Tasmanian tiger) and her suckling young which must be more than 3000 years old given the time of their extinction on the mainland.[11] Many scientists have claimed that the ancestors of the Australian Aboriginal people caused the extinction of dozens of vertebrate species, including the very large animals palaeontologists refer to as megafauna. Such an animal was the plant-eating diprotodon, which was the world's largest known marsupial. Diprotodons appear to have died out by 46,000 years ago—scientists are not yet completely certain of this date, but the evidence for this is mounting. [12] It is possible that people could have caused the demise of the megafauna and other animals directly by hunting, or indirectly through deliberately burning the land and bringing about permanent changes in the vegetation structure. [13] This is a view dismissed by some scientists, who believe climate change was a more likely cause of this. [14] Yet it is conceivable that both explanations may be true. It is possible that changing climates had a role to play in megafaunal extinctions, although the fact that episodes of climate change prior to the arrival of people, did not lead to the extinction of these megafauna would suggest that human impacts were more significant. My own opinion is that human impact on the flora and fauna, when combined with climate changes, would have pushed some vulnerable species towards extinction. Regardless of what triggered the high rate of extinctions for many of the larger animals in Australia, other animal species, such as some kangaroos, adapted to the new conditions imposed on them by becoming smaller, a process of selection and genetic alteration that biologists call 'dwarfing'. The physical stress upon animals imposed by a drier more frequently burnt landscape has possibly favoured smaller animals.

Although the dingo contributed to the extinction of some mainland species, it could not have been a factor in the extinction of the megafauna. The Asian dog, called the 'dingo' in modern Australian English, was a new placental predator which first arrived in Australia some time between 4000 and 3500 years ago. The dingo does appear to have been linked to the extinction of marsupial carnivores, such as the thylacine and the Tasmanian devil, on the Australian mainland. The manner in which this came about is unclear, as the dingo would not have been a direct threat to thylacines and devils, which are formidable aggressors. The dingo, nevertheless, probably had a faster breeding cycle and would have competed with them both for game. [15] It is thought that the persistence of the thylacine and devil in Tasmania until European settlement was probably due to the absence of the dingo there. The dingo could not have crossed the water distances to reach there, or even have come to Greater Australia at any time, without human assistance.

The easterly migration of the Austronesians, commencing a few thousand years ago, brought new technologies and organisms into the Pacific. It was their developed agricultural skills that allowed them to exploit the rich environments of the Indonesian archipelago. Nonetheless, the existence of already settled human populations, and possibly the physical environments of New Guinea and Australia, largely halted their progress south. In New Guinea, agriculture based on staple foods, such as taro and banana, has existed in the fertile highland valleys for at least 6000 years, and possibly began as far back as 9000 years ago while it was still connected to Australia. The northern and eastern Torres Strait Islanders occupying areas between New Guinea and Australia practised agriculture, but those of the south—and closest to mainland Australia—did not.[16] The territories of the Australian Aboriginal people, who had hunting and gathering subsistence strategies well adapted to the Australian continent over thousands of years of occupation, were safely beyond the reach of the Austronesians who were heavily reliant on tropical agriculture. In any case, in general the Austronesians do not seem to have created widespread settlements in places where people already lived. They do not seem to have replaced pre-existing populations, except in a few, localised coastal pockets of Melanesia.

For tens of thousands of years, the Australian landmass has been the home of people who are the ancestors of present day Aboriginal people. Due to rising sea levels they have lived until recently in relative isolation from other cultures. The landscape they first encountered, as a wilderness, has been altered through climate change, the extinction of some fauna and the long-term effects of hunting and gathering activities. Partly in response to these physical changes, the Aboriginal cultural landscape has been transformed through this period too. Aboriginal cultures are not static.

Two

Religious Landscapes

In the last chapter we dealt with a scientist's account of how Aboriginal people came to live in Australia. Aboriginal people and the Europeans who also eventually settled in Australia had—and continue to have—fundamentally different accounts of the creation of the world and how it was first peopled. They also had, and have, different views of themselves in relation to the physical environment. While Western Europeans today tend to think of themselves as separate from the 'natural' world, Aboriginal people consider that the social and physical aspects of their existence closely intermesh.

Furthermore, Aboriginal people believe that their spiritual Ancestors have given social relevance to the landscape, imbuing it with their power and humanising it. In Aboriginal thought land could never be seen as a total wilderness, although there are certainly concepts about which parts of their country are most productive.

The Dreaming

In Australian English the corpus of beliefs that forms Aboriginal religion is often referred to as the 'Dreaming'.[1] Central to this concept is that there was a creative period in the past when creator beings performed heroic deeds, the landscape was moulded and enhanced, and the customs followed by Aboriginal people laid down. The main beings in the Dreaming accounts are the spiritual Ancestors of the present-day Aboriginal community. These beings, who are considered to still influence Aboriginal Australia, possess all human traits, virtues, pleasures and vices. They may also die and be transformed. The Ancestors may often be manifested as animals and birds, but may also be plants, atmospheric and cosmological phenomena or even diseases. Aboriginal people perceive the Dreaming as collectively the Ancestors, the practices they introduced, and the tangible objects and places that they left behind in the landscape. Although it relates to past events, Dreaming knowledge is still of immense importance to present-day Aboriginal people for understanding the world.

The Dreaming mythology provides Aboriginal people with answers to the great universal religious questions of humankind—concerning the origin, meaning, purpose and destiny of life. The term 'Dreaming' represents a gloss of a range of meanings and can also loosely be defined as the whole body of mythology and associated belief and custom that provides some insight into Aboriginal religion. Although in some regions, such as Central Australia, Aboriginal people gain insights into their past and the relevance of parts of the landscape through actual dreams, the Dreaming and Dreaming Ancestors are not the products of dreams. The creative period itself is often referred to as the 'Dreamtime', but since its power is eternal, this term is best replaced by the 'Dreaming'.

Across Australia the 'Dreaming' period is known by a number of language terms: for example *Ungud* (Ngarinyin people, the Kimberley), *Wongar* (Yolngu people, northeast Arnhem Land), *Tjukurpa* (Western Desert region), *Altyjerre* (Arrernte people, Central Australia), *Bulurru* (Djabugay people, north-eastern Queensland) and *Kulhal* (Yaraldi people, Lower Murray region of South Australia). A related word in Aboriginal English is 'Law', which refers to the body of religious and cultural knowledge that is used to inform and direct Aboriginal society. Whenever I have asked Aboriginal people to explain the Dreaming they have mostly responded in the same manner: it is the story of their old ways, how the land was formed, what they used to do and what they learned from their grandparents' generation about their Ancestors.

The Dreaming relates to the past, present and the future, which are connected in a great cycle of time. To many Aboriginal people, the issue of whether their biological ancestors arrived in Australia 40,000 years ago or over 50,000 years ago is irrelevant, as they consider that they originated with the landscape. Indeed, several Aboriginal people whom I know are quite amused that a 'white fellow' would want to conceive such things in this quantitative manner. An elderly Western Desert man told me once that 'Walpala has nyiri. Anangu has Tjukurpa,' meaning, 'While Europeans have paper documents, Aboriginal people have the Dreaming.' Through participation in ceremonies and rituals, Aboriginal people can connect directly with the Dreaming. The Ancestors are totems for their clans, thereby providing a link to contemporary people. The Dreaming is the basis of customary law and remains the fundamental reality for many Aboriginal people.[2]

The initial Dreaming landscape as described in Aboriginal mythology is generally considered to be vast and relatively featureless, such as a plain of earth, the sea or sometimes just cloud matter. A number of spiritual Ancestors, often existing as an amalgam of human and animal forms, emerged out of the ether to set in course events that refined the space into an ordered landscape. Aboriginal people recognised that the Ancestors' activities created landscape features, such as wetlands and water holes, which later by chance benefited them as hunters and gatherers. Even more importantly, the Ancestors gave the land cultural meaning. For instance, Ngarrindjeri people in southern South Australia believed that the course of the Murray River was produced when a male Ancestor, Ngurunderi, chased a large Murray codfish down a narrow creek, forcing the banks to widen into the present form of the river.[3] He also made hills with his brush shelters, dug drinking soaks into the sand dunes, made his canoe into the Milky Way, his legs became peninsulas and his spirit went up to the Skyworld. Through knowing the feats of Ngurunderi, it is difficult to look at this landscape without reference to him. The landscape was his artefact.

The behaviour of the Dreaming Ancestors was essentially human and they suffered from the same calamities that their descendants did. For example, Ngurunderi performed some of his epic deeds while chasing his two runaway wives.[4] He also got into fights, had his nets torn by the water spirit and called on his kin for assistance. After passing through the known landscape of one group, Aboriginal people believe that many of their Dreaming Ancestors went on to other lands for more creations or entered the sky where they can still be pointed out. Many of the major Dreaming Ancestors interacted with each other. The Dreaming Ancestors are

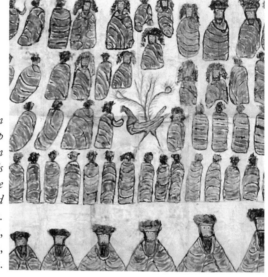

'Lyrebird dance', by William Barak of the Woiworung group of the Kulin people from southern Victoria. Barak's paintings of ceremonies are evidence of the rich artistic and ceremonial life of the region.
WATERCOLOUR: W. BARAK, CORANDERRK MISSION, VICTORIA, 1890S.

recognised as being forefathers of both the living Aboriginal people and of the plants, animals and natural phenomena that they created and were transformed into. Thus in complete contrast with Western European beliefs, Aboriginal beliefs make no sharp distinction between humanity and nature; both are closely linked. In the Dreaming, the land and its people have a common origin.

To Aboriginal people a part of the legacy of the Dreaming Ancestors is in the landscape, and their association with the land is marked by sacred memorials or 'sacred sites'. As the Ancestors travelled across the landscape, they left behind a trail that can be recognised by Aboriginal people in the form of mountains, waterholes, plant formations and other environmental and geographical phenomena. Such places and large landforms are tangible evidence to Aboriginal people that the Dreaming actually took place. They also provide connections that link living people with the Dreaming. The sacred memorials are focal points in the religious landscape around which Aboriginal people build a local identity. To Aboriginal people, sacredness is localised in the landscape, with most major geographical features to some extent related to the tracks of their Ancestors and the places they gave meaning to. For instance, in the 1980s during a site recording expedition I travelled with elderly Aboriginal people along the eastern edge of the Simpson Desert, where it appeared that every prominent sand dune, rock outcrop, soakage and large tree had some specific mythological relevance to the Muramura Ancestors, whose Dreaming Tracks crisscrossed the country. Their descriptions of the hundreds of places within this landscape made it alive with cultural and social relevance.

The term 'sacred site' has become more widely used since the 1970s, as anthropologists and lawyers have tried to distinguish places that are extremely significant to Aboriginal people in a total landscape that was predominantly the creation of the Ancestors. This has led to popular misunderstanding that Aboriginal religion has a finite, unchanging number of places of Dreaming importance. But, with the crossing over of many Dreaming Tracks made by a large number of Ancestors, the potential number of important places that are linked together through a web of Dreaming tradition is enormous.[5] In response to cultural and landscape changes, the significance and location of the sites may change too. In practice, Aboriginal people do not treat all sites as equally important. Amid the large number of sites in any given area, particular Dreaming sites are often considered to be of special significance to Aboriginal people for various ceremonial and religious reasons.

Myth is defined in Western European tradition in two main contradictory ways. First, it is construed as an invented or fictitious story. In this sense, myth is a false and trivial belief. This definition is often used by people, possessing the ideology of a dominant culture, who seek to describe what they consider to be the 'superstitions'—false suppositions—of subordinate cultures. The second concept of myth is as a 'traditional' belief, or a reflection of a culture, and allows for less emphasis on evaluating true/false aspects. It is this second concept I use when speaking of myths. Although Aboriginal myth provides the listener with an explanation of their world, the comparison of Aboriginal myth with a European notion of history as a systematic and chronological record of past events is confusing. (The Aboriginal English use of the word 'history' to mean the 'Dreaming' in some regions of Australia makes this more confusing to non-Aboriginal people.) Myth is much more than an Aboriginal version of history. All myths provide a view of the world that can be constantly explored and modified by culture. It follows that a particular myth can mean different things to different people, with many equally valid versions. Many of the myths have varying layers of meaning.

The local variations that arise in Dreaming beliefs do not necessarily challenge the pre-existing views, but rather allow the believers to collectively determine what is in common to them all and to introduce new possibilities. For example, since the 1940s some of the Pintupi people have moved hundreds of kilometres from their homelands around Lake Mackay west of Alice Springs to a northern mission settlement at Balgo in Western Australia. Here they discovered that one of their own Dreaming Tracks extended to this place too, having passed underground.[6] This realisation came through a man's vision. The Pintupi here were able to discover aspects of their culture that were considered either lost or never before known, although always perceived as lying just under the surface of existing knowledge. The basic foundation was seen as having always been there, but until recently not yet found by Aboriginal people. Such newly acquired knowledge helps incoming groups justify to local people their rights to live there. Through the discoveries that come about through dreams, visions, contact with other cultural groups and experience with 'new' landscapes, Aboriginal people can make adjustments to their religious beliefs and thus absorb change into their cultures. And while the Dreaming is not the direct product of dreams in the commonly understood sense, influential Aboriginal people have realised some deeper inner meanings with the help of actual dreams. Thus Dreaming beliefs provide more than a reconstruction of events—for Aboriginal believers they are the ultimate point of reference for everything and continue to set the scene for what is possible. The corpus of Dreaming mythology, as perceived by Australian Aboriginal people, may have some similar functions to European history, but nevertheless has a broader purpose.

Non-academic literature about Aboriginal Dreamings is of mixed value in understanding Aboriginal links to the landscape. In the past, Aboriginal myths have often been used as a source of plots for stories written for a non-Aboriginal audience. European writers borrowed outlines from Aboriginal myths to weave them into fairy stories created for European Australian readers. Other authors have written condensed versions of Aboriginal myths, but in doing so have reduced or removed altogether the geographical aspects of their source material, and in many cases not acknowledged that material.[7] Apart from ignoring the landscape, events that are portrayed without a cultural background to explain their significance give the uninformed reader a somewhat hollow view of the myth. Nevertheless, these popularised versions are not all bad in effect. The myths written in brief by the amateur ethnologist Charles P. Mountford, for example, were used as inspiration for the impressionist paintings of Ainslie

Roberts.[8] Mountford worked extensively across Central and northern Australia from the 1920s to the 1960s, mostly while based at the South Australian Museum. He had a particular interest in Aboriginal art and mythology. My own first interest in Aboriginal cultures as a child came through reading the joint publications of Mountford and Roberts in a primary-school library in the Adelaide Hills. These books encouraged an interest in Aboriginal mythology and an appreciation of the diversity of beliefs across Australia.

Sacred Networks

The religious landscape linked widely dispersed people. Membership of a group identified by the same totem sometimes included people who spoke different languages, spread throughout larger cultural regions. For instance, in Central Australia the anthropologist T.G.H. Strehlow recorded and mapped a number of people who were descendants of the Rain Ancestor: a Wangkangurru group at Parapara in the Simpson Desert; an Eastern Arrernte group at Aljoa on the Hale River; and a Southern Arrernte group at Iibora on the Lower Finke River.[9] Through recognising a common link to an Ancestor and by having ownership of sacred sites that are connected by a Dreaming Track, all these people considered themselves to be closely related in one sense. The Dreaming provided a grid of links across the desert between widely dispersed groups. (The Yarralin people of the Victoria River area of the Northern Territory refer to Dreaming Tracks in Aboriginal English as 'Strings' in recognition that they connect people together.)[10] To Aboriginal people these links were not just academic. For instance, as the soakages in the Simpson Desert dried up, the Wangkangurru people would have had rights to retreat to the permanent waters in their neighbours' country, such as that of the Diyari and Ngamini people, with whom they had close links through intermarriage and the sharing of sacred traditions.[11] With the absence of any long-term water source for most of the desert, access to areas outside the normal hunting and gathering territory was crucial. The efficiency of Aboriginal occupation of the whole landscape and the exploitation of its resources rested on the network of Dreaming connections and kinship links. Anthropologists variously refer to the individuals who have some degree of cultural responsibility over particular sites as 'custodians' and 'traditional owners'.

Aboriginal people often express obligations to land by stating where their 'country' lies and in some areas there is an individual who is recognised as 'boss' or 'manager' of it. The Dreaming landscape requires a human population to maintain it through ceremony and ritual.

Some landforms are intersected by the tracks of several Ancestral Beings. These places are considered highly important due to the nature of the Dreaming events that are believed to have taken place there. Dreaming Ancestors associated with Aboriginal sites clustered around Uluru (Ayers Rock) in Central Australia include the Mala (Hare Wallaby), Kuniya (Python), Lungkata (Blue-tongue Lizard) and Tjati (Red Lizard).[12] Their activities are recorded in landscape features. Knowing something of these mythologies gives a completely different experience to visitors, most of whom today regrettably come just to conquer 'the Rock' by climbing it. Some sites have prohibitions about who may approach them, for example restrictions based on initiation status or kinship group. Nevertheless, many sacred areas are regular camping places for their traditional owners. Through their intimate and extensive knowledge of the Dreaming, an Aboriginal person could never become truly lost in their own land. Many Aboriginal placenames celebrate aspects of the Dreaming that occurred there when the Ancestors travelled across the country. For example, the northern area of the Adelaide CBD was known as Tarndanya, which refers to Tarnda, the Kangaroo Ancestor who brought the body scarring practice to the Kaurna people of the Adelaide Plains.[13]

Living with Spirits

Spirits are considered to occupy particular places in the landscape. They are not the Ancestors of Aboriginal people and were believed to share the land with humans. For example, the Mimih spirits are believed to live in the escarpment of western Arnhem Land, known locally as the 'stone country'.[14] They are characterised as being very thin, as they live in the cracks of rocks. Although human-like in form, the Mimih spirits are not considered to be people. According to Aboriginal tradition, they originally taught the ancestors of the present Aboriginal groups how to paint in rock shelters. The famous Gunwinggu bark painters Yirawala and Kubarkku have made Mimih spirits well known to Europeans through their art.[15] Aboriginal beliefs in spirits contain within them crucial knowledge about the landscape, particularly about 'dangerous' places, which because of such things as sorcery, present a physical threat. For example, the 'bunyip' of south-eastern Australia is believed to typically live in freshwater bodies that are notorious for snags and for people drowning; bunyips are also associated with the bases of cliffs, near water, which Aboriginal people generally avoided through fear of contact with these spirits.[16] The bunyip spirit has entered Australian English to mean a general water being. The earliest information received from Aboriginal people on the appearance and behaviour of these spirits was so detailed that some European colonists believed that they existed as a species of animal. Other physical phenomena in the landscape were also linked to spirits. For example, in 1860 the missionary George Taplin heard the booming noises from Lake Alexandrina which Aboriginal people had attributed to the river spirit.[17] These sounds may have been caused by marsh gases. Some Aboriginal people living in the Lower Murray continue to firmly believe in the existence of these and other spirit beings.

Aboriginal adults across Australia often use the potential actions of spirit beings in threats to help control children. For instance, in the Western Desert children in particular fear the *mamu* or 'devil', which is believed to cause illness. The fear of malignant spirits is particularly strong during dark nights. However other spirits serve as omens, providing a means by which Aboriginal people can make predictions about the immediate future. For example, many Aboriginal groups I have worked with believe nocturnal hunting birds, such as owls and frogmouths, are spirits and that the appearance and call of these birds means that someone socially close to them is about to die. Birds, such as the willie wagtail, appear to have attracted the attention of Aboriginal people everywhere. In one of the Western Desert songs, the frenetic sideways movement of the willie wagtail is described as 'dancing like a man' in a ceremony.[18] In many parts of southern Australia Aboriginal people believe that any unusual behaviour they observed in this bird means that bad news is coming. A Ngarrindjeri woman of the Lower Murray talking about the willie wagtail several years ago claimed to me that 'Him good telephone that fella', referring to news that a friend or relative had died. To Aboriginal people anything unusual in the environment could be an important sign, but only if you have the cultural knowledge to interpret it. Particular 'clever' or spiritually powerful people are believed to have received training from knowledgeable elders to develop skills in reading these signs.

A child drawing a sand picture of a mamu, *or devil. These spirits, who are more dangerous at night, can usually only be seen by dogs.* PHOTO: N.B. TINDALE, OOLDEA, WESTERN SOUTH AUSTRALIA, 1940.

Aboriginal people also consider that some people have the ability, through spirit mediums, to sing a traveller's way shorter and easier. For instance, a colonist in the Murray River region of South Australia in the nineteenth century recalled an Aboriginal explanation of the small flattened out piles of stone resembling road metal that were placed at intervals along routes used by Aboriginal people.[19] He had been told, 'Well, you know, fellow sit down under those stones who has control of the earth, and when blackfellow very tired him give presents to that fellow.' The first offering made would be a bough removed from a nearby tree. If the traveller were a man, this would be thrown on the stones, the thrower saying, 'That is your spear.' A second bough would follow, 'That is your waddy, make ground come shorter.' Similarly, women would offer the underground spirit two boughs, the first representing a possum rug, the second a net. In this way, Aboriginal people along the river made the ground shrink and the length of their trip shorten. In Aboriginal Australia, distance is not generally spoken of in terms of precise standard measurements, but through experience. Before European people introduced vehicles to Australia, distance was normally described relative to such things as the traveller's thirst and the burden they carried, with the distance travelled in a single day (generally from 15 to 30 kilometres, depending on the terrain) being the main measuring unit.[20] Aboriginal people rarely travelled at night, except during a full moon.

Skyworld and Underworld

In Aboriginal Dreamings, many of the Ancestors both originated and terminated in the Skyworld, a place which Europeans would define as the cosmos or heavens. The spirits of dead people were considered by Aboriginal people to follow a similar path, to join with the Ancestors. The Dreaming accounts are full of descriptions of celestial and subterranean places that sound much like how one would describe a physical place. For example, explorer, anthropologist and geographer Alfred W. Howitt recorded that the Wurunjerri (= Woiworung) people around the northern side of Melbourne believed they '. . . had a sky country, which they called Tharangalk-bek, the gum-tree country. It was described to me as a land where there were trees. The tribal legends also tell of it as the place to which Bunjil ascended with all his people in a whirlwind.'[21] The land was named after the trees, which were said to be *tharangalk*, or manna gums. From the accounts of religious beliefs and customs across Australia, it is clear that Aboriginal people considered there were other realms within the perceived cultural landscape in addition to their own terrestrial regions, to which they could travel in spirit form.[22] Such regions are the Skyworld and the Underworld. The latter is also sometimes recorded as the 'Land to the West' or the 'World of the Dead'.

The existence of Aboriginal beliefs in the Skyworld as an image of the terrestrial landscape is common across Australia, although not as important in the Central Australian region. The Skyworld is considered to be a region that, to a large degree, is subject to the same laws as those of terrestrial regions. This was the Aboriginal opinion recorded by the German missionary Christian G. Teichelmann, who arrived at Adelaide in 1838, two years after the Proclamation of the Colony of South Australia, and commenced studying the religion of his intended converts. Teichelmann stated that the Kaurna people:

> consider the firmament [Heavens] with its bodies as a land similar to what they are living upon . . . It is their opinion that all the celestial

bodies were formerly living upon earth, partly as animals, partly as men, and that they left this lower region to exchange for the higher one. Therefore all the names which apply to the beings on earth they apply to the celestial bodies, and believe themselves to be obnoxious to their influence, and ascribe to them mal-formation of the body, and other accidents.[23]

Accounts that illustrate the connections between the Skyworld and the terrestrial landscape exist for other parts of Australia. In the Murray River area of South Australia, the magistrate, Edward J. Eyre, noted:

One old native informed me, that all blacks, when dead, go up to the clouds, where they have plenty to eat and drink; fish, birds, and game of all kinds, with weapons and implements to take them. He then told me, that occasionally individuals had been up to the clouds, and had come back, but that such instances were very rare; his own mother, he said, had been one of the favoured few. Some one from above had let down a rope, and hauled her up by it; she remained one night, and on her return, gave a description of what she had seen in a chant, or song, which she sung for me, but of the meaning of which I could make out nothing.[24]

To Aboriginal people their connection to the Skyworld is tangible and able to be experienced outside of death.

The connection between the human spirit and the Skyworld is broad, involving both ends of an individual's life cycle. For instance, in the 1930s Pinkie Mack, a Yaraldi woman of the Lower Murray, claimed that before birth 'children are said to be little, flying about in the air, dropped out of a bag and they could be caught'.[25] As well as being a place where the spirit, or a part of it, travelled to after death, the Skyworld was thought of as a place where greater knowledge could be attained.[26] For example, in the Adelaide area, initiates were ritually taken to the celestial region by their ceremonial leaders in order to gain sacred knowledge from the Ancestors who lived there.[27] Similarly, in south-eastern Australia, healers reputedly gained knowledge through crossing into the Heavens by climbing a tree.[28]

Aboriginal people perceived the Skyworld and Underworld as part of a landscape that was within their physical reach. In some parts of Australia, particular large trees, big sand dunes, large hills and mountains were thought to attract lightning strikes being so dangerously close to the Skyworld, and they were therefore avoided during storm seasons.[29] It was also possible to reach the Skyworld from the land, as Eyre noted. Reaching the Skyworld could be rewarded. For example, in the Adelaide area a man named Monana gained access to the Skyworld and became an Ancestor:

> [Monana] . . . was one day throwing large spears in various directions, east, west, north, south; when, having thrown one upwards, it did not return to earth. He threw another, and another, and so continued throwing; each spear sticking fast to the former one until they reached the ground, and he climbed up by them to the sky, where he has ever since remained.[30]

Monana was considered to be a mortal who, like Jack in 'Jack and the Beanstalk', had climbed up into the Skyworld. Here he realised immortality.

Similarly, the Underworld, through which the sun and the moon passed, was not far away. Blowholes on the west coast of South Australia were avoided for fear that a huge Snake Spirit called Ganba would come out and eat humans.[31]

After travelling through the Skyworld and ending up in the west, the sun and the moon as spirit beings were believed by Aboriginal people to return by distant routes to the east. Some Aboriginal people considered the path back as being to the south or north of their country, while others thought it was through an underground passage in the Underworld. Charles Mountford recorded the belief among the Tiwi people at Melville and Bathurst Islands that:

> At one time the moon-man used to return to the east by a road just under the southern horizon. But a nest of hornets, which lived along that road, stung him so badly that he changed his path and now returns to his home by a northern route . . . Most informants, however, said that the moon returned to the east through the same underground world as the sun-woman.[32]

Many coastal groups of southern and western Australia believe that the sun entered the Underworld by diving into the sea. In contrast, Aboriginal groups near Lake Eyre in Central Australia believed that it disappeared into the ground at a place called Dityi-minka, reputedly meaning 'Hole of

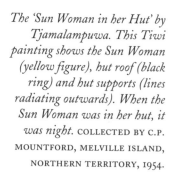

The 'Sun Woman in her Hut' by Tjamalampuwa. This Tiwi painting shows the Sun Woman (yellow figure), hut roof (black ring) and hut supports (lines radiating outwards). When the Sun Woman was in her hut, it was night. COLLECTED BY C.P. MOUNTFORD, MELVILLE ISLAND, NORTHERN TERRITORY, 1954.

the Sun'.[33] Similarly, people of the Kulin nation of southern Victoria believed that when the sun disappeared in the west, it entered a hole in the ground like that left behind by a large tree burned in a bush fire.[34] Another belief about the sun existed among people of the inland river systems of south-eastern Australia, to whom the sun was considered a fire created by a major Ancestor.[35] Here, the warmth of the day was equated with the strength of the fire and how much wood was left to burn. Presumably Aboriginal people believed more fuel was being gathered during the night.

To Aboriginal people the heavens were rich with meaning. This is illustrated in an account by an Aboriginal man named Billy Poole from the Lake Albert area of the Lower Murray, recorded by a South Australian colonist:

> When around the camp fire at night he [Billy Poole] told me the names of stars, and, more over, of constellations. He pointed out one group as an old man kangaroo with his arm broken; another group was a turkey sitting on her eggs, the eggs being our constellation Pleiades, another a Toolicher [toolache wallaby], a small and very prettily marked kangaroo peculiar to the district; another an emu and so on.[36]

The cosmic landscape was, to these Aboriginal people, populated with animal species that also occurred in their terrestrial landscape. It is sad that in the case of the *toolicher* this is no longer so, as this marsupial became extinct in the 1920s.

The stars, planets and constellations were considered actual Ancestors and spirits, not just symbols. Knowing the heavens as a record of the Dreaming was considered by many Aboriginal groups to be important, although the depth of this knowledge within the community probably varied. In south-western Victoria, the early colonist Dawson recorded that:

> Although the knowledge of the heavenly bodies possessed by the natives may not entitle it to be dignified by the name of astronomical science, it greatly exceeds that of most white people. Of such importance is a knowledge of the stars to the aborigines in their night journeys, and of their positions denoting the particular seasons of the year, that astronomy is considered one of their principal branches of education. Among the tribes between the rivers Leigh and Glenelg, it is taught by men selected for their intelligence and information.[37]

Through the identification of Ancestors in the Skyworld, it is clear that the cosmic bodies provided a record of the Dreaming.

With Aboriginal beliefs in the separate existence of the human spirit, the total landscape defined both the living and the dead. To study the world that individual humans created as thinking beings we must also include concepts that relate to regions that people could only reach in their minds. The Skyworld is one such place and the Underworld is another. The places to which people travelled in their imagination or as spirits upon their death and the sites where spirit beings live are important additions to the mapping of the total cultural landscape of the Aboriginal people. Different cultural groups may experience a landscape in different ways—physically in their perception of space, and culturally in the recognition of the values of land and its resources.

Three

Social Life

Although Australian Aboriginal people do not have a formal social hierarchy, as do many cultures in the world, there is nevertheless much internal differentiation within their society. In this chapter I consider the identity of individuals and the ways in which people come together to form groups. Aboriginal people are related to other members of their community through family ties, totems, ceremonies, 'tribes', clans, sections, subsections, moieties and languages. Apart from formal links to these groups, Aboriginal people typically live in small bands of mixed and changing membership, which have a range or territory they move within. The size and composition of Aboriginal groups depends on the ability of the land within an area to support them economically. The clan links of an individual to particular sites or estates may not match the area they generally hunt and gather in. These relationships may change through the course of a person's life, with gender playing a role too. Aboriginal links to the landscapes are built upon all these social and cultural relationships.

Knowing your Kin

All societies have formal rules and practices that regulate relationships between people. In Aboriginal Australia, kinship determines access to resources and connections to the landscape. Indeed within Aboriginal communities, kinship connections form the basis of most types of relationship. Before Europeans arrived, the Aboriginal world was such that all true strangers were by definition outside of the kinship system, therefore putting them in a problematic position with respect to the Aboriginal community. Anthropological studies of kinship involve mathematical formulas, which can appear complex to lay people. Nonetheless, attaining a deeper understanding of Aboriginal social and cultural life requires a working knowledge of the systems that structure kin relationships and must be addressed here.

Aboriginal families are composed differently from those of Western Europeans. In everyday life, Aboriginal people moved around in bands which were groups of flexible membership, made up of people in various social relationships. Bands came together during ceremonies and for economic activities, such as food gathering and trading.[1] The Aboriginal people who camped together at the same hearth were generally a man, his wife or wives and young children.[2] Camps nearby might contain young unmarried men, and others might have older relatives, such as parents of the adults. Anthropologists Ronald and Catherine Berndt described the situation for the Gunwinggu people of western Arnhem Land during their fieldwork from the 1940s to 1960s:

> . . . the population in and around the larger or most popular [camping] sites ranged from a single nuclear family to constellations of fifty or so, and more on special occasions. Quite often a combined camp was made up of one or two polygynous [multiple wife] families plus parents of any or all of the spouses and other relatives temporarily attached to them. When the husbands were not close brothers or when fathers and adult sons were not in the same camping complex at a given time, at least a few such men (brothers, fathers, sons) were likely to be somewhere in the vicinity.[3]

In Aboriginal societies, many men would have two or more wives who would collectively gather food and care for children. Young girls approaching puberty were generally given to middle-aged men in marriage, while widows were passed to younger brothers of the deceased. Wives gained without community consent, either through theft or elopement, were often the cause of conflict between the Aboriginal groups involved.

Aboriginal people do not have hereditary chiefs, although older men and some elderly women have considerable personal authority in their community. Relationships between Aboriginal and European people on the frontier could depend on such prominent people. For instance, in the 1930s and 1940s, the anthropologist and biologist Donald Thomson worked with a middle-aged Aboriginal man named Wongo in north-eastern Arnhem Land which was then beyond the frontier of European settlement.[4] Thomson's own political standing among the local Aboriginal people rested on the strength of his relationship with this person. Wongo's power and influence was according to Thomson due to a number of factors: his own personality; the support of his grown sons; and his twenty-two wives. Although Wongo's group had been in a decline in terms of warriors, Wongo had gained through political manipulation many more wives than was regarded as usual. Older people, who had gathered a considerable amount of cultural knowledge and experience through participation in ceremony, were often both greatly respected and feared by their community.

Within Aboriginal society everyone who is likely to interact, whether close relatives or people more distantly related, are classed as kin and have a particular term that conveys this relationship. Nevertheless relationships within the family group are paramount. To people who stand outside the Aboriginal kinship system, it is difficult at first to understand the kin terminology, even when English is used, as it is based on a family model that differs greatly from that of modern Western European people. In many Australian systems the category of what in English would be termed as being an 'uncle' includes the mother's brother, but not the father's brother.[5] The special bond between mother's brother and sister's son leads to the uncle in this relationship taking his nephew's side in fights and arguments, as well as assisting him with food and shelter. Similarly, the equivalent of an 'aunt' is the father's sister, but not the mother's sister. Other kin categories contain a large number of people. For example, all sisters may fall into the one category, meaning that a person refers to all their mother's sisters by the same term in their language as they do for their biological 'mother'. This also applies to in-laws, so that a woman will also refer to her sister's husband using the same word as for 'husband'. In some systems, grandparents and grandchild are classified together under the one term. In Aboriginal communities it is virtually impossible for a child to become orphaned, regardless of the deaths of their biological mother and father.

Aboriginal people use extended kin categories to politically incorporate themselves into a wider group. Diplomacy ceremonies exist to establish or reaffirm connections between different Aboriginal groups.[6] They are held on a variety of occasions, which also function for trade, to create political alliances or to commemorate dead relatives. During my fieldwork I have also witnessed less formal situations when visiting Aboriginal people have met a local group and have then gone to extraordinary lengths to identify a relationship for them, through a distant relative. In this manner, visitors are given an identity upon which relations could be built. In order to make these connections, Aboriginal people from different kinship systems work out complex formulas to translate between the various kin categories. In northern and Central Australia, the increasing movements of Aboriginal people since European settlement has spread the need for these bridging systems.[7] In earlier times, individuals who could not establish a firm relationship were likely, as strangers, to be treated with suspicion and blamed for any inexplicable trauma suffered by the hosts.

The willingness of Aboriginal people to incorporate new individuals into their kinship system is demonstrated by looking at how European people have been attached to a local group. While Donald Thomson was working for the government in Arnhem Land in the 1930s and 1940s, Wongo regarded him as *gaminyarr*, meaning 'daughter's son'.[8] This not only specified a relationship between Thomson and Wongo, but also strategically established relationships with everyone else in the community. Similarly, the museum researcher Norman Tindale was given a totemic classification of Brown Hawk by his Arrernte and Luritja informants.[9] Tindale later told me that he actively utilised this identity when approaching Aboriginal people throughout the desert.

Not all Europeans who were linked to Aboriginal people through kinship appreciated that their actions were governed by formal rules. Europeans who were adopted into Aboriginal society would on occasion suffer if their subsequent behaviour was deemed unacceptable according to the local kinship system. In one extreme case prior to 1931, Aboriginal people living on the edge of the Tanami Desert in Central Australia killed a white shepherd who had, after taking one Aboriginal woman as a wife, broken their marriage code by attempting to take another woman of the wrong kinship group.[10] This is a stark illustration of how deeply Aboriginal concepts of ownership, sharing and the law are built upon their rules of kinship.

Aboriginal people use the extended kin categories to politically incorporate themselves into a wider group. Kinship ties are also established through totems, those Dreaming Ancestors who are considered to have genealogical links to living people. This means that all natural and supernatural phenomena that together form the Dreaming are categorised among kin. Among the Pitjantjatjara people of the Western Desert, biological descent is not of primary importance in deciding rights to land, which are instead mainly determined by the birth location and the Dreaming Ancestors associated with that location.[11] For their northern neighbours, the Pintupi, the conception site is considered more significant in this regard.[12] The conception site is the place where it is determined that the Dreaming Ancestor entered the mother in order to become part of the unborn child.

When Aboriginal people today speak of 'visiting country', they are generally referring to the spiritual homes of the Dreaming Ancestors with whom they are closely associated. Some people have several links to totemic Ancestors. For example, in the Lower Murray region of South Australia the primary totem assigned to a child depends on the clan into which they are born.[13] Clans are land-owning groups and clan members typically marry outsiders, people from other clans. In the Lower Murray members were responsible, through ceremony, for maintaining a particular territory. Clan membership is determined through the father's line, although people have some affiliation with the clans on their mother's line. While not all Aboriginal groups have totems for their clans, for those that do or did, the totemic links to land possessed by every individual was an asset to their wider community, providing greater access to resources in the landscape.

In many regions the Aboriginal community and the cosmos is perceived to be divided into two halves, called 'moieties' by anthropologists.[14] Rules associated with the moiety system provide a general guide to behaviour. In north-eastern Arnhem Land the moieties are called Dhuwa and Yirritja, with children entering the moiety of their father. In some desert regions ritual life is organised on the basis of moieties that are comprised of people from alternate generations. Many Central Australian societies divide themselves into two moieties in different ways for different purposes, either derived from the father's line, mother's line or from the same generation. This basic division is important for ceremonial organisation, although it rarely requires people gathering solely along these lines. In societies that possess moieties, it is a rule that an individual's spouse must come from the other moiety. Other societies have section systems that are based on four classes, or subsection systems with eight basic divisions, which are all essentially subdivisions of the moieties. In parts of Central Australia, Aboriginal people generally refer to the section and subsections as 'skin' groups and these often appear in their names.[15] As with the moieties, sections and subsections are the basic units involved in kinship and marriage ceremony.

Although Australian Aboriginal kinship systems are diverse, they all serve to regulate whom a person may marry and whom they should avoid.[16] The favoured spouse is a classificatory 'cousin' or a 'grandparent', although one who is biologically distant. In many groups, 'mothers in-law' and 'sons in-law' actively avoid each other, getting children to act as intermediaries when passing objects such as food between each other. Any close interaction between people who should avoid one another would lead to what is known in Aboriginal English as 'shame', and the practice of avoidance is considered a sign of respect. I recall during my fieldwork in Cape York Peninsula the embarrassment of a young Wik man who claimed, when asked, that he did not know the name of an elderly woman in the small group he was travelling with. In English he eventually said 'mother in-law', which clarified the situation. In this case the embarrassment was brought on by an outsider asking questions, but generally there would be no overt tension between the two such people in an avoidance relationship. Through their kinship connection, people from other categories are permitted to have 'joking' relationships, allowing for horseplay and verbal challenges to occur in public. During some ceremonies, ritual breakdown allows for more open relations between individuals who are normally in avoidance.

The centrality of Aboriginal kin classifications is such that it is difficult to understand Aboriginal language and customs without a basic knowledge of it. Personal names as used by Europeans do not feature strongly in kin-based societies. Nicknames are far more commonly used, with real names—which may relate to one's Dreaming Ancestor or to an important site—often being kept secret, except for restricted ritual use.

Codes of behaviour, as determined by kinship, cover all areas of life, from hunting and gathering, access to land-based resources, birth rituals, initiation, marriage, access to Dreaming knowledge, mourning practices and death. Membership of a kin group in part determines an individual's voice on particular issues. For example, in many parts of Australia groups of people who are related through the father's line control access to certain totemic sites in the landscape. In these communities this is balanced by a group of mother's relatives who are responsible for organising such critical life events as initiation, marriage and mourning. Kinship plays a much more central role in Aboriginal society than it does for Western Europeans. In practice, 'strangers' may eventually become kin if they are present in the community long enough to establish social relations. In common with all societies, actual behaviour between people depends on a combination of the closeness of the kin relationship, the sharing of personal histories and individual personalities.

Tribes and Clans

In all societies, there are numerous different models employed to identify groups of people in relation to their distribution across the landscape. There are also many different ways that individuals may choose to connect with other people and places, which vary according to situation. The manner in which people can be mapped is therefore complex. For Western Europeans the set of communities that individuals belong to is determined by such things as where a person lives, where they were educated and what primary languages are spoken. While this is also to some extent true for Aboriginal people, in their case the land and the sites within it emerge more prominently as an element of their identity.

The fact that individual Aboriginal people had close associations to particular pieces of land was recognised from the beginning of British settlement when it was noted that the Aboriginal man Bennelong had inherited Goat Island in Sydney Harbour from his father's line even though his ownership was not what Europeans understood ownership to mean.[17] The clan was the fundamental unit dictating ownership to tracts of land, rituals and sites over much of Australia with the exception of the Western Desert. Most clans are named and were based on descent from a single Dreaming Ancestor.

However, in everyday life, Aboriginal people were not restricted to moving around as a clan where all members were identified with a particular Dreaming Ancestor. Instead, they assembled in various groupings, the composition of which depended on the situation.[18] When hunting and

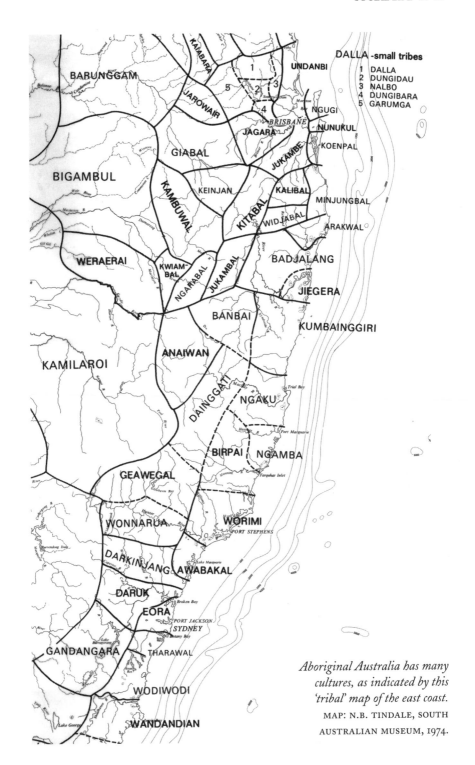

BARUNGGAM

KAIABARA

UNDANBI

DALLA -small tribes
1 DALLA
2 DUNGIDAU
3 NALBO
4 DUNGIBARA
5 GARUMGA

JAROWAIR

NGUGI

BRISBANE

JAGARA

NUNUKUL

KOENPAL

GIABAL

BIGAMBUL

KEINJAN

JUKAMBE

KALIBAL

MINJUNGBAL

KAMBUWAL

KITABAL

WIDJABAL

ARAKWAL

WERAERAI

KWIAM-BAL

NGARABAL

JUKAMBAL

BADJALANG

JIEGERA

BANBAI

KUMBAINGGIRI

KAMILAROI

ANAIWAN

DAINGGATI

NGAKU

BIRPAI

NGAMBA

GEAWEGAL

WONNARUA

WORIMI
PORT STEPHENS

DARKINJANG AWABAKAL

DARUK

EORA
PORT JACKSON
SYDNEY

GANDANGARA

THARAWAL

WODIWODI

WANDANDIAN

*Aboriginal Australia has many
cultures, as indicated by this
'tribal' map of the east coast.*
MAP: N.B. TINDALE, SOUTH
AUSTRALIAN MUSEUM, 1974.

gathering, Aboriginal people moved about in bands. These were formed around one or two older people and consisted of members from several clans or land-owning groups. Membership could change from time to time and bands were linked to other bands and wider groups through the sharing of some cultural characteristics. Each band had a hunting and gathering territory or range, which would normally take in the 'country' or estates of several clans. People usually had a range of rights to 'country', with some individuals having connections to land derived through four grandparents originally from widely dispersed groups. While the father's father's line was often favoured in determining rights to land, circumstances may mean that people activate rights to other countries, such as that belonging to their mother's mother.

Clan members were typically widely dispersed across the landscape. People sought marriage partners from other clans. Each band therefore had members from several clans, thereby legitimising their hunting and gathering activities over an extended area. For example, in the Kimberleys land ownership generally depended on descent rather than conception site or birthplace. A woman continued to be part of the land-owning clan of her father, even when living away with her husband's group.[19] In northern and Central Australia these relationships are still a lived reality for many Aboriginal people. In northeast Arnhem Land, the clan is identified with a particular language. A person's 'country' is a tract of land, or sometimes a set of sites, to which an individual has strong spiritual and historic connections that are recognised and given some legitimacy by the rest of their community.

For much of the twentieth century, the 'tribe' was considered by Europeans to be the main unit of Aboriginal cultures, where biological, cultural, political and linguistic identities were all thought to merge as one.[20] Some authors would describe a large group of related 'tribes' as a 'nation'. The problem with the 'tribe' concept is that it does not in fact describe the situation on the ground, with groups tending to come together in diverse ways with more complex links to the land usually based on the clans. When holding ceremonies, people from a large range of cultural backgrounds, sometimes including persons who speak different languages, do come together at one place. The term 'tribe' is usually used as a handy means of labelling large groups of Indigenous people formed on traditional lines, however we must look beyond this simplistic concept to appreciate the complex range of relationships that Aboriginal people have with the landscape.

Languages and Signals

Aboriginal people often choose language differences to discriminate between various groups with which they come into contact.[21] Land-owning groups may be identified by a particular language. The language of a person is commonly used to identify their 'tribe'. Nevertheless, members of a band may speak a variety of languages and dialects, because of population movements and through marriage practices that take clan members into other groups. Therefore, the recognised speech of the 'country' may not be the language that is generally spoken. Language differences between neighbouring groups may be slight or dialectal. For example, the Pitjant-jatjara dialect of the Western Desert language is named from the word they use for 'coming, be going somewhere', *pitjantja*.[22] This contrasts with words used for the same concept in other languages, such as *yankunytja* in Yankunytjatjara. The difference in vocabulary between these two dialects is slight, although there are much greater variations between the dialects of more distant people in the Western Desert. In spite of the difficulty of determining what makes a distinct language in many parts of Aboriginal Australia, linguists estimate that the number of languages in existence when Europeans arrived was somewhere between 150 to 650.[23] The most commonly accepted number is between 250 and 300 distinct languages, and probably twice as many dialects. Between eight and twelve of these languages were spoken in Tasmania.

Linguists recognise families of languages that have a common origin and are structurally similar in many respects, although not necessarily mutually intelligible. The majority of Australian languages, from Cape York Peninsula to Perth, appear to be related. Linguists suggest that they are part of one ancestral language family, known as Pama-Nyungan.[24] The name consists of two words for 'man': *pama* from Cape York Peninsula and *nyunga* from near Perth. The four languages in Australia with the largest number of contemporary speakers are from this group: Western Desert (includes Pitjantjatjara spoken in the Musgrave Ranges), Warlpiri (Tanami Desert), Mabuyag (Western Torres Strait) and Arrernte (various dialects in the Macdonnell Ranges/Finke River system). A large number of languages in northern Australia, from the Kimberley to the western Gulf of Carpentaria, are sufficiently different to be called Non-Pama-Nyungan. Nevertheless, at a broad level there is some relationship between all Australian languages, with most of them having forms for 'I' that begin with *ng*, such as in the widespread form *ngali*. The reason there may not be a single proto-Australian language from which all modern forms derive might be because the ancestors of the Australian Aboriginal people came in multiple waves spread over thousands of years. Given the amount of change a language undergoes within even the span of a thousand years, and the great antiquity of human occupation in Australia the origins of Aboriginal languages are difficult to determine.

None of the Australian languages can be described as primitive, as all of them were, and in some cases still are, highly developed means of communicating complex ideas and concepts relevant to the social and physical environment. As a unique code for interpreting the cultural landscape the complete loss of any language is a tragedy. As cultural changes occur, the language is pushed into new directions. For instance, many Aboriginal languages originally did not have terms for a numbering system beyond five, limited to the fingers on each hand, although if they had to, Aboriginal people could count higher in multiples of five. Nevertheless, the ability to count like Europeans was rapidly gained when a new economic system was imposed.[25]

In addition to the spoken forms of language, Aboriginal people utilise body language like everyone else. There are also sign languages and other signals used on secret occasions during particular ceremonies and rituals. In the case of sign language, a non-Aboriginal person must learn these subtle messages in order to be part of a conversation between Aboriginal people. Hand signals, often described in Aboriginal English as 'finger talk', are used when communicating with speakers of foreign languages and when speaking orally is not practical or allowed.[26] For example, in 1853 it was recorded by Alfred W. Howitt that seventeen Wirangu-speaking people from the arid region far west of Lake Torrens in South Australia travelled to Elder Range to the east near Wilpena Pound in order to find drinking water:

> Here they fell in with the Arkaba blacks, who received them very kindly and hospitably for about a fortnight, when the appearance of rain induced the visitors to take departure homewards. They did not understand a word of each other's language, and it was merely by gestures that they managed to communicate with each other.[27]

In 1897 anthropologist Walter Roth described 198 different hand signs used by Aboriginal people in north-western Queensland, and there were probably many more.[28] These signals covered terms for categories of people, various plants and animals, artefacts and some basic nouns and verbs, and allowed for silent conversations to take place. For the Warlpiri and Warumungu people of Central Australia, hand signs are numerous and elaborate enough to be considered an auxiliary language.[29]

There are numerous social situations that favour the use of sign language. Aboriginal men use hand signals during hunting trips to indicate the identity, direction and behaviour of animals sighted, when any noise would disturb game.[30] There is also an element of politeness involved in the use of hand and body movements; information conveyed in this manner removes the need for shouting across a crowded camp. In other situations, it also removes the need for some speaking. As I quickly discovered during my early Central Australian fieldwork, desert people possess distinctive hand movements that they use as car passengers to indicate preferred speed and direction to the driver in relation to obstacles on the road. In some ceremonial occasions, categories of people that are not allowed to communicate directly with each other often still speak via their hands. Furthermore, during the night people will use hand signals and other motions to silently alert others to the presence of malignant spirits roaming around about the camp.

Aboriginal people also use smoke signals to give neighbours advanced warnings of the movements of widely dispersed groups. A group will send out a signal to other bands to tell them in which part of the landscape they were camping. Smoke signals are also used to bring larger groups together and for seeking permission to visit. Some Europeans have suggested that different forms of rising smoke stacks were a code.[31] However, more reliable reports suggest an open system of interpretation, with the messages conveyed tending to be ones that were agreed beforehand between the sender and receiver. Alfred W. Howitt gave the following account for the Yuin people of a coastal New South Wales region:

> To communicate with friends at a distance a sheet of bark would be rolled up and stuffed full of bark and leaves. Being then set on fire to at the bottom and held straight up, a column of smoke ascended into the air. They preferred this to a hollow tree, but in either case the signal would have to be arranged for beforehand, so as to be understood.[32]

The American archaeologist Richard A. Gould described a similar event witnessed during his Western Desert fieldwork in the 1960s. It was prearranged among the hunting and gathering party Gould was following that a woman who had been sent off alone would send a smoke signal if she found ripe fruit among sand dunes to the north.[33] If she found none, then there would be no signal. In the event, the smoke was seen in the distance and interpreted as meaning that the rest of the party should go over and gather the food. Similarly, in the Moreton Bay district of Queensland, a fire was commonly used to announce the arrival of visitors.[34] Aboriginal hunters and gatherers are constantly alert for all types of signs in their environment. Camping places are often chosen on the basis of their view of the horizon, which allows the band the best position to observe smoke from campfires and deliberate vegetation burnings, and thereby follow the movement of other groups.

Children

In Aboriginal Australia, people progress through various life stages, with some transitions being highly formalised. Infants are often encouraged to speak by using a simplified form of the local language called 'baby talk' in Aboriginal English. Children are kept on the breast until three or even five years after birth. Prolonged breastfeeding helps keep down the birth rate. Mothers and other female kin generally look after all the children, until the time of their initiation.[35] All children are treated with much indulgence. Food and social taboos are not enforced and apart from when extremely rude to elders, the children are rarely scolded. After living and working with Aboriginal people for several years, the anthropologist Donald Thomson claimed: 'Childhood among the Australian Aborigines is the happiest time of their lives.'[36]

Play is a universal aspect of human life. Each culture has its own set of games, some of them unique. While play serves as entertainment and a means by which children begin to learn how to socialise, among hunters and gatherers there are also survival skills to be learned. Many of the amusements for children have an educative function as well. Aboriginal children play with toys that involve spinning, rolling, floating, blowing, rattling and throwing using spinning tops, marbles, small watercraft, whistles, rattles and projectiles.[37] Children also play house, with small

*Arrernte women holding a baby in a wooden cradle. Caring for babies and small
children is the responsibility of several female relatives.* PHOTO: F.J. GILLEN &
W.B. SPENCER, ALICE SPRINGS, NORTHERN TERRITORY, 1895.

shelters and in some areas with clay breasts to feed babies. Women and girls
use their fingers or fork-shaped sticks for illustrating stories in the sand.
Similarly, women use string games or 'cats-cradles', to help illustrate stories
that provide details of the landscape and the life within it. Examples of
string toys in the South Australian Museum include two men fighting, a
spider, turtles mating on a log, a yam, a perentie lizard and a fishing net. In
the desert, young boys practise 'play about' ceremonies during the evenings,
in preparation for their participation in adult ceremonies after their initiation, at about sixteen.[38]

The adults make small versions of weapons and gathering implements
for use by children. Youngsters are taught to track from an early age. A male
child following his father on a short hunting trip would be taught to
recognise the tracks of animals and the prints of individuals in their group.
A toy that was once widely played with by boys and men in Australia and
the Pacific, but rarely used now, was a play-stick, known in many Aboriginal languages as either a *wit-wit* or *kukuru*.[39] The players hurled the
play-stick, either underarm or overarm and it would bounce off the ground
or through the grass. The aim of the game was to cover the longest
distance. The *wit-wit* was sometimes thrown over 350 metres. In southern

Boys throwing toy spears at bark targets. Although playing, the skills they develop are important for adult life. PHOTO: N.B. TINDALE, WARBURTON RANGES, WESTERN AUSTRALIA, 1935.

Australia, another group game was football. The ball was generally made of strips of possum skin tightly rolled around a folded up piece and stitched together with sinews, although the scrotum of an 'old-man' kangaroo was also used.[40] The aim was to retain possession, with the participants organised into two opposing teams, based on social connections—kin class, totem, or country. Other games developed skills in throwing spears. Youths in the Western Desert and Kimberley regions cut a bark disk from a tree and threw spears at it while it rolled along the ground. In the southern coastal regions, a sponge was rolled as a target.[41] All of these action games exercised children and sharpened vital skills they would require as adults.

Rites of Passage

Initiation ceremonies mark the transition of young Aboriginal people from childhood freedom to adult responsibility and prepare them for greater participation in the ritual life of the culture.[42] In Aboriginal English the process is referred to as 'make him a young man' or 'put through the Law'. In general for the initiates it involves some level of estrangement from previous friends and relatives. Having gone through these particular 'rites

Bark target used during spear throwing practice. COLLECTED BY N.B. TINDALE, ERNABELLA, SOUTH AUSTRALIA, 1933.

of passage', people gain more authority in their community, as well as more obligations and responsibilities, including marriage. In most Aboriginal societies both boys and girls go through some form of initiation ritual, although initiation is generally more prolonged for males. The structure of the ceremonies varies from region to region, sometimes involving operations upon the body. For instance, the decorative scarring of the body and upper arms was formerly common throughout Australia, and publicly signified the adult status of both men and women.[43] The scarring, which was often incorrectly termed 'tattooing' by Europeans, was not obligatory, with people able to refuse it. In some parts of Australia, scarring implied membership of a particular group of people. Although no longer widely practised, Aboriginal people from these regions are able to recognise their kinsmen in old museum photographs through the body scarring patterns. Scarification could also indicate mourning for close relatives.

Initiations usually proceed in stages occurring over several years, each with different markers. Initiation status could be indicated through knocking out the front tooth, removing part of the little finger and nose-boring to hold a bone ornament.[44] Today, senior Aboriginal custodians regard the details of some of the other operations upon the body as too culturally sensitive to talk about openly. The roles of community members during the ceremony are dictated by kinship, and immediate relatives, in particular the parents, may not have direct input into such events. Once initiated, Aboriginal people are taught to see the landscape in a new more informed way. Privately, initiated men refer to each other by personal names that may refer to Dreamings and associated places. These names are given at the time of their initiation ceremonies.[45] Through the possession of greater knowledge, the connections between places and Dreaming stories are given a heightened meaning.

Aboriginal people believe that the individuality of a person's spirit ends at death, with the totemic essence merging with the Dreaming Ancestors who are embedded in the landscape.[46] The mortal component of the spirit is considered to remain hovering around the place of death and taking comfort from the depth of sorrow of its living kinsmen. This part of the soul is considered to eventually fade, or as the Western Arrernte people of Central Australia believe, to be extinguished by lightning.[47] In some remote communities today, female relatives of the deceased show their grief through wailing, gashing their heads, painting their faces white and cutting off their hair, while the men of certain kin relationships slash their thighs with knives.[48] In parts of northern and Central Australia, older women

Aboriginal women in many areas painted themselves white to show they were mourning for a deceased relative.
WATERCOLOUR: G. FRENCH ANGAS,
MURRAY RIVER, SOUTH AUSTRALIA, 1844.

have closely shaved heads to indicate mourning. In the past, this practice was encouraged by the need for human hair to make ritual objects when mourning the death of close relatives. Most deaths, excepting those of the elderly or very young, were considered to be caused by sorcerers, and inquests were often held to determine the person or persons believed responsible for the death.

Aboriginal mourning ceremonies are often elaborate affairs that last over many months.[49] It would be incorrect to see these ceremonies as primarily involving the disposal of the dead. As well as ensuring the spirits of the deceased are directed into the afterworld, mourning ceremonies are occasions to acknowledge the Dreaming Ancestors and to re-establish the social order. In many parts of Australia, the body of the deceased goes through stages involving two burials, with the final resting place being a site directly related to their Dreaming Ancestor.[50]

Gender, Age and Taboos

The contribution of women to all areas of the life of hunters and gatherers in Australia was not often fully recognised by the first European recorders. When it was mentioned in the historical accounts, the role of female gatherers tended to be characterised as secondary to that of male hunters. For example, in 1841 the German missionary Christian G. Teichelmann stated that when the Kaurna people of the Adelaide Plains were travelling: '. . . the men start first, carrying nothing but a small net bag and hunting implements—the women, burdened like camels, follow, gather & prepare on the road vegetable food for the night, whilst the men are looking out for meat . . .'[51] Similarly the amateur anthropologist Daisy Bates described the lot of Aboriginal women in pitiful terms. In Aboriginal society, she claimed, 'There is no glorification of maternity, no reverence of woman as woman, in the dark mind of the aboriginal.'[52] Such accounts have generally taken gender division much too far by suggesting that in all aspects of Aboriginal cultures women were subordinate to men. Early recorders of Aboriginal life thought that Aboriginal women were also 'inferior' to Aboriginal men in the area of sacred knowledge.[53] This opinion was undoubtedly attributable largely to the patriarchal society that the writers came from, and in part to the views of the male Aboriginal informants themselves. The portrayal of Aboriginal men as 'violent brutes' and women as abject 'pawns' or 'slaves' was a major humanitarian argument used by missionaries who wanted to modify or reject pre-European Aboriginal society.[54]

Female anthropologists have corrected many of the earlier assumptions about the position of women in Aboriginal society. Catherine Berndt, who with her husband Ronald Berndt, worked all over Australia, warned that it is wrong to assume that the labour of women was completely subordinate to that of the men.[55] She considered that hunting and gathering was a cooperative enterprise. The responsibilities of women were significant, being the major food providers on a daily basis and the main carers of children. Nevertheless, there would have been time for cultural activities for women too. The anthropologist, Phyllis M. Kaberry, who, in the eastern Kimberley, made the first major anthropological contribution to establishing the status of Aboriginal women in their society, wrote: 'It is true the woman provides the large part of the meal, but one must not automatically assume that her work is more onerous. Actually it is less so than the men's, as I can speak from experience.'[56]

In spite of the gender division of food production, most categories of food can be procured by either sex if an opportunity presents itself. When camped at one place, the women set off daily with their children to gather food, comprising plants, small burrowing animals and in some regions, shellfish. The men generally forage separately from the women. Groups of women and children, who are away from the camp gathering food, generally avoid all contact with men. Male members of the band are often away several days while seeking wide-ranging game species, such as emu and kangaroo, although these activities are generally undertaken less frequently than women's gathering. The male and female economic roles in Aboriginal communities are therefore separate, but nevertheless highly complementary. With the bulk of the food gathered by women, wife-obtaining practices, both through 'sister' exchange and 'stealing', have important economic consequences in terms of labour supply for the band.

Gender has a major impact on cultural prohibitions, commonly called 'taboos'. For example, among the Pitjantjatjara of southern Central Australia, men alone hunt and fight with spears, with no females, apart from young children, being allowed to touch or even to pretend to throw a spear.[57] Here, it is the work of the men to make all wooden implements, except the digging-stick, which women make themselves. The symbols of the spear and digging-stick are often used to depict men and women in Central Australian art. Similarly, in the Lower Murray of South Australia women avoided particular large trees that were ritually consulted by men before hunting commenced.[58] The trees were therefore treated as dangerous by the women, although the knowledge of their existence and purpose was not kept secret. The extreme separation of the male and female realms ('men's business' and 'women's business') is a distinctive characteristic in parts of the Central Australian and Kimberley regions.[59] Nevertheless, for much of the rest of Australia, there is a large degree of publicly acknowledged sharing of ceremonial knowledge and practice between men and women, even when there is gender division in the performance of some rituals.[60]

In many parts of Australia, the division of secret sacred aspects of Aboriginal ritual and ceremony is predominantly according to age and knowledge rather than gender. Older people in Aboriginal society are regarded as reserves of important knowledge concerning the Dreaming and the physical resources of the landscape. By virtue of their survival experience, older people in a society are often considered to have immense spiritual power. This gives elders considerable authority over younger people.

Taboos are applied in many circumstances and not just in relation to gender. In Aboriginal Australia periodic restrictions are put on the use of certain words, such as the name of a dead person, which is completely avoided until a lengthy period after their death. This was not just out of respect for the deceased, but because of the need to leave the spirit behind in peace. Alternative terms are used in this case, or at least a gloss. Writing of South Australia in 1847, the early traveller and watercolourist George French Angas noted: 'When an individual dies, they carefully avoid mentioning his name; but if compelled to do so, they pronounce it in a very low whisper, so faint that they imagine the spirit cannot hear their voice.'[61] Likewise in 1837 the convict-explorer turned police constable Jorgen Jorgenson noted that among Tasmanians, 'Nothing could offend an Aborigine so much as to speak of or inquire about his dead friends or relations.'[62] This taboo sometimes leads to the names of living people being periodically avoided or possibly even changed altogether. As some of these names are based on plant and animal terms, these are also temporarily changed. The Pitjantjatjara people, for example, use the name *Kunmanara* for anyone who shares the name of a deceased individual, and *kunmanu* for a shared object name, until a suitable mourning period is over.[63] Aboriginal people did not tend to give personal names to their babies until they had grown to walking age, through fear of spirits finding them and stealing the newborn away.[64] In this case, kinship terms would be used instead.

Part II

MATERIALS *of* CULTURE

Four

Hunting *and* Gathering

European observers have in the past considered that Australian Aboriginal people had a passive relationship with the environment. It was thought that they responded in an ad hoc manner to whatever resources were found, aimlessly roaming about the landscape waiting to see what each season would bring them by way of food and resources. One of the first Europeans to encounter Australian Aboriginal people was William Dampier, who visited the Kimberley coast of northern Australia in 1688. He thought them to be worse off than the Hottentots he had seen in the Cape Colony of southern Africa. Dampier stated that the Indigenous people of New Holland (Australia) were 'the miserablest People in the World . . . They have no Houses, or Skin Garments, Sheep, Poultry, Fruits of the Earth, Ostrich Eggs, &c . . .'[1] In 1770, James Cook reached a similar conclusion: 'They seem to have no fixed habitation, but move about from place to place like wild beasts in search of Food, and, I believe, depend wholly upon the Success of the present day for their Subsistence.'[2] From the point of view of Europeans who liked well-ordered urban and rural landscapes, early visitors, such as Dampier and Cook, considered the new continent to be a wild and unsettled place, and to British eyes, 'terra nullius', without legal owners.[3]

In spite of these European perceptions, the Australian landscape was already humanised before British colonists arrived. To Aboriginal Australians it was full of cultural and social meaning, and it had been physically altered by them through millennia of hunting and gathering practices. Aboriginal use and perception of the landscape was according to patterns developed through long occupation, only now being appreciated by European researchers.

Aboriginal Population

To develop a geographical backdrop to study Aboriginal occupancy, it is necessary to consider the Australian landscape and climate. In spite of their shared history as part of a combined landmass, the regions of New Guinea and Australia differ geographically in major ways. New Guinea is an island spread over 2250 kilometres along an east-to-west axis and at its widest north to south is over 670 kilometres. It is mountainous, with a range of tropical environments. Australia is the smallest of the world's continents, extending about 4000 kilometres east to west from the Pacific to the Indian Oceans, and about 3700 kilometres north to south from the Torres Strait to the southern tip of Tasmania. Unlike New Guinea, Australia is a land of generally low relief. Some of the land surfaces, particularly in the west, form part of the oldest landmasses to be found anywhere on the planet. The northern third of Australia sits beyond the Tropic of Capricorn, where the monsoonal weather belt produces a wet summer and a relatively dry winter. The eastern seaboard is reasonably wet due to the presence of the Great Dividing Range. To the west of the mountains, the Murray–Darling River system drains 910,000 square kilometres and at this size can be compared to the Danube of Europe and the Indus of Pakistan, although it carries a much smaller volume of water to the sea. In the south, the Australian and Tasmanian coastlines front the Southern Ocean. Here, the anticyclonic weather belt generates rainfall that predominantly falls during the winter months, resulting in a temperate climate.

The dry interior of Australia, dominated by the Western and Central Deserts, covers two-thirds of the continent. Large areas of the desert region are covered by sand dunes that extend in parallel arrays. Rainfall in the interior relies on storms originating from either of the two major weather belts. Rainfall is unpredictable throughout the central region, resulting in little or no rain in some years and floods in others. There have been times since the ancestors of the Aboriginal people first arrived in Australia when the deserts have been much wetter. Presently the inland region is arid, with some drainage systems, such as that centred on Lake Eyre, having no outlet to the coast and for the most part a land surface below sea level.

We will never know the size of the entire Aboriginal population as it was in 1788 when the British settlers first arrived in Australia. Apart from an unknown number of people living in remote regions beyond the frontier, many of the early official Australian census reports did not even list Aboriginal people, as they were not considered to be full citizens until 1967. Early colonial officials were confused over the size of the Indigenous population, which was nomadic and in decline through European diseases and frontier conflict. For instance, in 1845 the explorer and Aboriginal Protector on the Murray River Edward J. Eyre remarked:

> . . . there is scarcely any point connected with the subject of the
> Aborigines of New Holland, upon which it is more difficult to
> found an opinion, even approximating to the truth, than that of
> the aggregate population of the continent, or the average number
> of persons to be found in any given space.[4]

Estimates for the whole of Australia range from the conservative 250,000 to more speculative figures of over a million people. In the early twentieth century, anthropologists estimated the total population of pre-European Australia as about 300,000, or one person for every 19 square kilometres across the continent.[5] Actual population numbers of course would have varied with the area. In higher rainfall areas less space was required to sustain populations (1.25 to 8 square kilometres per person in Arnhem Land) than in arid regions (31 to 88 square kilometres per person in Central Australia). The former convict and later a policeman in Tasmania Jorgen Jorgensen estimated that there would have been from 2000 to 3000 Aboriginal Tasmanians before Europeans arrived, although the archaeologist Rhys Jones puts the figure at between 3000 and 5000, which means one person to every 13.5 to 22 square kilometres.[6] The coastal and riverine areas of Aboriginal Australia tended to have the highest number of people. South-eastern Australia is particularly rich in such environments.

The density of hunters and gatherers was not just subject to the availability of food; there were also cultural factors that would have limited population size.[7] Inter-group conflict and accidents all had an impact on keeping the Aboriginal population levels down.[8] Many children suffered fatal burns from rolling into fires made for night-time warmth. Aboriginal mobility favoured smaller populations, leading to infanticide and possibly senilicide during times of severe physical stress in extreme environments.[9] The capability of the land to support people is ultimately determined during its harshest cycles, such as droughts and floods. There is still no total population figure that is readily accepted by all scholars for Aboriginal populations when Europeans first arrived.

Food and Medicine

Aboriginal hunters and gatherers limited their short-term impact upon the landscape through dispersing themselves thinly and by constantly moving according to season. Although they were nomadic, there are documented cases of Aboriginal people actively assisting in the long-term production of food. For instance, the Yugumbir people of south-eastern Queensland collected edible marine cobra worms (a molluscan borer) from waterlogged timber before throwing the wood back into the sea for next season's worms to grow and multiply in.[10] At Port Lincoln in South Australia, Aboriginal people took care not to destroy nests of food species of bird.[11] Aboriginal people also replanted undersized tubers and other plant fragments to encourage the growth of food. Aboriginal people on the west coast of Australia in the late nineteenth century were known to 'invariably re-insert the head of the yams so as to be sure of a future crop'.[12] A similar practice was recorded of the women of Flinders Island in north-eastern Queensland.[13] At Sunbury in Victoria there once existed numerous mounds that were caused by the 'accidental gardening' that occurred while Aboriginal people gathered *murnong* (yam daisy).[14] The gatherers would have realised the effect they were having on the numbers of edible roots in the ground. When I was working with elderly Aboriginal people of the southeast of South Australia during the 1980s, one species of yam was described to me as having a main '*pakanu* [grandfather] potato', which was taken for eating, and 'grannies [grand children]', which were left for the next year. Digging would have assisted in the dispersal and replanting of undersized tubers for future collecting, as well as helped prepare the soil for plant growth.

There are two main categories of food recognised by Aboriginal people: animal and vegetable, described in the Western Desert language as *kuka* and *mai* respectively.[15] A similar distinction exists in many other Aboriginal languages, including Wik-Ngathan spoken in north-western Cape York, where animal foods, including eggs, are termed *minh*, while all vegetable food is *kuthel*.[16] The number of food species used by Aboriginal people across Australia was immense in comparison to the foods brought to the country by the first Europeans. Nevertheless both animal and plant foods are highly seasonal. In some areas the proportion of animal food in the overall diet varies through the year from being a major source to a minor one. Meat sources include insects, crustaceans, shellfish, fish, reptiles, birds and mammals. Aboriginal people utilise a wide variety of plant parts: fruits, seeds, nuts, sporocarps (seed-like growths from ferns), foliage, stems, galls, gums, roots, rhizomes, tubers and fungi.[17] When available, animal food would be generally preferred, over more reliable plant food sources, which are either less palatable or more time-consuming to prepare.[18]

An Arrernte woman with her child, balancing a food-collecting dish on her head and holding a digging stick. A woman might spend most days like this with her local group, collecting food and caring for children. PHOTO: F.J. GILLEN & W.B. SPENCER, MACDONNELL RANGES, NORTHERN TERRITORY, 1896.

The seasonal abundance of food sources allowed for a surplus to be produced for trade and provided an opportunity for visitors to come to share in feasts. Due to their economic and social importance—in facilitating trade and attracting significant visiting groups—Aboriginal people actively managed and protected these resources. For instance, individual wattle trees that exuded large quantities of edible gum during the warmer seasons were claimed as the property of particular Aboriginal families in western Victoria.[19] In southern Queensland and northern New South Wales, the seasonal availability of the nut from the bunya pine (*Araucaria bidwillii*) brought in Aboriginal groups from a wide area to hold ceremonies.[20] Plant foods had an importance that went beyond subsistence; as well as being traded they were planned for, as Aboriginal hunters and gatherers negotiated the landscape in order to make most of the surplus food when it came into season.

The role of the Australian dog, known in Australian English as the dingo and warrigal, as a hunting aide for Aboriginal people has been a matter of some debate.[21] The dingo arrived in Australia between 4000 and 3500 years ago. Its distribution is restricted to mainland Australia, its access to Tasmania cut off by rising of sea levels about 10,000 years ago. From many accounts the dingo does not appear to have been used extensively for hunting, but was certainly kept as a pet and hunted as a food source. Tamed dingoes kept the camp clean and provided warmth to people during the night. They also provided their owners with a warning of approaching strangers and were believed to keep bad spirits away at night. The dingo was described by P. Beveridge in 1883 as:

> . . . used for the running down of game, and although not particularly speedy, are found useful in following wounded animals not sufficiently maimed to allow of their being easily overtaken by the hunters. In the cold nights also these animals are of singular good service, as they tend in no inconsiderable degree to keep up the temperature . . .[22]

In the arid zone, wild dingoes performed a service to Aboriginal people by locating and digging open water soakages.[23] It is likely that the use of the dingo for hunting in many areas was secondary to their roles as blanket, cleaner, pet and a source of meat.

Although in some areas the dingo appears to have been a useful companion to Aboriginal people, this was not universal across Australia. The biologist and anthropologist Donald Thomson claimed:

From my experience I am confident that few if any Dingoes live very long in native camps. Nor are those that are captured as a rule ever very strong dogs. They are generally taken when very young. Most of them that I have seen are weak and emaciated . . . The natives assure me that most of the Dingoes that they have captured go bush when they grow up. I am convinced, from my own experience of the rarity of real Dingoes even in remote camps in the interior of eastern Arnhem land, of the truth of this fact.[24]

After a day of hunting and gathering, food was brought back to the main camp for the rest of the band. Although the foraging groups in most cases would have eaten some food during the day, there were other people who may have stayed behind at camp. Older people in the group controlled the distribution of food, and kinship obligations were important in determining the way in which food was shared. Daisy Bates reported the division of kangaroo meat in the Swan River district of the southwest of Western Australia on occasions she was there:

The leg and hind quarter was the portion of the *yogga biderr* (old grandmother of some influence) belonging to the family of the hunter. The hunter kept the forequarter for his family. The tail and part of the back were given to the relations-in-law, the thigh was given to 'uncles', the back and entrails to the grandparents. The hunter did not divide the game he had caught, he usually handed it over to his father or some older relative to distribute.[25]

Some Arnhem Land paintings in rock shelters and on bark are lined to show how various animals were butchered. Reporting on Aborigines of Port Lincoln in South Australia, C. Wilhelmi recorded that in general the game was divided up so that the men ate the adult male animals, the women ate adult female animals and children ate small animals.[26] In this way, the hunting success was spread within the group, although not necessarily evenly. At most times, Aboriginal people ate very well, using a wide variety of foods with a heavy reliance upon plants. Apart from periods of hardship, such as those brought on by prolonged drought and disease epidemics, it is likely that in 1788 the Aboriginal people were generally far healthier than were the newly arrived British colonists in Sydney.

When they did get sick, however, Aboriginal people had, and in some

Warlpiri men using the adze on the handle of a spearthrower to help butcher a cooked kangaroo carcass on a bed of leaves. PHOTO: N.B. TINDALE, COCKATOO CREEK, NORTHERN TERRITORY, 1931.

regions still have, complex systems of medical practices, diagnoses and remedies to refer to. These derive from their understanding of medicine and the 'Law' (see chapter 2), and often link behaviour to injury and illness.[27] Aboriginal healers have considerable social standing in their community. Resolution of sickness and apportioning blame for injuries often involves rules of revenge and punishment. Healers use specialised ritual equipment and wear various ornaments and clothing that make them stand apart from others in their community. The healers are not always men, and particular women are also recognised by their community as midwives.[28] The properties of Aboriginal medicines are sometimes analysable by pharmacologists.[29] Scientific research into the Aboriginal pharmacopoeia has turned up several remedies worthy of more development. Nevertheless, the effectiveness of some Indigenous 'medicines' is related more to the powers of the Dreaming than to chemical properties alone. An individual can appeal to totemic Ancestors or spirit familiars in order to combat an illness brought on by bad spirits or sorcery, or due to breaking the Dreaming 'Law'. The role of the healer, sometimes called a 'clever man', is particularly important in sorting out illness considered to be from these causes. Many Aboriginal people still use their traditional medicines to supplement European methods of treatment. [30]

To Aboriginal people, certain pigments have spiritual powers. Ritually, red ochre is associated with the blood of humans and of the Ancestors, being a symbol of fertility, regrowth and power.[31] During initiations, novices are sometimes smeared with red ochre to herald a symbolic death and their passage from the world of children to that of adults.[32] Their grieving mothers might cover themselves in white pipeclay as a sign that they are in mourning for their children. In parts of Victoria, powdered red ochre was mixed with fat and applied to burns with a swab of animal fur; it was also stirred into a solution of boiled wattle bark for treatment of other skin disorders.[33] Aboriginal people placed much faith in the spiritual essences in ochre. For instance, during the early years of European settlement in South Australia, it was reported that a deaf and dumb Aboriginal man and another who suffered from palsy were being kept completely covered with a mixture of red ochre and fat as a form of treatment.[34] From time to time, while in the course of my work at the South Australian Museum, Aboriginal people have requested certain types of ochre from the collections, particularly material from recognised mythological sites, in order to treat a sick relative in an Adelaide hospital. I also know people who use smoke from campfires to purify others they believe have come across a bad spirit, which may be causing bad luck during activities such as hunting and sport. Smoke is thought to drive away bad spirits.

Plant-based narcotics and stimulants were used extensively across Australia to relieve pain and for ritual and recreational purposes. In Central Australia, bags of the narcotic *pituri* ('pitcheri', *Duboisia hopwoodii*) were highly prized as trade items.[35] Although the plant is common in the arid zone, the main *pituri* plants that were harvested

Woven vegetable-fibre string bag used to carry the narcotic, pituri, *for trade.*
H. DUTTON COLLECTION, LAKE EYRE BASIN, SOUTH AUSTRALIA, AROUND 1900.

came from the Mulligan River area in south-western Queensland. After it was dried over a fire, the *pituri* was broken down into fine fragments for personal use or trade. It was mixed with alkaline wattle ash to make a biscuit, known in Australian English as a 'quid' or 'plug'. These were repeatedly chewed, and kept behind the ear or stored in a pouch when not being used. For trading purposes *pituri* was packaged into bags woven from string or made from marsupial skin. The trade in *pituri* was extensive, covering the Lake Eyre Basin region and across western Queensland. In the collections of the South Australian Museum there is a red cloth bag of *pituri* that was traded from Cooper Creek near the Queensland/South Australian border ending up at Quorn in the southern Flinders Ranges, a distance of over 700 kilometres away.[36]

Managing Resources

In Australia, there is much historical evidence to show that Aboriginal people actively harnessed the resources of the environment. Coastal and riverine zones were sometimes modified for fishing, as noted by William Dampier in 1688. Dampier described stone fish traps in use by the Bardi people of Karrakatta Bay, north of Broome on the Kimberley coast.[37] The use of such fish traps was widespread across Australia. Although many have been destroyed, examples can still be seen in the Darling River at Brewarrina, in central New South Wales.[38] In the late 1830s, an early South Australian colonist observed fish traps in the creeks of the eastern escarpment of the Mount Lofty Ranges. He described their operation by the Aboriginal people who 'build a dam into the river, high enough to let about a foot [31 cm] of water stream over it. Because of this dam, the fish in their run must come close to the surface of the water, where the savages stand in readiness to spear them.'[39]

In coastal zones, weirs of brushwood constructed at creek mouths caught fish left by receding tides.[40] Many museums have large wicker baskets from northern Australia which have an entrance funnel which operated like that of a European crayfish pot, letting fish in but preventing their exit. These fish traps were strategically placed in mangrove inlets or tidal creeks to catch fish returning to the sea with an outgoing tide. At Martin Well near the Coorong in South Australia, Aboriginal people constructed drains 100 metres in length to contain small fish.[41] Here, the fish were easily netted in fine close-mesh nets. There were even larger trench constructions at Lake Condah in western Victoria, which were to encourage eels from the swamps.[42] By modifying the flow of water, Aboriginal people could control the movement of fish and make them easier to catch. In Aboriginal Australia, fish poisons made from plants were widely used in lagoons and other relatively small bodies of water.[43] The poisoned fish were collected after they floated to the surface.

Aboriginal people also stored surplus food for their future use. In the McArthur River district of the southern Gulf of Carpentaria region, Yanyuwa people used the labour-intensive practice of grinding up cycad nuts and cooking large dampers.[44] This food was dried and used later during ceremonial events when large numbers of people converged at one place, most of the vistitors being unable to gather their own food each day. In parts of Central Australia, strips of kangaroo flesh were dried on hot stones for putting aside.[45] The skins of several species of *Solanum*, which Europeans call 'desert raisins' or 'bush tomatoes', were dried and skewered on sticks for later use, at which time they were soaked in water or ground into a paste.[46] Across the arid zone there was a widespread practice of storing excess grass seed.[47] In 1870 while Christopher Giles was engaged in the erection of the Overland Telegraph Line near the Finke River:

> . . . he came upon a depot of aboriginal property, consisting mainly of bags of these seeds [nardoo sporocarps] ready for grinding into flour for food. The seed, which was about 1cwt. [about 51 kg], was garnered in bags, some made from the legs of trousers, and others made from socks and the sleaves of shirts stolen from his party.[48]

In earlier times this food would have been stored in wooden bowls. Extra food, when properly prepared and contained, not only prolonged its availability, but also provided a surplus for engaging in trade.

Aboriginal people believe that in hunting and gathering they were involved in the same activities as their totemic Ancestors once engaged in. The anthropologist, T.G.H. Strehlow, recorded that in the mythology of the Northern Arrernte in Central Australia: 'The gurra [bandicoot man] ancestor hunts, kills, and eats bandicoots; and his sons are always engaged upon the same quest. The witchetty grub men of Lukara spend every day of their lives in digging up grubs from the roots of acacia trees.'[49] Their descendants hunted a wide variety of game.

Through ceremonies celebrating and re-enacting the actions of their Dreaming Ancestors, Aboriginal people help to maintain the abundance of economically important plants and animals. These ceremonies were sometimes called 'increase ceremonies' by early anthropologists.[50] Through their religion Aboriginal people have various other ways to spiritually maintain the environment. As Alfred W. Howitt related:

> There is a spot at Lake Victoria [= Lake Alexandrina], in the Narrinyeri [= Ngarrindjeri] country, where when the water is, at long intervals, exceptionally low, it causes a tree-stump to become visible. This is in charge of a family, and it is the duty of one of the men to anoint it with grease and red ochre. The reason for this is that they believe that if it is not done the lake would dry up and the supply of fish be lessened. This duty is hereditary from father to son.[51]

Aboriginal people believe that their resources will decline through any lack of observance towards rituals set down in the Dreaming. It was and is a source of sorrow and shame for particular totemic groups if the species for which they were responsible became rare or locally extinct.

Religious prohibitions protected some places through their spirit associations. In the McArthur River district of the southern Gulf of Carpentaria region, the Yanyuwa impose a ban on hunting in the country of a person recently dead, which also enables game in that country to increase in numbers.[52] Similarly, on the western side of the Gibson Desert in Western Australia, the Mardudjara people completely avoid Lake Disappointment, a large salt lake that becomes a haven for waterbirds after heavy rains, believing that it is the home of the Ngayunangalgu spirit beings, which live underground and will eat humans if they trespass in the area.[53] Hunting prohibitions near many of the totemic sites would have served to create refuges for certain game species. For instance, one ecologist in Central Australia noted that the red kangaroo was protected around certain Dreaming sites that happened to occur in some of the best habitats for this species.[54] Although this is not deliberate conservation, the mosaic of hunting and refuge areas in the landscape would have been of some benefit to the fauna that had temporarily been hunted out of other parts of their normal range. Aboriginal movement patterns in general, according to season and recent weather patterns, would also have helped soften the impact of their hunting and gathering activities upon the environment.

From the earliest European experiences of the Australian continent there has been concern about the spread of fires from deliberate or accidental lightings by Aboriginal people. One South Australian colonist reported of the Adelaide Hills during early February 1837 that 'the natives had set fire to the long dry grass to enable them more easily to obtain the animals and vermin on which a great part of their living depends'.[55] A local newspaper in 1839 recounted that an Aboriginal man named Williamy had been charged with firing the grass in the parklands of Adelaide. His release, it reported, was due to lack of proof of malicious intent, the authorities recognising that Aboriginal people considered it 'a necessary and laudable practice annually to burn off withered grass on their hunting-grounds to facilitate and hasten the growth of the young grass of which the native animals are so fond . . .'.[56] This was a major concession, given that it was then a capital offence back in England to light fires that destroyed property. A newspaper report from the Port Lincoln area of the lower Eyre Peninsula in 1841 stated: 'Independently of the danger which follows in the wake of a tribe of natives carrying fire-sticks through ripe grass, two or three feet high, they always set fire to scrubby places, whenever a small patch is found, in order to hunt.'[57] Similarly, European settlers in the southwest of Western Australia were concerned that Aboriginal practices of burning the vegetation to collect food were threatening their property.[58]

Aboriginal people also used fire to open up the country by removing the understorey to allow easier travelling and to promote the future growth of grass for game species. In the account of his exploring, Edward J. Eyre remarked at length on the wide open plains that he found to the north of Adelaide. He appears to have been puzzled by them, particularly when there were remnants of large growths of timber nearby. In other places, the dense mallee-type vegetation had pockets or grassy openings that to Eyre were like 'oases of the desert'. He suggested that 'the plains found interspersed among the dense scrubs may probably have been occasioned by fires, purposely or accidentally lighted by the natives in their wanderings'.[59] It is interesting to note that Eyre considered these grass plains to be an improvement on the dense mallee scrub, as they provided feed for his horses and were easier to traverse. Aboriginal people also preferred not to walk through dense prickly thickets if they could avoid it. And at least some of the plant foods eaten by Aboriginal people would have benefited from the opening of the understorey and the build up of ash produced from regular burnings.

Although some Aboriginal burnings were opportunistic and directed at flushing out game, others had more structure. Aboriginal people knew that they could manipulate the environment to produce food and actively used firing as a resource management tool.[60] The Yanyuwa of the southern Gulf of Carpentaria region burnt their hunting territories, the first fires starting in the early dry season.[61] Before starting a fire the permission of the traditional owner, determined by clan membership, was required. Indigenous Tasmanians deliberately burned the vegetation to convert closed rainforest vegetation into open sclerophyll forest.[62] They considered sclerophyll forest a better food-producing environment for them. Biologist Tim Flannery, has suggested that Australian hunters and gatherers in antiquity first took up burning practices when megafauna, such as Diprotodon, became extinct, in order to control the build up of the vegetation that was no longer being eaten by large herbivores.[63]

Fires caused by hunters and gatherers differed significantly from naturally occurring fires in terms of their seasonality, selectivity, frequency and intensity.[64] They also resulted in a mosaic pattern of differing types of vegetation on the land. Ecologists understand well how in many parts of the Australian bush the type of plants you find on a given spot depends, among other things, on the frequency of fires and how long it was since it last burned. The mosaic pattern, once lost, is difficult to reproduce. Animals such as the hare wallaby and bilby in Central Australia that are thought to depend on mosaic vegetation, are believed by some ecologists to have become almost extinct as a result of the cessation of Aboriginal burning practices. Frequent burning of small areas also created firebreaks. In Central Australia it has been claimed that the cessation of the Aboriginal burning regime has led to the eventual outbreak of more damaging fires.[65]

Archaeologist Rhys Jones has described Aboriginal manipulation of the environment through the use of fire as 'fire-stick farming'.[66] In using their ecological knowledge to deliberately bring about changes favourable to their hunting and gathering practices, Aboriginal people practised what has been termed by anthropologists 'proto-agriculture'. This kind of farming occurred not only with the use of fire. Aboriginal women digging in the 'yam grounds' would have promoted the future growth and spread of particular food plants, such as *murnong* yam daisies (*Microseris lanceolata*) in south-eastern Australia and *warran* yams (*Dioscorea hastifolia*) in the southwest of Western Australia, by dispersing tubers and trampling them into the loose soil.[67] The shell mounds of northern Queensland, created by the build-up of cooking-fire remains from Aboriginal camps, are places that favour the establishment of vine forests.[68] To Aboriginal people, the plant resources associated with the shell mounds include foods, medicines, and raw materials for artefact making and the construction of shelters.

A number of researchers have argued that the Aboriginal impact on the Australian environment over the tens of thousands of years they have dwelt here is such that there were few, if any, true wilderness areas left by the time Europeans arrived.[69] The Aboriginal hunting and gathering mode of living was fundamental to the creation of the Australian landscape that Europeans claimed in 1788.

Five

Aboriginal Artefacts

The objects that Aboriginal people make vary considerably from region to region, due to climate, topography, custom and the availability of materials. Many of the items of material culture discussed here—the tools, weapons, shelters and the like—at first glance appear 'simple'. However, closer investigation shows that they are made in many different regional styles using technologies well suited for the challenge posed by living in the variable Australian environment. The nomadic lifestyle of Aboriginal people means that the implements they carry are generally lightweight and few in number, in contrast to those of some sedentary horticulturalist societies in nearby Papua New Guinea. In some parts of Australia, such as the tip of Cape York Peninsula in north Queensland, Aboriginal people were well aware of many objects and practices used by people in Torres Strait and southern Papua further to the north—such as bows and arrows and horticulture—but did not adopt them as they would have hampered their own lifestyles. Although there is not one standard set of tools for the whole of the continent, there are broad regions within which Aboriginal people use similar types of artefacts.

Museums collectively contain many thousands of examples of Aboriginal tools. In spite of this abundance, every curator who has ever attempted to put on an exhibition of Australian Aboriginal culture will know that their collections are not unbiased surveys of Indigenous artefacts. There is a strong weighting towards more robust and spectacular-looking objects, such as the club, boomerang, spear and shield, at the expense of such things as fragile ornaments and the more mundane-looking digging-stick and fire-making apparatus. European collectors also neglected large objects, such as watercraft, harpoons, dugong nets and shelters, simply because of their size and awkwardness in storing them. Historical accounts of early European observers also tended to favour the interests of the observer, to the detriment of providing a balanced overview. These biases must be kept in mind when describing hunting and gathering practices from museum-based and historical sources of information. This chapter focuses on the material belongings of Aboriginal people, relying in large part on the artefacts of the South Australian Museum. It does not present an exhaustive list of the artefacts used, but concentrates on major object categories.

Hunting and Gathering Kit

In past Aboriginal Australia, women and men engaged in separate, but complementary, hunting and gathering activities. As a result, they used and saw their landscape differently. Women tended to move about in small groups during the day to gather food, while caring for babies and young children.[1] They generally concentrated on gathering food sources such as fruit and seeds from above the ground, and tubers, grubs, lizards and small mammals from underground. Men focused on hunting highly mobile game, such as kangaroos, wallabies, emus, ducks, crocodiles and turtles. Women, therefore provided much of the required daily food, while men concentrated on less predictable food sources, such as meat from larger animals, brought in after successful hunting expeditions.

Digging-sticks

The digging-stick was an essential item in a woman's daily food-gathering kit. In colloquial Australian English digging-sticks are sometimes referred to as 'yam-sticks'. They were made from wood and were generally between 40 centimetres and a metre in length. Their bevelled or pointed ends were especially useful in digging out water soakages in sandy country and for keeping soakages clear of debris.

Arrernte family in front of a bough shelter, with a woman grinding seed and a man smoothing a spear shaft. Men and women had different but complementary roles.
PHOTO: F.J. GILLEN & W.B. SPENCER, MACDONNELL RANGES, NORTHERN TERRITORY, 1896.

Digging-sticks could also be used as clubs and jabbing spears when fighting, or for threshing edible seeds from branches. They were made by using adzes and scrapers on hardwood such as eucalypt or acacia.[2] Aboriginal women always carried their personal digging-stick when leaving camp to hunt and gather. Donald Thomson claimed that among the Pintupi people of the Western Desert 'The digging-stick is regarded as a woman's own personal property—an individual possession—and would not normally be borrowed or used by another woman.'[3] The digging end of the tool was kept ground to a fine edge and care was taken not to chip it. In Western Desert dot paintings a woman is often symbolised by the *wana*, a large wooden digging-stick.

Containers

Being nomadic Aboriginal people required a means of carrying their belongings. In Australian English, Aboriginal carry bags and sometimes baskets are generally called 'dilly bags'. This is based upon the Aboriginal word from the Jagara language of the Brisbane area: *dili*, meaning a bag made from grass.[4] In southern Australia, bags were sometimes made from kangaroo and wallaby skins turned inside out and stitched up at the neck and limb openings. These could carry both water to camp or loose plant material, such as the *pituri* narcotic, for trading. In the Flinders Ranges, Adnyamathanha men used the skin of a kangaroo scrotum for carrying personal items, while, in the Hahndorf area of the Mount Lofty Ranges, kangaroo entrails were made into carrying bags.[5] Apart from bags, Aboriginal people used baskets, bowls and buckets made from plant fibre, wood and bone, for carrying loads, straining food, cooking, scooping fish and as cradles for young babies.[6]

In many regions of Australia, Aboriginal people relied on the wooden container, known in Aboriginal English as a 'coolamon' or 'pitchi'. These terms are based on Indigenous words for containers: *gulaman*, from Kamilaroi in eastern New South Wales, and *pityi*, from Arrernte in Central Australia.[7] In the Western Desert, women tended to each carry a number of wooden containers of various sizes: for digging earth, scooping and carrying water, as baby cradles, winnowing dishes and for carrying gathered food. These were also sometimes upturned and used as a pillow or worn as an eyeshade. In some regions wooden containers were generally carried balanced on the head—resting upon a circular head-pad made of string— or supported on the hip. Containers were also made from other materials, depending on local availability. For example, in Tasmania, small containers were made from dried bull kelp, tree bark and abalone shells with their holes sealed with clay.[8]

Clubs

When away from camp, Aboriginal men always carried their main weapons in case of a chance encounter with a food animal or a sudden attack by human aggressors. Special weapons, such as bark shields, were sometimes prepared for fights organised to settle disputes, and were discarded after use. The use of European terms, such as clubs and spears, to describe Aboriginal weapons and hunting implements has obscured the different styles and functions of these tools. Clubs were primarily used as weapons, but many types were also used by some people as percussion instruments and as dance-sticks in ceremonies.[9] Some Aboriginal groups used a range of clubs variously designed for throwing, stabbing, slashing and clubbing. Long straight clubs—or fighting-sticks—were used like a truncheon and for warding off opposing blows. The broad sweep of objects that could be functionally classed as clubs also includes some boomerangs, which could be used as handheld weapons.

Wangkangurru men demonstrating the use of murrawirri *boomerang clubs in fights organised to settle disputes. These objects were not thrown, but used as staves.*
PHOTO: G. AISTON, NORTHEAST SOUTH AUSTRALIA, EARLY TWENTIETH CENTURY.

Typically, a basic club measured from 40 to 100 centimetres in length and was carved from a single piece of hardwood. In some areas, large sword clubs were made with two edges, for example in north-eastern Queensland rainforests, where they were used in combat along with large softwood shields. Across Australia, the head shapes were the most variable part of the club: being cylindrical, cone-shaped, bulbous, hooked, hatchet-like, resembling a mace or with a jabbing spearhead. In a few regions, clubs were the main weapons and more varied in design than spears. This was the case in the northeast of South Australia, where clubs ranged from the relatively small banana-shaped club, *koondi*, and boomerang-shaped club, *kirra*, both about 70 centimetres long, up to the large boomerang-shaped weapons, *murrawirri*, that approached 2 metres in length.[10] The large *murrawirri* were not thrown and were too awkward for hunting; instead they were used in organised combat and for exchange as highly valued items. They generally belonged to senior men and were objects of prestige. Like many wooden artefacts, clubs were made hard through firing and were treated with ochre and animal oil to prevent weathering. They were also often decorated with incised designs, longitudinal fluting and painting.

Recently Aboriginal men have given accounts of how in the 'wild times' (before European settlement) a man would seldom have been caught out in the open without at least one club to defend himself. Similarly in camp a man would keep a club within his reach at all times. An attacker may be a single man or a group of ten or more men on a raid. For organised fights, several clubs would be required. In the Lower Murray region of South Australia, a shoulder harness made from sedges was used to carry several clubs into battle. In some Aboriginal groups, clubs were considered by their owners to have had special sorcery powers that could be used to inflict pain and death on humans.

Small throwing clubs were used to bring down birds and animals. In some parts of Australia, throwing stones, chosen for their size and weight, were used instead of clubs or throwing sticks to kill birds and animals from a short distance.[11] Throwing stones, which were generally water-worn pebbles of a size that fitted the hand, could also be used as a weapon against people.

In Australian English clubs are often described using a variety of terms derived from Indigenous languages. Although the words have undergone some change, their origins are still apparent: 'waddys' from *wadi*, meaning 'a stick of wood' in the Dharug language of Sydney; 'wirri' from *wirri*, meaning a club in the Kaurna language of Adelaide; and 'nulla nulla' from *ngala ngala*, meaning a club, also from the Dharug language.[12]

Boomerangs

For thousands of years, Aboriginal people across Australia have used bent, flattened throwing sticks now known globally as 'boomerangs'.[13] The word for boomerang appears to have come from a combination of the Aboriginal words *bumarit* and *wumarang*, from the Dharug language of the Sydney region.[14] Boomerangs were used for fishing, hunting, fighting, playing and in ceremonies. They ranged from commonly recognised returning types to curved fighting sticks that were never thrown. The main forms were hunting, returning, sharp-angled fighting, sword club and hooked. Different types of boomerangs were used across Australia, varying in form, use and meaning depending on local conditions. The true returning type was mainly used in south-eastern Australia to knock down birds. The broad Kimberley and hooked Central Australian types were generally used for fighting. In Arnhem Land, boomerangs were not used for hunting, but rather as musical 'clapsticks'. Since European settlement, the boomerang, along with the kangaroo and emu, has become an iconic

Arrernte man about to throw a boomerang, while holding a shield for defence. This type of boomerang flew in a swerving line, but did not return.

PHOTO: F.J. GILLEN & W.B. SPENCER, MACDONNELL RANGES, NORTHERN TERRITORY, 1890S.

image of Australia and a sought-after tourist item. This has resulted in boomerang-making spreading to parts of Aboriginal Australia where boomerangs were formerly not used.

Spears and Spearthrowers

To early European observers, spears and spearthrowers were much under-rated tools, with an effectiveness that was not at first appreciated. Watkin Tench, an early colonist in the Sydney region of the eastern Australia, recorded in 1788 that:

> On first setting foot in the country we were inclined to hold the spears of the natives very cheap. Fatal experience has, however, convinced us that the wound inflicted by this weapon is not a trivial one, and that the skill of the Indians [Aboriginal people] in throwing it is far from despicable.[15]

Like boomerangs, spears were used by Aboriginal people for hunting, fighting and in ceremonies as well as for fishing.[16] The length of Aboriginal spears varied between 1 and 3 metres, with heads either barbed or just sharpened to a point. In some areas there was little difference between the spears used for hunting and those used for fighting, although

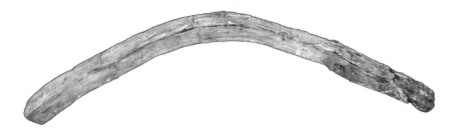

The returning boomerang in Australia has ancient origins. This perfectly preserved example came from a peat bog and is estimated at being between 9000 and 10,200 years old. COLLECTED BY R.LUEBBERS, WYRIE SWAMP, SOUTH EAST OF SOUTH AUSTRALIA, 1973.

in other areas several types were put to different uses. Three- or four-pronged spears were generally used for fishing and were sometimes hand-thrown, rather than launched from a spearthrower. In the case of fighting, some spear types were designed to do maximum damage. Anthropologist Walter Roth stated in 1909 that the *pi-lar* spear used in the Brisbane area:

> Was made from nine to ten feet [2.7 to 3 metres] long, and used for fighting at close quarters. Sometimes old ones were nicked very nearly through, about two inches [5 centimetres] from the tip, for some fellow they had a special 'down' on, so that when stuck in, it would break off and remain behind. At other occasions one or two stingaree [stingray] barbs might be stuck on with beeswax and twine for a similar purpose.[17]

Ceremonial spears were often so heavily decorated that they could not be easily thrown. For example, the hardwood spears used in Pukumani ceremonies on the Tiwi Islands were not made for throwing; they have very large heads with finely carved barbs and are heavily painted.[18]

Spearthrowers are known in Australian English as 'woomeras', derived from an Aboriginal word, *wamara*, from the Dharug language of the Sydney region.[19] They act as an extension of the thrower's arm,[20] and varied in size and shape across Australia, depending on local traditions and the type of spear used. For example, in Groote Eylandt Aboriginal people used two types of spearthrower: a fishing model that had a flat blade which made a soft hiss when moving through the air, and a rounded style for hunting wallabies, which was silent when used.[21] The typical Western Desert spearthrower served as a fire saw, a small dish, a hook for pulling things closer and had a stone blade attached for cutting and scraping—rather reminiscent of the Swiss army pocketknife in its applications! Some Aboriginal groups, including the Tasmanians and the Tiwi people, did not use spearthrowers, hurling all their spears by hand. Their isolation from mainland groups may explain why they did not receive the technology.

Shields

In many parts of Australia, shields were used as defence from clubs and spears.[22] There were two main types: a broad style made from a lightweight wood or from tree bark; and a narrower, heavier shield, typically made from hardwood and chiefly used for parrying blows from clubs. Broad bark shields, which were green and able to absorb shocks, were restricted in use to south-eastern Australia and were made for deflecting spears thrown in organised fights. They were of limited use, as they became brittle as the bark dried. Broad shields common in the Daintree to Mulgrave River areas of northeast Queensland were made from the buttresses of wild fig trees and decorated with painted totemic designs. They were designed for protection from the blows from long sword clubs. Because of their size and beauty, these objects have long been valued by European artefact collectors. In Central Australia, the relatively large shields made from beantree softwood

Yidinjdji men made large shields, painted with totemic designs, from fig-tree wood.
PHOTO: N.B. TINDALE, YARRABAH, NORTHERN QUEENSLAND, 1938.

A Wangkangurru man and boy using a spindle to manufacture fur string, which was used for making ornaments. PHOTO: G. AISTON, NORTHEAST SOUTH AUSTRALIA, EARLY TWENTIETH CENTURY.

were not only for protection against heavy spears, but also served as a base upon which a fire saw was used, for starting fires. Narrow club-parrying shields, which were triangular in cross section, were restricted to south-eastern Australia. They were made from hardwood and with extra bulk due to their shape, they were able to withstand blows from heavy clubs.

Watercraft

Watercraft were used to reach environments for fishing and to hunt animals such as dugong and turtle. Before European settlement, Aboriginal watercraft ranged from floating platforms of weed and loose bark used for crossing creeks and lagoons, to larger and more robust seagoing outriggers made from tree trunks.[23] Aboriginal people used bark canoes and small reed rafts to travel across the relatively quiet inland waters of the Murray–Darling Basin, but these were not suitable for rough seas.[24] Due to a lack of seagoing watercraft, the ability of southern mainland Aboriginal people to reach offshore islands was reduced to those places that were generally within swimming distance from the mainland. Those groups who did have vessels capable of sea voyages included Tasmanians who made what have been described as a 'canoe-raft', for use on inland streams and also some limited ocean travel.[25] These were made of a few large bundles of bark or rushes tied together, and were propelled with punting poles. The Tasmanian watercraft were about 4 or 5 metres long and could carry up to six people. The most robust vessels, however, were to be found in northern Australia, where the Macassans introduced sea-going dugouts to people in the Kimberley to Gulf of Carpentaria regions, and Torres Strait Islanders introduced them to Cape York groups.[26] The Torres Strait dugout canoes themselves were traded into the Strait from southern Papua—in particular from the Fly River mouth—where suitably large trees grew. That northern Aboriginal people were aware of the existence of large watercraft before the arrival of Europeans is evident in the representations of Macassan praus and dugouts which feature in some of the more recent Aboriginal rock art and on bark paintings.

In addition to the tools discussed here, Aboriginal people also utilised a wide variety of other artefacts, many of which are not normally associated with them. These included game nets for hunting mammals and birds, lures and decoys, fish traps and egg scoops, hooks for extracting borer grubs from wood, and a variety of nooses and snares, and are discussed in more detail in Part 3. Through looking at artefacts we can gain some insight into the social dimensions of Aboriginal life. Individual makers had, and have, their own styles and users preferred objects of certain form, size and weight, and made from particular materials.

The large variation found in Aboriginal artefacts is evidence that they were not made and used by 'primitive' people.

Toolmaking Materials

Aboriginal people used a wide variety of materials to make artefacts, including stone, bone, teeth, shell, fur, hair, sinew, skin, seeds, wood, bark, ochre, beeswax, resin and plant fibre. The archaeological record today consists of artefacts and other remains of human activity found on the surface or buried in the ground. It tends to favour stone, bone and shell artefacts—those artefacts that are inorganic or decompose very slowly—over more fragile objects made of plant fibre, fur, hair and skin. Given the wide variety of materials from which artefacts were made, although not preserved archaeologically, it is somewhat misleading to describe

Aboriginal cultures as part of the 'stone age'. Furthermore, it is also misleading because while there are cultures who use stone to make artefacts—such as Aboriginal peoples—the concept of the 'stone age' also implies ancient times ancestral to our modern times. Yet as Aboriginal people and other Indigenous peoples around the world have shown, these cultures are of the present and in this sense as modern as any other culture.

Since the early twentieth century, archaeologists have developed methods of differentiating artefacts from naturally occurring stones shaped by weathering or natural breakage.[27] This can be determined by the angle of shaping and by the type of stone. Aboriginal people generally manufactured stone tools by either flaking or grinding. Flaked stone provided sharp edges in a variety of shapes and sizes useful for cutting and scraping implements. They can be used as weapons, to carve wood, for surgical procedures and to cut carcasses. Hard siliceous stones, such as chert and flint, were favoured for making flakes, due to their property of breaking evenly in all directions. Durable and easily recognisable, flaked stone artefacts are what we often think of as the archaeological record.

The need for high-quality stone from which to make good tools formed the basis of a trade system,[28] although stone tools were not as important in all parts of Aboriginal Australia. When the British arrived in Australia, Aboriginal stone technology was heavily utilised in parts of the Kimberley and Central Australia, where there are many sources of fine stone. It was less significant in other places, such as some coastal regions of northern Cape York Peninsula where suitable stone was scarce and almost completely ignored in favour of shell, bone and wood.[29]

Bones from wallabies, kangaroos, birds and large fish were used across Australia to make a number of specialised tools. These included bone points used in basketry, net making, surgery and for removing kernels out of pandanus fruit. The fine carving on wooden objects was performed with an engraver: typically a possum tooth still fixed to the jaw that served as a grip, or a kangaroo tooth mounted on a wooden handle. Animal teeth were also often used to make body and head ornaments. Shells were used as knives, scrapers, drinking cups, vessels for cooking and warming resins, weights on spearthrower handgrips and as ornaments. Animal skins were made into carry bags and cloaks, although their use was not universal across Aboriginal Australia. Kangaroo and wallaby tail tendons were also used for tying parts of a weapon together, such as to fix a barb onto a spearhead.

Plant fibre, obtained from grasses, bark, leaves and stems, was and continues to be used for making string and for weaving into mats, baskets, nets and bags.[30] In the past, basket-making techniques were also used for mosquito and fly guards in Arnhem Land, and fish traps, cloaks and coffins in parts of southern Australia. A large variety of woody materials were used for making artefacts, not just from trees, but also from vines, bamboo and shrubs.[31] In the case of trees, wood was sometimes taken from the roots rather than branches or the trunk—such wood was often harder. The wood was generally carved while still green and kept buried in damp sand until the object was finished. The working edges of wooden tools, such as digging-sticks, spear points, boomerangs and clubs, were hardened over fire. Aboriginal people used beeswax, plant gums and resins as glues and cements for making and fixing artefacts.[32] The manufacture and use of adhesives provided an efficient means of holding things together, producing strong and durable artefacts. Stone blades and points were fixed on to spear heads, axes, fighting picks and adzes.

Ngarrindjeri men duelling using clubs and narrow shields.
PHOTO: UNKNOWN PHOTOGRAPHER, LAKE ALEXANDRINA, SOUTH AUSTRALIA, ABOUT 1900.

Throughout the millennia of their occupation of Australia, Aboriginal people adopted new hunting and gathering strategies and tools, which archaeologists can detect in the archaeological record.[33] During the last two hundred years, Aboriginal people have been quick to acquire the use of new materials from Europeans, even if the contact was indirect through trade. For example, the first use of glass by Aboriginal people in southern South Australia predated European settlement. At Yorke Peninsula, Aboriginal people claimed that they used glass to make knives from bottles they had found washed up on the beach many years before Europeans came to live there.[34] Shortly after European colonisation, the Tasmanians also used broken glass to make sharp-edged tools.[35] While in the Hahndorf area of the Mount Lofty Ranges during the 1830s, Aboriginal people used broken bits of glass to replace pieces of flint on the point and two sides of their spearheads.[36] Here they also dyed their hair with the dampened dust created by rubbing two red house bricks together. In these examples, Aboriginal people were using new materials according to pre-European traditions.

In Central Australia during the late nineteenth century when the Europeans expanded their settlement into the region, Aboriginal people made hatchet heads from the metal removed from the bases of telegraph poles, packsaddles and horseshoes. Similarly, adze blades were made from sharpened steel files or shearing blades. In the Top End of the Northern Territory, stone spearheads were being replaced by iron obtained from Macassans in the mid-nineteenth century and later from Europeans.[37] Across northern Australia, Aboriginal people started using metal nails to make fishhooks to replace those of bone. In the Western Desert, from the early twentieth century, shiny plates of tin were made into pendants, resembling those made from pearl shell. Aboriginal people also used bitumen pitch as an adhesive in place of plant resin. To Aboriginal toolmakers, the use of new materials for old ways does not involve a denial of their traditions, but rather the more efficient use of the resources available. Today, Aboriginal people in remote parts of Australia usually go hunting with rifles and gather with digging-sticks made from an iron rod or crowbar. This in itself is not evidence of loss of hunting and gathering knowledge, although the skill for making earlier types of tools is declining in many areas. Like Europeans or any other peoples in the world, Aboriginal people change and adopt new material items and knowledge through the course of their lives. These changes, however, are always undertaken in a context of their own cultural experiences and expectations.

Camp Life

Space around the Aboriginal camp in remote central and northern parts of Australia is still organised such that each family group tends to have its own area for sleeping around a central fire, although additional fires may be placed between individuals and couples.[38] The camping area is like a house without any roof or walls, and yet with spaces allocated for particular people and activities. There are generally different housing structures for daytime activities, when men and women tend to be apart, and for late afternoon and night-time activities, when the family unit comes together. When several groups camp in close proximity, each group will set itself up on the side closest to its home territory.[39] This is a defensive strategy to allow for quick departure and to easily accommodate incoming kin. Often, a number of younger men will camp together a short distance from their family groups, as a measure of their independence.

Shelters

The form and structure of Aboriginal shelters is diverse, depending on the area and season. Generally, when the weather is mild, a minimum of shelter is used. For overnight camps, a simple circular or U-shaped windbreak is constructed from dense plant material for protection against cold winds. They are quickly made from branches or bark. I have on occasion slept inside a windbreak constructed by Aboriginal people, and it is surprising how efficiently the cold wind is deflected, leaving a pocket of warm air in the centre. During seasons of cold or persistently wet weather, more substantial housing structures with roofs are produced. Aboriginal people do not move about much at these times and invest more time in building shelter. A wide variety of techniques are employed in their making, including using logs or branches, thatching, plaiting grass, plastering with clay, weighting the roof with soil, using split cane ties and threading foliage into wall rails. In the past, rock shelters were sometimes used for camping as well. Tree platforms are used to hold objects, like food containers, above the ground where scavenging animals, such as dogs, will not get them.

In Australian English there are a number of words for an Aboriginal bush shelter that are derived from Indigenous terms: 'mia-mia', from *maya-maya* in the Nyungar languages from Perth to Albany; 'wurley', from *wadli* of the Kaurna language of Adelaide; 'gunyah', from *ganya* in the Dharug language of Sydney; and 'humpy' or 'umpy', from *ngumbi* in the Jagara language of Brisbane.[40] The generalised meaning of these words does not do justice to the wide variety of housing employed. For example, the domed shade of the Western Desert region is made of curved poles arranged in a circular plan and thickly covered with spinifex grass. While providing shade, this type of shelter also allows cooling breezes to pass through, but keeps out most of the flies that are common after summer rains. In Arnhem Land, sleeping platforms are constructed, with a fire burning underneath to keep mosquitoes away. Aboriginal people may construct several types of shelter through the course of the year, depending on the season and locality of the camp.

Food Technology

Aboriginal people gained a living from the land in many ways, with techniques that varied across Australia. Also, people who used fishing technology along the coast in summer used different hunting and gathering strategies when they moved inland during winter. Although hunting and gathering strategies were crucial for survival, the preparation of food was also important. For instance, a larger population of Aboriginal people was able to live in arid Australia than otherwise would have been the case, because of the inhabitants' ability to release the energy in grass seed and in the seed-like sporocarps of the nardoo, a semi-aquatic fern of the southern inland waterways.[41] Here, such foods were seasonally abundant, although the process of making food was laborious. Food preparation at the camp involved winnowing raw seeds to remove husks and dirt, then grinding the seeds into a softer form before cooking. Seeds were winnowed using wooden containers with a grooved inner surface to assist in the separation. In Australian English this action is described as 'yandying', based on the Indigenous word *yandi*, meaning 'winnowing dish', from the Yindjibarndi language of the Pilbara in Western Australia.[42] Grindstones, or millstones, are usually flat pieces of hard, coarse stone. The grinding action is produced by rolling an upper grindstone of a comfortably handheld size, across grass seed or sporocarps on the lower grindstone, typically a slab about 50 by 30 centimetres across and about 4 centimetres thick. Water is generally applied to the ground material during milling when seeds were dry to start with.

In the past, the use of grindstones was common from the northern reaches of the Murray–Darling system across to the Pilbara in Western Australia.[43] Throughout Australia, stone mortars were used to pound edible roots, nuts and fruits into a paste for making cakes which were cooked on a fire. Wooden mallets were also used for mashing roots into paste.

The size of the grindstone varied with locality and food sources. In the Murray Valley, where wattle and other shrub seeds were treated, smaller grindstones and mortars were needed than was the case for treating grass seeds or sporocarps in the desert regions.[44] Likewise, in parts of the Western Desert, small stone mortars were required for cracking quandong kernels, the hard seed cases of kurrajongs, and for preparing leaves for chewing tobacco.

A coil of string was used on the grindstone to keep the meal from scattering during grinding.[45] Grindstones were generally left at camp sites near seed sources and water. Being fairly large, most grindstones were not carried around by their owners, but left at campsites for seasonal use. On Groote Eylandt in the Gulf of Carpentaria in the Northern Territory, the large mortars used by women for preparing burrawang nuts were buried in the ground during seasons when they were not being used.[46]

Grindstones eventually wear out through decades of grinding. Some of the larger stones in museum collections have several grooves in them, some of which are worn through to the other side. The value of these devices to life in Australia was such that much of the arid zone was only made habitable in the long-term with the use of seed-grinding technology.

Fire

Fire is an integral part of Aboriginal life and culture, being essential for cooking and keeping warm. Past Aboriginal people made fire through methods that employed friction and percussion.[47] The use of firesticks in a rotating motion—one stick rotating inside a hole in another—to produce fire is widespread across Australia. Norman Tindale described this process:

> Fire making is practiced using a dry grasstree flower stalk, the 'male', twirled into a split section of the same stalk, in which usually a notch has been cut. This is the 'female'. Tinder is placed below the notch which supplements the hot powdered pith engendered by the rotary

process. When a spark appears it is deftly transferred to a ball of dry, teased grass or other easily ignitable matter.[48]

Tindale added that fine grit was sometimes placed in the female part of the apparatus to help fire-making by increasing friction.

Firesticks were long lasting, producing many fires before being worn down. In tropical regions, the difficulty of making fire in a moist environment was overcome by using longer sticks, which had more turning force. In northern Queensland, the ends were kept dry in a protective sheath made of beeswax and orchid fibre decorated with red abrus seeds. The Aboriginal people of Central Australia also used the edge of their hardwood spearthrowers and boomerangs as fire-making saws.[49] Sawing them rapidly to and fro across a dry branch or the face of a softwood shield created an ember. The fibrous dried dung of the kangaroo was used as tinder, with dead grass and leaves to feed the growing fire.

The use of percussion methods to make fire, generally by striking flint against 'ironstone' or iron pyrites, was used in southern Australia.[50] This technique used sun-dried, powdered kangaroo dung, fungus, bark and sandalwood scrapings as tinder, which was kept dry by wrapping in possum fur. In the Coorong area of South Australia, Norman Tindale's Tangani informant Clarence Long told him that fire-making flint came by way of trade from south of Cape Jaffa in the southeast of South Australia.[51] The flint came from a place in the Mount Lofty Ranges to the north of the Coorong. In the cold and wet regions of south-eastern Australia where fire-making was sometimes difficult, fire was often transported smouldering within slow-burning bracket fungus that was removed from the trunks of trees. Firemaking would otherwise be difficult in these conditions. Elderly people, who tended to stay around the camp, had the responsibility of keeping the fire going. In the bark canoes and reed rafts of the Murray–Darling Basin, fire was maintained in a clay hearth or carried on board within a wooden container lined with clay. This fire provided not just warmth, but attracted fish to the watercraft at night, and these could be cooked on the fire for a quick meal.

Cooking

Aboriginal people prefer to eat healthy and well-fed animals. Pre-European Aboriginal cooking techniques did not involve maintaining very high temperatures, due to the type of containers they had available. While some food, such as small marsupials, lizards, molluscs, witchetty grubs and small birds were broiled in ashes, much of the food was cooked in earth ovens. A western Victorian colonist, James Dawson, described Aboriginal cooking as follows:

> Ovens are made outside the dwellings by digging holes in the ground, plastering them with mud, and keeping a fire in them till quite hot, then withdrawing the embers and lining the holes with wet grass. The flesh, fish or roots are put into baskets, which are placed in the oven and covered with more wet grass, gravel, hot stones, and earth, and kept covered until they are cooked.[52]

He went on to note that larger animals, such as emus, wombats, turkeys and kangaroos, were cooked in the same manner, but with stones placed at the bottom of the oven. Some types of stone, such as sandstone, have heat-retaining properties that are important for underground cooking ovens.[53] At places where suitable rocks were unavailable, cooking stones were sometimes made from baked termite mounds, or from clay gathered from the ground or from mud-dauber wasp nests.[54] Cooking stones were generally left at the campsite.

Present-day Aboriginal people who cook with earth ovens use particular plants as wrapping and seasoning, avoiding those that may impart a bad taste. In parts of the Victoria River area of the Northern Territory, for example, Aboriginal people place large wads of native lemongrass (*Cymbopogon bombycinus*) in the stomach cavities of kangaroo carcases before cooking them.[55] Specific woods are sought to make the ashes and coals of a cooking fire, and ovens are dug in soils that will not taint the food.

There was some regional variation in cooking style. For example, in the Western Desert and in southwest Queensland, the carcases of kangaroos and wallabies were cooked unskinned.[56] This is in contrast to the southern mainland areas where the skin was removed, often for making cloaks and bags, and the animal body wrapped with plant material and then sealed in the preheated earth oven. In Tasmania, the kangaroo was cooked in earth ovens with the skin on, but rubbed all over with the contents of the stomach and intestines to prevent burning.[57] Kimberley man, the late David Mowaljarlai explained how the exposed leg bones of a kangaroo being cooked in an earth oven act as a timer: 'When it's pure white and the hands bend, it's cooked.'[58] Lizards were encased in clay before being covered by ashes for cooking.[59] When ready, the clay was peeled off, taking the skin with it. In northern Australia, fish were wrapped in paperbark before being placed in an earth oven, thereby keeping the flesh clean. Digging-sticks or a pair of small sticks would be used as tongs to move small items of food through the heat of the fire. The built-up remains of Aboriginal cooking fires, commonly found as middens near inland lakes, major rivers and in coastal dune systems, are primarily composed of ash, bone and shell material.[60]

In some northern coastal regions, large seashells placed in the ashes of a fire were used as containers to warm water and to heat fat and resins, and for making oil. In the Encounter Bay region of South Australia, Aboriginal women caught tadpoles with a fine net and cooked them in large abalone shells placed over the fire.[61] Fine nets were also used to collect bogong moths, which were a major seasonal food source, in the high country of South Australia. The moths there were lightly cooked, so as not to burn them, on low-smouldering fireplaces.[62]

Clothing

Past Aboriginal people generally wore little or no clothing for protection from the elements, regardless of the region they lived in. Minimum clothing was in the form of aprons and pubic fringes made of bark and hair/fur strings, which were worn by both sexes.[63] These were sometimes further decorated with a variety of materials including feathers, plant down and ochre, with additions of dried animal tails, bones and bird heads. Items of dress generally indicated to the community the initiation and marriage status of the wearer.

In all parts of Australia, animal grease was rubbed onto the body to make the skin shine. It probably also served as a form of protection against the elements.[64] During cold weather at the beginning of the dry season at Groote Eylandt in the Northern Territory, for example, Aboriginal people rubbed their bodies and faces with grease mixed with powdered charcoal or ochre. At hot times, grease also protected the skin from sunburn and dry winds.

During the cold seasons of temperate Australia, Aboriginal people in some areas kept warm with cloaks made from a variety of materials.[65] In the southwest of Western Australia, an early colonist reported:

> . . . their dress consists simply of Kangaroo Skin, made into a Bookra or cloak, which is worn at all seasons, and seems well adapted to keep out the wet in the rainy season, in addition to which the women have one small bag made of the same material, with a sling to throw over their shoulders, in which they carry their little child . . .[66]

When European blankets became available through missions and ration depots, these were similarly used.

Skin cloaks were generally either single kangaroo skins, or pelts made from segments of possum or wallaby skin stitched together with sinew.[67] The marsupial skins were partially tanned in some areas by being pegged onto saltpans,[68] and in south-eastern Australia, scoring on the inner side, which made the skin more flexible, was done in a decorative geometric pattern.

The Aboriginal artefacts described here are the main ones that Aboriginal people used to provide themselves with the basic needs of food, water, protection and shelter from the elements. In order to maintain a lifestyle that involved high mobility, Aboriginal hunting and gathering tool kits were small but versatile. The historical record shows that a wide variety of materials were used in their manufacture, although the archaeological record does not equally reflect all of them. Over tens of thousands of years, Aboriginal people shaped the Australian landscape by the use of the digging-stick, club, spear and fire-making apparatus.

Six

Art *of the* Dreaming

In pre-European Aboriginal society, there were no firm distinctions between art and non-art, or 'fine art', 'decorative art' and 'craft', as has existed in recent Western European art traditions. What Europeans define as Aboriginal art, music, storytelling and dramatic performance are integral parts of cultural and social activities. The imagery used by Aboriginal people draws meaning from their extensive knowledge of the Dreaming which is used to interpret and explain their world. The painting of sacred designs is a visible reference to the religious forces that Ancestors placed within the landscape. Aboriginal people sing or paint their 'country', as a statement of their close connection to their land. There are distinct regional expressions of art, incorporating a range of identifiable motifs and designs. Similarly, there are differences in performance and musical styles across Australia.

Space and Colour

Aboriginal people today record and display the events of their Dreamings in art, in celebration of Ancestors whose actions are recorded in the land itself. Aboriginal art thereby provides a record of Dreaming Ancestors, describing their exploits and creations. It also represents spirit beings, which occupy the land alongside people. Individual paintings may refer to the complete epic journey of an Ancestor, linking many places that were visited during the Dreaming period, or they may refer more directly to a particular place or a single event in the Dreaming. Much of Aboriginal art reflects directly on cultural links to land, to the extent that the European observer often treats individual paintings as 'maps'. This is especially marked in Western Desert dot and Top End X-ray paintings, which appear to have a three-dimensional quality to them, as if they are the product of an aerial perspective.

Europeans and Aboriginal people have a different perspective on space. Although Aboriginal people can be precise when explaining their landscape verbally, as artists they do not generally put importance on showing the relative distance between places or the actual physical size of a site. Europeans and Aboriginal people also have a different sense of orientation for their paintings. Pre-European forms of Aboriginal art were on irregular surfaces such as rock faces, the ground, inner surfaces of bark huts and on human torsos. The angle the artwork was viewed from was equally variable, ranging from the vertical plane to the horizontal. Therefore, unlike Western European traditions in which paintings are hung or viewed at eye level, or in relation to architectural features, in Aboriginal art there is generally no overall sense of up/down, north/south or east/west. Nonetheless, cardinal points, such as major Dreaming sites, are important. What orients Aboriginal art are not so much the Euclidean or spatial dimensions that typically directs the canvases of European art, as Aboriginal affinity with the Dreaming ancestors, events and beliefs that ultimately shapes the work and life itself.

Aboriginal people have a keen perception of direction, even if it is not obviously represented in their art. I say 'obviously' because in effect much Aboriginal art, whether abstract or not, is rich in spatial cues: animal tracks are not randomly distributed on a rock wall or bark painting, but move from one strategic or key place to another; waterholes are precisely positioned as testimony of Ancestral movements across the landscape; and indeed individual figures are located in specific places precisely because of their Dreaming location and movements in the landscape.

In Aboriginal art the Skyworld and Underworld may also be drawn as extensions to the terrestrial landscape, which complicates the perspective. In some cases we can understand Aboriginal perceptions of direction as based on the observed movements of celestial bodies and the prevailing directions of the seasonal weather. For instance, in Aboriginal languages, many of the terms for 'west' refer to the 'direction to which the Sun travels', whereas the 'east' often refers to 'dawn' or 'moon', and in at least one group the term for 'south' is related to 'cold'.[1]

The size of elements in their paintings, such as hills, animals and humans, are relative to their cultural importance and are not to scale. In the dot painting tradition of Central Australia, several painters may collaborate to produce an individual piece, particularly if it is large and associated with ceremony. In such cases, several Dreaming events and sites are often depicted, each with its own orientation. The mythological space experienced by Aboriginal people, and geographical space recognised by European mapmakers, both relate to the landscape. Nonetheless, Aboriginal art differs from maps by being primarily directed at charting the significance of the Dreaming, rather than illustrating topographic relationships.

The diverse nature of Aboriginal links to the Dreaming landscape means that a group of artists from a single community will have among them many differing totemic affiliations with the land. All artists have their own set of Dreaming relationships to draw upon when painting, which reflects their perspective to the surrounding landscape. Individual paintings often feature many sites and several Dreamings. The artwork in the Western Desert dot painting tradition tends to utilise a small group of symbols, each of which may represent a variety of objects or phenomena, to present a graphic image of complex concepts relating to Dreamings.[2] In this tradition, concentric circles often represent important Dreaming sites. Whether they indicate a waterhole or a hill will vary according to the Dreaming Ancestor concerned. The viewer cannot begin to read this art without knowledge of the Dreaming landscape to which it refers.

Being recognised as having the right to paint a particular Dreaming design usually implies some form of ritual authority and often the traditional ownership of the land and of the sites themselves. In cultures such as the Warlpiri of the Tanami Desert in Central Australia there are *kirda* who 'own' a particular country and *kurdungurlu* who are guardians that make certain that the country is looked after.[3] These roles are determined through kinship: the *kirda* through the father's line and *kurdungurlu* through the mother's line. While the *kirda* are painters of their land, its sites and Dreamings, it is the *kurdungurlu* who ensure that this is done properly in accordance to their traditions. The designs themselves are believed by the artists to have originated with the Ancestors and Aboriginal people access the power of the Dreaming through replicating the designs and styles set by the Ancestors. In eastern Arnhem Land artists paint the totemic designs that belong to their clan.[4] This system ensures a form of copyright, with artists displaying their rights to their country, which are gained through their kinship and the possession of ritual knowledge acquired through participation in ceremony. In many other areas, artists can paint their own Dreaming, but not one for which they do not have a primary association. The decorative styles are therefore not just 'art', as seen by Europeans, but Aboriginal expressions of their place in their culture and in the cosmos.

The Aboriginal palette was based on four basic colours—relating to the materials available to make paint red, yellow, white and black. Whether a colour is bright and shiny or plain and dull is significant,[5] with brightness and shininess representing the power of the Ancestors embedded in the object. For example, the Anbarra people of the Gidjingali language group in Central Arnhem Land recognise two colour classes that are denoted by the terms *gungaltja*, which refers to light colours, including bright red, and *gungundja*, which is applied to dark and dull colours.[6] The names of the four minerals used to make pigments (*rrakal*—white pipeclay, *gunyimiga*—charcoal, *djuno*—red ochre, and *dulgo*—yellow ochre) are applied to describe objects that have similar hues. In the Tanami Desert of Central Australia the Warlpiri believe that the four basic colours (*karntawarra*—yellow, *yalyuyalyu*—red, *kardirri*—white and *maru*—black) used for ritual purposes originated from an elemental fire.[7] As with the Gidjingali language, a distinction is made between shiny and dull forms. For instance, the Warlpiri accordingly refer to pipeclay, which is comparatively shiny, as *ngujunguju*, whereas chalk, which is not, is called *karlji*.

Some colours are associated with specific Dreamings and certain kinship groups, as anthropologists Chris Anderson and François Dussart explained in relation to the Warlpiri:

Each Dreaming or Dreaming segment and its related subsection group is associated with a specific set of colors and color sources. Thus, among the Warlpiri at Yuendumu, black and white (charcoal and pipeclay) belong to Emu Dreaming and to the jampijinmpa/nampijinpa, jangala/nangala subsection groups; yellow is associated with Snake Dreaming and the jakamarra/nakamarra, jupurrurla/napurrurla subsections.[8]

The colours chosen for paintings are therefore reflective of the order imposed by the Dreaming. In Aboriginal Australia, shiny and iridescent objects are typically held to be both attractive and potentially dangerous. Refraction of light into the colour spectrum is found in a number of naturally occurring objects: shells, particularly pearl; new snake skin; rainbows; bright feathers, such as on rainbow lorikeets; and crystalline rocks. This property is associated with fertility and the ability to produce water; and on objects, whether created naturally or made by humans, it reflects the Ancestral forces present within them. According to Aboriginal aesthetic senses it is highly desirable for the body paint used at ceremonies held at night to be strong and to have shimmering properties.

Many of the naturally occurring pigments in Australia are based on minerals.[9] Ochres, which range from yellow through to orange and red, can be obtained on a visit to a particular mine or quarry, or if access to such a site is not possible, then by trade. The red forms are generally made from iron-rich minerals, such as haematite. Not all ochre is considered to be of equal value, due to a combination of physical and cultural properties. Apart from its lustre and shine, ochre originating from particular Dreaming sites gains extra power by symbolising such things as the blood of an Ancestor.

Yellow pigment can be made from limonite and goethite, which are also iron minerals. White paint (pipeclay), is made from a variety of calcium-based substances, such as kaolin clays, gypsum, calcite and burnt selenite. In the Kimberley region the rare mineral huntite is used to make white paint. The colour black is generally made from charcoal, but was also made from naturally occurring psilomelane (manganese dioxide), especially on Groote Eylandt in the Gulf of Carpentaria where it is available in the ground.

Aboriginal artists also make paint from organic materials, such as bird excreta. Pigment can also be made from particular coloured spores, fruits and roots. These vegetable sources of paint are often for more ephemeral uses, such as body and face painting. In northern Australia, substances such as egg yolk, bees wax, honey, plant resins and the juice of orchid bulbs serve as paint fixatives.[10] Ochre is also mixed with animal grease and oil for the treatment of wooden artefacts, such as clubs and spearthrowers. For ceremonial occasions, the soft down from bird feathers and plants are often stuck onto objects and performers to enhance a design. The loose down floating from these designs during performances helps spread the power of the Dreaming. Since European settlement in northern Australia, blue paint has sometimes appeared in rock-art galleries and on artefacts. This was made from Reckitt's Blue, a chalk-like blue washing compound which became an Aboriginal trade item in parts of northern Australia.

Paint brushes are made from tied hanks or wisps of human hair, bark fibre and leaves or from a chewed wooden stick.[11] In some cases it is sprayed on by the mouth. Wooden 'combs' are also used in northern Australia to paint large numbers of evenly spaced dots, which saves the artist time.

Early Art Traditions

The cultural landscape was, and continues to be, symbolically represented by Aboriginal people in many ways. In discussing Aboriginal art tradition it is useful to categorise according to media used, although the artists themselves would not have made the same distinctions.

Rock Art

Rock art sites occur unevenly across the Australian landscape. Although the art they contain was often considered 'primitive' by many early recorders—and this is now understood to indicate European prejudices rather than Aboriginal artistic abilities and intentions—a wide diversity in style demonstrates that there have been numerous traditions in Australia which collectively stretch over 40,000 years of rock painting, stencilling and engraving. It is estimated that there are presently over 100,000 surviving rock painting and engraving sites in Australia.[12] This represents only a small fraction of all the rock art ever produced by Aboriginal people. The painting traditions associated with some Aboriginal rock art, particularly in northern and Central Australia, continues through to today.[13]

The use of 'rock art' to describe these traditions is not without problems, with some scholars preferring 'rock pictures' because of the uncertainty of defining 'Aboriginal art' in the absence of detailed knowledge of the cultural circumstances that produced it. Christopher Chippindale and Paul Taçon have similarly suggested that we should signal some conceptual distance between Western notions of art, which are produced for a market economy, and Aboriginal rock art by symbolically writing the latter as 'rock-art' with a hyphen.[14] For convenience, rock art is divided by European students of it into two main categories: pigmented art or 'pictographs', made by applying paint to a rock surface, and extractive rock art or 'petroglyphs', made by cutting into a rock surface to remove layers to form a pattern. Over the millennia, pigments wash off with rain, the surfaces of rock engravings erode and flake, and whole rock-art galleries may collapse due to earth movements. (Although in a few locations where Aboriginal rock art is extremely ancient, pigments have by chance chemically bonded with the rock surface and become permanently fixed.) Ancient coastal sites are particularly vulnerable, not just to weathering but to sea level changes. Undoubtedly there are ice-age art sites that are presently under the sea. The present distribution of rock art is therefore a product of such things as the local environment, as well as the cultural history of Aboriginal occupancy in the region.

In general, from the few accounts recorded directly from Aboriginal artists, it is known that rock art sites collectively contain images of people, Dreaming Ancestors, animals, plants, human-made objects, cosmic phenomena, and make references to particular sites. In some rock-art galleries, paintings from many periods overlap each other, producing a collage of imagery. Due to the passing of time and to population movements, both before and after European settlement, Aboriginal people sometimes find themselves custodians of painting sites, or of individual

Rock engravings exposed on a cliff face along the coast at Mount Cameron West, Tasmania. PHOTO: N.B. TINDALE, NORTHWESTERN TASMANIA, 1936.

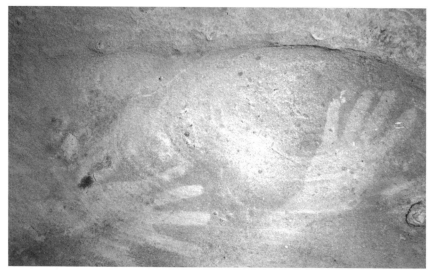

Stencils, which were made by spraying pigment from the mouth over the hand placed on the rock surface. PHOTO: N. BLUNDEN, BLUE MOUNTAINS, NEW SOUTH WALES, 1963.

paintings, that were created by other people, and therefore with art whose original associations were with a different cultural landscape, although this art is still treated as part of the local cosmology.

There is much speculation and controversy among students of rock art over the original intended meanings of specific bodies of art. Determining 'meaning' in the absence of a record of the artist's intentions or a direct association with the traditions depicted is obviously difficult. In many cases later people have their own interpretations of the work of earlier people. For example, anthropologist Norman Tindale claimed that certain rock carvings located west of the Macdonnell Ranges 'can be interpreted as the front-facing representations of the Giant bird, *Genyornis*, at a site which still bears the reputation [among Aboriginal people] of being a *tjukurupa* [Dreaming] place of the Kalaia or emu Being'.[15] An interesting case concerns a rock art site of Panaramittee in arid mid-north South Australia recorded by photographer and museum ethnologist Charles Mountford, in the 1920s. Mountford claimed it included a depiction of a crocodile head.[16] Yet these animals would not have existed there for many tens of thousands of years at least. The depiction provides tantalising evidence that crocodiles occurred over a greater range during a wetter climatic period in the distant past but it is also possible that the artist saw such an animal at a site many hundreds of kilometres away and engraved it entirely from memory. Many years after Mountford's publication, the anthropologist Ronald Berndt published a detailed explanation of the same rock art, told to him earlier by Barney Waria (Warrior) of the Ngadjuri people. Challenging Mountford's interpretation, Berndt's source stated that the design was of a 'magic object', of which he described the meaning.[17] This would seem to show clearly how the interpretation of ancient cultural iconography changes, as the culture and landscape are transformed over time. We will never truly know the intended meaning of any of the old rock art.

Further complicating the issue of meaning is the fact that items of art may have different meanings under different contexts of visitation and use. For example, in Wardaman country around Katherine in the Northern Territory, specific paintings mean one thing to groups of women, men and children at times when the site is openly visited, but these same paintings mean completely different things when initiated men contemplate particular Dreaming stories at those sites.[18] In other words, a painting or engraving does not necessarily have just one meaning, but can have multiple meanings depending on the context of interpretation. We see much the same thing happening in other societies around the world—for example, the Southern Cross constellation can be thought of as an emblem of Australia, as a compass by which to find south at night, to initiated Aboriginal souls the footprints of an eagle, and for some as reminiscent of the cross of Christianity.

Sculpture

Across Australia, there are a number of sculptural traditions that predate European settlement. In comparison with Asia and Melanesia, which have extensive wood carving traditions, large sculpture was significant to only a few Australian Aboriginal groups. Tree trunks carved with abstract designs are found in parts of eastern New South Wales and were associated with Aboriginal initiation and burial rituals.[19] They often occur in groups that grew on 'bora grounds' where ceremonies were held.

Northern Aboriginal people have the most pronounced sculptural traditions in Aboriginal Australia, perhaps due to the influences of Asian and Papuan cultural traditions. Three dimensional pole sculptures play a major role in the Pukumani mourning ceremony of the Tiwi people today living on Melville and Bathurst Islands in the Northern Territory.[20] These ceremonies are held as a series of mortuary rituals that release the spirit of the recently dead. To outsiders, the distinctively carved burial poles, erected vertically near the grave, have become widely recognised symbols of Tiwi culture, and are often made today for sale to art galleries and museums. The poles are cut from the trunks of ironwood trees, and can be up to 3 metres in length. The mythology behind the Pukumani is based on the Purruka-parli Ancestor who in Tiwi Dreaming first brought them death.

In northeast Arnhem Land, Aboriginal people carve ceremonial poles and log coffins, which are highly decorated and, as a result, were sought after in the past by museums and art galleries.[21] Similarly, in north-western Cape York, the Wik sculpt animal forms for some of their ceremonies. These represent such Ancestral Beings as Saara the Seagull, the Apalach Brothers and the Two Young Women from Cape Keerweer, who have major ceremonies held in their honour.[22] The works are made from wood and beeswax, and then painted. The dots used to decorate the Apalach figures are a strong feature and are symbolic of the shimmering of light on clear water.

Bark Paintings

The earliest western Arnhem Land bark paintings to be collected by Europeans date to the late nineteenth century. These include a set of early paintings discovered in 1884 by Captain F. Carrington while he was engaged in a survey of coastal rivers of the Northern Territory.[23] At Field Island, near the mouth of the South Alligator River, he found paintings on the inner surface of the bark-slab roof of a wet season hut. The paintings consist of several layers of figures, some painted over earlier work that had been scraped off. The bark painting art styles in the Top End are directly related to the extensive rock-art galleries found elsewhere in the same region. Tindale noted the connections in northern Australia in 1921 during a trip to Groote Eylandt in the Gulf of Carpentaria off the coast of eastern Arnhem Land. Observing the link between sand drawing and the paintings on rock and bark slabs he wrote:

> The tracing of designs and pictures on the ground is a common pastime at night around the camp fires . . . Hunting and fishing episodes are roughly sketched, the artist meanwhile narrating the story of the happenings he depicts. In similar fashion illustrations

are painted in colours in an enduring form on the walls and roofs of rock-shelters during the enforced leisure hours of the wet season. Not only are paintings done in the rock-shelters, but any bark hut which has been occupied for some time contains such pictures.[24]

Like other media bark paintings convey information about the landscape. Some from Arnhem Land concern major Dreaming Ancestors, such as the Djang'kawu and the Wagilak Sisters, or feature spirit people, such as the *Mimih* of the western Arnhem Land escarpment. Food animals, such as kangaroos and barramundi, also appear in paintings, as do images of past contact with people such as Macassans or European buffalo hunters.

Beginning in the early twentieth century, European interest in the distinctive Top End bark paintings, and later in Central Australian dot paintings, has led to the development of a lucrative international market for Australian Indigenous art.[25] Prior to the arrival of Europeans, people directly painted onto bark 'canvases' and in time the artworks were left to deteriorate—after a few years straightened sheets of bark tend to curve back to the curvature of the trees from which they came. But increasing European interest in bark paintings has created demand for long-lasting artworks. To overcome this problem Aboriginal artists from northern Australia began to secure the ends of bark paintings with transverse wooden prongs, thus inhibiting the bark from curving and providing a useful example of artistic innovation in the face of changing contexts of artistic production and display.

Through the twentieth century, Aboriginal artists used what were to them 'new' media, such as ceramics, glass, paper, hardboard and canvas for their paintings. At least initially, many of them still painted within their traditional styles. Since the 1970s commercial paints have introduced a new palette of colours to Indigenous artworks. As more Indigenous people become involved in producing European-style 'fine art', the category of Australian Aboriginal art will embrace not just the earlier traditional forms, but include more conventional artforms that contain Aboriginal themes. Significantly also in recent years 'fine-art' galleries around the world have embraced non-traditional Australian Aboriginal art, a change in attitude that was made possible by the realisation of Aboriginal art's depth of meanings. Aboriginal artwork continues to provide a spectacular record of Aboriginal beliefs, cultures and everyday life.

Wanjina Beings often appear in rock art galleries in the Kimberley. Wunambal people have painted a Wanjina on the reverse side of this bark container.

COLLECTED BY J.B. BIRDSELL,

SCOTT STRAIT, KIMBERLEY,

WESTERN AUSTRALIA, 1953–4.

Performance Art

In Aboriginal Australia, people hold ceremonies that sometimes involve widely dispersed groups coming together at a single place. Ceremonies may be either sacred and ritualised or secular less formal events. They may be elaborate, with groups coming from a large area to converge at a single place, or they may be very simple. European Australians refer to Aboriginal dance ceremonies, which are accompanied by singing and rhythmical music, as 'corroborees'. This Australian English term is derived from *garabari*, a word from the Dharug language of Sydney.[26] In sacred ceremonies dancers will often act out events from a particular Dreaming, while secular ceremonies and dance may relate to more everyday events such as hunting and gathering. Some sacred ceremonies involve music, performance, special decorations relevant to the Dreaming Ancestors and headgear. At larger events, occurring over several days, there is opportunity for groups to organise marriages and to engage in trading.

Some ceremonies were part of cycles, with episodes traded or simply passed from group to group across great distances in a recognised sequence. For instance, in the Adelaide region, the Kaurna people from time to time held a ceremony called the Kuri, which was passed to them from the north, before being relayed onto Murray River peoples to the east.[27] One observer

The Kuri dance was a part of a public ceremony that was taken to the Adelaide Plains area by Aboriginal groups living to the north. WATERCOLOUR: G. FRENCH ANGAS, ADELAIDE PLAINS, SOUTH AUSTRALIA, 1844.

in 1844 regarded this public ceremony as unrivalled in its drama. It was held at night under moonlight with a backdrop of campfires. The male performers were painted in white pipeclay and had dried gum leaves tied to their legs just above the knee, which made a loud crackling noise at each step. A number of objects decorated with feathers and human hair string were used. The Kuri ceremony provided the occasion for cultural and social exchanges to take place among a wide group of people. The name, Kuri, also refers to a circle, being a reference to how the ceremony travelled across the landscape. In another example, in 1901–02 the Mudlungga dance was reported to have travelled south from around Mount Isa in western Queensland to near Lake Eyre in northern South Australia.[28]

Over much of past Aboriginal Australia, formal musical events consisted of group singing accompanied by various kinds of percussion, using materials such as hardwood and bamboo, with natural musical qualities.[29] Paired tapping sticks, also known as 'clap-sticks', set the rhythm and were often decorated with totemic designs associated with a ceremony. Boomerangs were also used for tapping, the user knocking the points of two of them together. Bunches of leaves tied above the ankles and knees of the performers, or held with shaking hands, produced a rustling sound which accentuated movement. As with most aspects of life there were regional variation in dance and music. In northern Queensland, the Wik people, for example, beat Papuan-type skin drums in 'island style' songs

Young Wik women dressed in the mortuary dress of the Ancestral Quail Women who came from Cape Keerweer. PHOTO: U.H. MCCONNEL, ARCHER RIVER, NORTHERN QUEENSLAND, 1933.

during events such as 'house opening' or 'tomb opening' ceremonies. Across northern Australia, whistles are made from the nuts of palms and other plants. In some regions, women used specially prepared animal skin pads, described as 'pillows', filled with feathers and rags or stretched skins across their legs for tautness, for beating out a sound to accompany singing and dancing.[30] Aboriginal people also added to their singing by hand clapping, stamping, buttock and thigh slapping. Both men and women performed during ceremonies, their roles determined according to custom.

One of the unique musical instruments attributed to Aboriginal people is the aerophone, also known as the 'drone pipe' but more commonly now as the 'didjeridu'.[31] Once restricted to the northern zone, from the southern Gulf of Carpentaria, across Arnhem Land to the western coastal Kimberley, it is now common all over Australia, including in south-eastern Australia, which did not have a pre-European form of this instrument. However, a smaller type of wind instrument, described by some early European observers as a 'trumpet', was used in parts of Central Australia. There is some evidence, gained from surveying artefacts depicted in dated rock art, which suggests that the didjeridu is a relatively recent introduction to Australia.[32] European interest in this instrument has encouraged its spread across the continent. The origin of the word 'didjeridu' is probably recent and imitative of the distinctive noise it makes. In western coastal regions of the Northern Territory, Aboriginal groups have tended to call this instrument 'bamboo', based on the material from which it was chiefly made. In northeast Arnhem Land today, Aboriginal people more commonly use the Indigenous term *yidaki*. Hardwood examples from the north also exist, with mangrove and Eucalyptus wood naturally hollowed by wood borers and termites being the most commonly used material of this kind.

There is no standard style of didjeridu. Those made out of solid wood tend to have a rim sealed with beeswax to soften it for the mouth. For a player to maintain a constant sound during a performance requires the breathing skills of a glass-blower. The acoustic behaviour of each individual instrument depends on the length of the tube and the shape of the hole bored through it. Most didjeridus from the Kimberley to Gulf of Carpentaria regions where they were used when Europeans first arrived range from between 1 and 1.6 metres in length. In Arnhem Land, the didjeridu is used in ceremonies of the Gunapipi and Djungguwan cults, being representative of the voice of the Ancestors. Here the chief participant during a performance is a song 'owner', who beats two tapping sticks together while singing. Although other singers may be part of the ensemble, it is rare that there is more than one didjeridu player operating at one time, although for particularly large instruments, requiring a major effort to play, there may be a relay of blowers. In Arnhem Land, a didjeridu player may also beat a stick against the instrument or alternatively flick the tube with his finger. A resonator made from a baler shell might also be utilised.

Some early Aboriginal traditions have been incorporated into the musical repertoire of post-European Australia. In the early twentieth century, gum-leaf bands in south-eastern Australia produced a popular form of Aboriginal music.[33] Touring Aboriginal bands played tunes by blowing through or across gum leaves. Some researchers believe that the gum leaf was a device for people without a front tooth—which was commonly ritually removed—to assist them whistle. The Yolngu-style didjeridu from northeast Arnhem Land has more recently become the sound of Indigenous Australia, and as an iconic artefact is second only to the boomerang.

The twentieth century experienced a growth in non-Aboriginal interest in Indigenous art, which has stimulated many pre-European art traditions— to the extent that many artists transferred to different media. The land and its Dreamings—both expressing Ancestral beings and events—were central features in most forms of art, and they continue to be themes today. In addition, however, Aboriginal historical and social themes now also find their way into the 'fine art' produced by Indigenous Australians. Aboriginal people continue also to perform ceremonies in honour of the Dreaming forces that made their 'country'. Key components of ceremonies, such as singing, dancing, storytelling, painting on bodies and on objects, all combine to help draw power from the Dreaming. So interwoven are these elements, that it is difficult to consider Aboriginal art in isolation from other expressions of their land and cultural traditions. The art of the Dreaming has varied across Australia and through time. It continues to change, influencing Indigenous and European Australians in new ways.

Part III

REGIONAL DIFFERENCES

Seven

Living *in a* Varied Land

Aboriginal people lived on a continent where their physical resources, such as food and materials, were widely distributed across both space and time. By maintaining their mobility, hunters and gatherers were generally able to overcome the problem of spatial dispersal and seasonality. Nevertheless, no single territory occupied in this way by one Aboriginal group would have provided everything that was required. Trading was the means by which goods located in restricted areas could be distributed throughout a much larger region.

Aboriginal Traders

Hunting and gathering societies are rarely thought of by Europeans as having extensive trade networks which moved commodities and established links between people across the landscape. Nevertheless, such economic systems existed in Aboriginal Australia, and in the north Aboriginal people made connections with Melanesian and South East Asian peoples. [1] Their trading goods included raw materials, manufactured items and cultural knowledge.

Aboriginal trade systems facilitated not only the exchange of materials but also cultural ideas across the land. While the landscape shaped Aboriginal technology it did not entirely confine it, and trade helped distribute material to overcome local shortages. Aboriginal people often required raw material for making their tools that was not available in their country. The need of such things as quartzite stone (for spearhead blades and knives), pitjuri or tobacco (to make a narcotic), lengths of straightened wood (as spear shafts), shell and ochre (for decoration and ceremony) and resin (for hafting stone tools) was often satisfied through trade.[2] Finished artefacts, such as boomerangs, clubs, ornaments and tools, as well as prepared and preserved food and narcotics, were also exchanged. Grindstones originated from a few major quarry sites and in the arid zone were essential tools for preparing the life-sustaining grass seed. However, goods were not the only things of material value. At large ceremonial gatherings there were songs, dances and Dreaming accounts to exchange. These occasions were also the opportunity for making marriage agreements. Trade also removed some of the threat of outside groups trespassing to collect necessary items.

Trade occurred in different ways: when people met in small groups along their borders; during special organised trading expeditions; and at large ceremonial events, which were organised during good seasons when the country could support many people for initiations and collective hunting and gathering events.[3] Trading expeditions occurred during times of plenty, when a surplus had been generated and the movement of groups of people along recognised pathways, such as particular watercourses, did not result in hardship to the local groups.

Some earlier writers did note the existence of Aboriginal trade. In 1911, for example, A.C. Stone wrote:

> The [Lake] Boga tribe had no difficulty in obtaining any quantity of reeds ('Jarruts'), used for making reed spears ('Charram'), which were exchanged for grinding and tomahawk stones or other raw material, which could not be found in the district, and which was necessary for hunting or decoration.[4]

The Lake Boga tribe were from northern central Victoria. Similar trade practice was recorded elsewhere. The Bibbulmun people of southwest Western Australia, for example, traded with their northern neighbours at 'exchange fairs', called *manja boming*.[5] The items that were sent to them from the north included pearl shell, ochre, various types of wood, cordage, weapons, grease and ornaments made from human hair and feathers. In exchange, the Bibbulmun people traded various fur strings and head ornaments, war spears, boomerangs and axes. The social contact necessary to enable bartering would have helped maintain good relations between local bands, and trade appears to have been based on the notion of equal relations, rather than attempting to gain the upper hand over an exchange partner.

Because of the long distances over which trade occurred, complex social arrangements were involved, sometimes between many culturally and linguistically differing peoples. The Kimberley area of northern Australia provides a good example of this and of changes over time. Exchange cycles there have three main components: the movement of women through marriage, the distribution of trade items, and the exchange of ritual objects.[6] Pearl shell moves from the coast to the interior, while certain types of ritual objects move from the interior to the coast. Trade occurs across groups that have different traditions. Pearl shell, for example, which is publicly worn in the Kimberley, gains more cultural and economic value as it travels further away and is regarded as being less public by certain inland groups. The fluted beantree shields from the Macdonnell Ranges area of Central Australia, which are often decorated with Dreaming designs, travel along the trade route as far west as Lagrange on the south coast of the Kimberley. Objects obtained from Europeans have been incorporated into this exchange system, sometimes replacing other items. Motor vehicles and European money now assist in the movement of objects and tape recorders also have a role in the transmission of messages.

The protocols surrounding the trade in ochre are another example of the complexity of trade. Ochre was a major trade item, with prepared cakes in trading parcels crossing vast distances. Access to mines and control of the trade was governed by complex rules.[7] In the north-eastern corner of South Australia, Aboriginal men of the Diyari, Tirari, Wangkangurru and Arabana groups went on long trade expeditions south to the ochre mines at Pukardu (Bookartoo) in the Flinders Ranges.[8] The expeditions occurred over a period of two months and involved the participants travelling about 500 kilometres to the country of the Guyani people near Parachilna. Trade based on this source of red ochre connected people from as far north as southwest Queensland, west to the Macdonnell Ranges, as far east as Tibooburra in western New South Wales, and possibly as far south as the

Adelaide Plains and Port Lincoln. The ochre at this main site still exists today. It is not bright red, but rather a metallic pink that is remarkably shiny when applied to human skin.

The red ochre expeditioners to Pukardu sent ahead message sticks—small decorated wooden objects that act like passports—to advise the mine custodians of the imminent arrival of the travellers, and proposing the exchange of various goods to provide them with access. Gifts from the north included black manganese pigment, boomerangs, spears, firesticks, feather down, nets and grass seed (food) in bags. In spite of the existence of local pigment sources at home in the north, the mythology of Pukardu made this a more desirable source of ochre. Pukardu ochre represented the blood of the Ancestors. Using it therefore connected an individual with the forces of the Dreaming. Aboriginal men in the expedition would hold ceremonies with the clans whose country they passed through along the way to and from the mines. Upon the expeditioners' return, the red ochre was used to decorate bodies and objects for the large ceremonies of the desert people. Stone from the Innaminka area of north-eastern South Australia for making grinding stones and the narcotic pituri from southwest Queensland were also part of this trade system.

Special kinship relationships were established to facilitate trade. Many trade practices were associated with quite elaborate rituals, and more formal relationships were established to facilitate the trading. For instance, Lower Murray people had the *ngia-ngiampe* custom of exchanging ornaments, called *kalduke*, which were made from human umbilical cords gathered at birth.[9] This trading relationship encouraged potentially hostile groups to be allies. This exchange practice also produced agents through which trade in materials could occur. The missionary George Taplin recorded that an Aboriginal man, Jack Hamilton, who lived a short distance up the river from Lake Alexandrina in the Lower Murray:

> . . . once had a *ngia-ngiampe* [partner] in the Mundoo tribe [based at the Murray Mouth]. While he lived on the Murray he sent spears and *plongges*, i.e., clubs, down to his agent of the Mundoo blacks, who was supplied with mats and nets and rugs to send up to him, for the purpose of giving them in exchange to the tribe to which he belonged.[10]

Trade, through *ngia-ngiampe*, linked the 'tribes' along the Murray River with the Lower Murray groups near the sea.[11]

Striking stone flakes off a core. Stone suitable to make tools was widely traded from particular quarry sites. PHOTO: G. AISTON, NORTHEAST OF SOUTH AUSTRALIA, EARLY TWENTIETH CENTURY.

Trade relations were also expressed in terms of permission to visit sources of rare and highly valued materials in another group's territory. For instance, in western Victoria a local clan known as Wurundjeri-willam governed access to the stone for making hatchets at Mount William.[12] These blades were traded over a wide area, possibly as far towards the west as the Coorong in South Australia.[13] When Europeans arrived, the right to operate the quarry belonged to a man called Billibellary and in his absence to his nephew. Anyone else wanting access to this place required his permission. In another example, Lake Alexandrina people sought access to the large river red gums (*Eucalyptus camaldulensis*) in the territory of their northern neighbours, the Peramangk, in the southern Mount Lofty Ranges in order to cut canoe bark.[14] Whip-stick mallee spear shafts were given in exchange for use of these trees, which were absent from lower regions of the Murray Basin.

Seasonal Practices

In the daily search for food, water and materials for making artefacts, Australian hunters and gatherers made use of a continent with variable seasons. Making a living meant reading the signs in the landscape: when to move, where to move and what to take. Aboriginal people possessed a wide variety of food-procuring techniques and had seasonal access to a diversity of plant and animal foods. However, obtaining food successfully meant understanding the local environment and keeping up with its changes. That knowledge is a form of intellectual property that was common around Australia, although varied.

European settlers to Australia have generally tried to classify the Australian climate and environmental changes according to the temperate Northern Hemisphere model of four seasons with which they were familiar. These equal temporal periods have little relevance to most of Australia. Compared to Europe and North America, Australian summers are generally longer, winters are shorter and variable, the concept of autumn vanishes in the absence of dominant deciduous vegetation, and spring seasons are hard to identify. The first British colonists arriving in Australia were confused and dismayed with the different seasonal pattern they encountered. During recent years, there has been a growing awareness of Aboriginal seasonal 'calendars', and appreciation of them as more relevant, and reflecting to a greater extent the nature of the Australian environment.[15] Adoption of Aboriginal models of seasonal change is beginning to occur in monsoonal Australia, where a number of detailed studies of Aboriginal seasonality have been produced; this knowledge is increasingly being used to help manage national parks particularly in relation to firing the vegetation.[16]

The term 'calendar' is used to describe the temporal divisions of a year, although Aboriginal perceptions of seasons often span greater periods, particularly in arid regions which have irregular rainfall. Most seasonal calendars used by Aboriginal groups have more than four seasons and are locally based using cues and cycles in each environment. Different temporal periods are identified or signalled by distinct faunal, floral, mythic and totemic associations, climatic events and patterns, and varied by intermittent landscape firings and floods. The movement of celestial bodies in the Skyworld was important too. For example, to the Kaurna people of the Adelaide Plains the arrival of the star Parna, at the end of the hot season, indicated the change of season and that it was time to build large and waterproof huts in the Adelaide foothills.[17] As with interpretations of the cultural landscape in other contexts, there is no single correct seasonal model that all people living in a region would recognise. For example, men and women,

Depending on the season, Wik women hunted small game and turtles, fished with nets and gathered mud shells, roots and fruits. PHOTO: U.H. MCCONNEL, ARCHER RIVER, NORTHERN QUEENSLAND, EARLY 1930S.

each with specific strategies for obtaining food, would have different activities tied to seasonal changes, and would be alert to different signs.

Aboriginal movement patterns were not only regulated by season, but also tended to occur along certain corridors in the landscape. The first European settlers found well-worn paths or tracks in some areas when they arrived in Australia. The visibility of these corridors suggest that they were frequently used by the local people when hunting and gathering and when moving camp. One major track made by Encounter Bay Aboriginal people in South Australia ran from Hindmarsh Valley to Willunga, a distance of over 25 kilometres. In western South Australia, Aboriginal tracks ran between water sources, connecting the coast with the arid interior,[18] while in Tasmania, Aboriginal 'roads' were used through dense or swampy country, but were not required in open woodlands, where travel was much easier.[19] In western Victoria, Aboriginal paths linked places, such as ceremonial grounds and important eel fishery sites,[20] and in northern Queensland, walking tracks, called *djimburru*, crossed the ranges and were used by Djabugay people when seasonally moving between the coast and the tablelands of the interior.[21] European settlers observed such tracks in frequent use by Aboriginal people in the early days of the colony, and made use of the tracks themselves. Less than a metre wide, the Hindmarsh Valley–Willunga track was used by Europeans initially for foot and horse traffic.[22] Eventually, however, it was widened for use by horse-driven coaches. Many Aboriginal tracks have their courses preserved today as bitumen roads.

Different Country

Aboriginal people possessed intricate ecological knowledge of their environment, such as flora, fauna and land associations, and the breeding cycle of a wide range of animals. In parts of Australia where the impact of European settlement has been greatest, particularly in temperate Australia, much of this knowledge has been lost forever. Regrettably, few Europeans in the past recognised the depth of this knowledge and its potential application. Making a record of the local Aboriginal language, A. C. Stone, an early resident of Lake Boga in northwestern Victoria, lamented that, 'It is not an easy task to get behind the aboriginal mind and to gain his entire confidence . . . but having gained his confidence it becomes surprising to find the vast knowledge possessed of the flora and fauna of his surroundings, and the tales and sometimes weird traditions of his tribe.'[23]

In the late twentieth century, botanists, in particular, came to recognise the value of Indigenous knowledge of the environment. While much of the knowledge from hunters and gatherers died out before it was properly recorded, we can gain some insight into how Aboriginal people saw the landscape by looking at Indigenous placenames. Europeans have often incorrectly interpreted Aboriginal placenames. Contrary to popular opinion, most of the Indigenous place names that persist today, albeit in altered form, do not simply mean 'meeting place'. In fact, they generally refer to environmental properties or to aspects of the Dreaming associated with the site. For example, the name of Wooltana Station in the Flinders Ranges was popularly considered to be an Aboriginalised version of 'wool place'.[24] However, linguistic research indicates that this is a poor translation of the local Aboriginal placename Uldhanha, derived from *uldha*, 'a small leafy branch' or 'bunch of leaves'.[25] Aboriginal placenames contain a wealth of information concerning the landscape.

In addition to placenames for discrete areas, Aboriginal people had landscape terms for ecological zones in the environment. For instance, Kalumburu people in the northern Kimberley have numerous terms relating to parts of the landscape distinguished by difference in vegetation, water drainage and soil type.[26] In their language, for example, *djindi* refers to dense jungle-like vegetation surrounding permanent fresh water; *balambala* is for flood plains; and *geningard* for waterlogged sandy soils found in sandstone outcrops. Similarly, the Gooniyandi (Konejandi) people lived in the desert country of northern Western Australia, mainly along the watercourses of the *walibiri*, or river country.[27] The open plains where they hunted kangaroos are called *pindiri*, and the hilly country where they found euros is *kawaro*. The scrub-covered country is *tiwinji* and the open forest is called *kerele*, which also means 'trees'. In southern South Australia the Tangani people had a different word for each recognised environment zone or regional landscape they utilised—*lerami* for inland scrub and swamp; *tenggi* for the landward Coorong shore; *pandalapi* for Coorong lagoon; *natunijuru* for the coastal sandhills; *paringari* for the seaward Coorong shore; and *yurli* for the ocean beach.[28] Each recognised landscape represented a set of potential resources and seasonal uses, which influenced people's movement over the landscape.

While Aboriginal people frequently visited particular ecological zones, there were others that were largely avoided or visited only briefly when hunting. Aboriginal people in the Fleurieu Peninsula region near Adelaide, for example, avoided the wet sclerophyll forests of the stringybark gumtrees (*Eucalyptus obliqua* and *E. baxteri*) in the high rainfall areas of the main spine of the Mount Lofty Ranges.[29] On both sides of the ranges the foothills were mainly covered with forests of river red gums (*Eucalyptus camaldulensis*) and South Australian blue gums (*Eucalyptus leucoxylon*). On the western escarpment were hunting grounds for Aboriginal groups living predominantly on the Adelaide Plains, whereas the eastern escarpment was the territory of groups ranging towards the Murray River. Although the ranges were crossed with Aboriginal pathways, there is little historical or archaeological evidence to suggest any prolonged use of the transitional zone. Having grown up near Mount Lofty in southern South Australia, I spent many fruitless hours of my youth looking for evidence of Aboriginal occupation in caves and rock shelters. Given how little Aboriginal people used this landscape, it would have been remarkable if I had found anything. Similarly, the Tasmanians had a riverine/coastal technology which required seasonal access to the coast. Up to a third of the land mass of Tasmania was not generally used by them as it was dense mountain forest.[30]

The close connection between Aboriginal people and land is demonstrated by the adoption of landscape terminology in the naming of individuals in the Aboriginal community. In the Adelaide area German missionaries Teichelmann and Schürmann recorded that each man had a strong kinship connection with a particular piece of land, defined as his *pangkarra*. The territory appeared to be that of a locally based descent group or clan. They explained, 'As each pankarra [= pangkarra] has its peculiar name, many of the owners take that as their proper name, with the addition of the term burka; for instance Mulleakiburka, Karkuyaburka, Tindoburka, etc.'[31] One prominent example of this is Mullawirraburka, known to Europeans as King John, whose Aboriginal name literally translates as 'dry-forest-old man'.[32] His name refers to an area of mallee vegetation typically found in areas inland from Aldinga, a town on the southern outskirts of Adelaide. He being 'old' is a reference to Mullawirraburka being a senior custodian of the clan territory.

Terms relating directly to the landscape also label some Aboriginal groups. The Adnyamathanha people of the Flinders Ranges, for example, explain the meaning of their group name as 'people of the rocks'.[33] The name of the Barkindji people from the Darling River region of western New South Wales was recorded from Aboriginal people to mean 'river people'.[34] Across Australia there are Aboriginal people who, in addition to other more formal ways of identifying themselves, make a distinction among themselves according to whether they live inland or near the sea. For example, today some northern Australian Aboriginal people still refer to themselves according to whether they are 'Fresh water' or 'Salt water People', quite apart from other distinctions they make between themselves, such as according to clans, kin and language groups. In the case of the latter, these people assert their rights to the sea.[35] This division between people on the basis of whether their country is predominately fresh or salt water appears to have been widespread, with implications for hunting and gathering styles and cultural traditions, and was superimposed upon a much more complex system of Aboriginal land ownership.

To Aboriginal people, the landscapes they perceive and live upon are full of meanings and possibilities. They provide the means to define the people and resources associated with them. Their uneven distribution of resources produced a trading economy, which had implications for the transfer of cultural knowledge. They called forth from Aboriginal people placenames that in turn helped define their recognised features, and grouped and identified the people themselves.

Eight

The South

The division of the landscape into just three climatic zones—the temperate south, the central deserts and the monsoonal north—does not do justice to the cultural and environmental diversity in Australia, but it serves the purpose of comparing regional adaptations of hunting and gathering strategies across the continent. The temperate region of Australia, which covers both the southwest and southeast, has many water courses and lakes. This reliable water supply meant Aboriginal population levels were high in comparison with other parts of Australia. It is no accident that the Europeans first chose southern Australia to settle, as this was a landscape with a climate most like that of Britain. It was made more European-like by the British as they introduced plants and animals from their homeland. Of course, European perceptions of the physical environment, based on agricultural potential and similarity to homelands, differed greatly from contemporaneous Aboriginal views.

Geographers have classified parts of the temperate Australian region, particularly the areas between Adelaide and Melbourne, and around Perth, as 'Mediterranean lands' because of its climatic similarity with coastal North Africa and southern Europe.[1] European trade possibilities were important in assessing the potential economic value of each new colony. In 1836 South Australian colonist John Morphett stated that South Australia 'in many places reminded me strongly of the Delta of the Nile, and other rich plains in Egypt'.[2] In the 1830s, the temperate regions of Australia promised much for farmers, with the Murray River a means of moving produce to lucrative markets. The coastal zone and inland river systems were the first parts of the Aboriginal landscape to be absorbed by Europeans. The impact of this on local Aboriginal cultures was enormous. The early dispossession of their lands in the south, followed by rapid depopulation, means there is a relative paucity of anthropological studies of Aboriginal traditions and customs in these areas, as well as a much changed landscape. It also means the job of describing earlier Aboriginal hunting and gathering practices is quite difficult. In this chapter historical accounts are therefore used to a greater extent to describe occupancy of the region than is the case for the rest of Australia.

Hunting and Gathering in the South

Through their movement, Aboriginal people positioned themselves in the landscape in order to take maximum advantage of the availability of seasonal resources, including food types that are restricted to particular habitat zones. Seasonal indicators, including the flowering of certain plants and the movements of star constellations, were used as a guide to move on. The temperate regions supported the highest Aboriginal population groups, due to the abundance of food found along the coasts and inland river systems. However, not all parts of the country were suitable for large numbers. For example, some of the Australian high country, even the relatively small Mount Lofty Ranges, appears to have been only sporadically visited, and then mainly by hunting parties.

Aboriginal groups living in the temperate regions had an enormous variety of food seasonally available. It is therefore likely that they did not have any true staples, to the extent that horticulturalists elsewhere did.

Plants

From the historical record, it appears that tubers of the bulrush (cumbungi or broad flag-reed, *Typha* species) and the yam daisy (*Microseris lanceolata*) were among the foods most depended upon by Aboriginal people living in temperate Australia.[3] Although once common, the yam daisy has

A large hut with a wooden frame and a windbreak extension, with fishing nets and spears. PHOTO: S. SWEET, LAKE ALEXANDRINA, SOUTH AUSTRALIA, ABOUT 1880.

disappeared from many regions through being trampled out by European grazing stock.

Tubers were generally a food source that had a longer season of availability in contrast with other food categories, such as gums, fruit and seed. Tubers of some plants had the added advantage of being a source of fibre, for knotting into nets and bags, and for binding spearheads onto their shafts. As well as the bulrush, the mallow (*Lavatera plebeia*) was a source of root fibre. The use of these major food sources therefore helped produce the material to make the devices necessary for activities such as fishing, collecting and hunting.

Some sedges were also important food sources found in abundance on river flats. For instance, the walnut-sized club rush (*Bolboschoenus medianus*) corms were prepared by being roasted and pounded between stones into a thin cake.[4] In the Murray district of the southwest of Western Australia, wooden 'pats' (flat boards with a handle) were used to pound up roots, as millstones were unknown in this area.[5]

At times of the year when food was more difficult to collect, such as during the cold and wet season when people stayed close to their fires, Aboriginal people in the coastal and riverine areas appear to have chiefly relied on roots and tubers, which the women mainly collected from nearby waterways. When particular types of fruit were in season, such as the native apple (*Kunzea pomifera*) and pigface (*Carpobrotus rossii*) during the warmer months, considerable effort was taken in their collection. Whenever possible, a surplus was gathered for preserving for later use and for trading.

At times of physical stress, such as during a prolonged summer drought or a particularly cold, wet spell, Aboriginal people would go outside their preferred practices, resorting to gathering what is known in Aboriginal English as 'hard time food'—foods requiring many hours of processing or that are considered to have an unpleasant taste. The cooked root bark of mallee trees was a 'hard time' food, eaten when other foods were not available.[6]

Aboriginal people in southern Australia did not heavily utilise sources of edible seed, such as from grasses, although it is known that some wattle (*Acacia* species) seeds were used.[7] In some riverine areas, sporocarps (seed-like structures) of the nardoo fern (*Marsilea* species) were eaten.[8] Aboriginal people commonly ate 'sheoak apples', which are the whole female cones from various sheoaks (*Allocasuarina* and *Casuarina* species).[9] Before the cones harden they are red and can be either consumed raw or cooked. Sheoak apples, and some other foods, were described in Aboriginal English as 'blood medicine', meaning that they were taken as a tonic. Another commonly used food in Southern Australia was the fruit of the native apple.[10] The fruit was dried before being pounded into large cakes for later trade, such as in exchange for basalt axe heads which originated from the volcanic plains of Western Victoria. During the summer time, large numbers of Aboriginal people camping along the coast collected this apple, which is the size of a current. Due to its pleasant taste and the large quantity available, this food species had immense social and economic importance to Aboriginal groups living in the temperate zone.

The fruit of the quandong (*Santalum acuminatum*) was widely used across Aboriginal Australia, and has the distinction today of being one of a few Indigenous fruits that is the basis of the Australian 'bush tucker food'—that is, Indigenous food produced commercially. In the southwest of Western Australia, eastern New South Wales and south-eastern Queensland, Aboriginal people made food from cycad fruit (*Macrozamia* species), but only after extensive processing to leach out the poison. This involved washing the pulp over several days before baking it into cakes.[11]

The nectar of several species of heavy flowering plants provided Aboriginal people with the basis for making a sweet beverage. The flower cones of the native honeysuckle (*Banksia* species) were soaked all day in water held in wooden or bone containers, for drinking in the evening.[12] The flower stems of the grasstree (*Xanthorrhoea* species) were similarly used.

The Aboriginal perception of nectar as a rich food source is suggested by the Kaurna language term, *paitpurla*, which is broadly used to mean nectar, animal fat and whale blubber.[13] Other flowering plants that produce copious amounts of nectar, such as species of gums (*Eucalyptus* species) and bottlebrushes (*Melaleuca* and *Callistemon* species), were also collected and used. Edible gum, particularly from the golden wattle (*Acacia pycnantha*) was a significant food source during the summer and was soaked in water to soften it and eaten as a tonic.[14]

Aboriginal people used Australian thistles (*Sonchus* species) in what they refer to in Aboriginal English a 'blackfellow's salad'.[15] The leaves and roots were stripped and discarded, with only the supple stem eaten. Sick people, in particular, used this food as it was regarded as a tonic. A few Aboriginal people in southern South Australia still use thistles in this manner. In times of food scarcity, Aboriginal people ate the green tops of the Australian stinging nettle (*Urtica incisa*) after baking them between heated stones.[16] Without this treatment, these leaves would cause considerable pain if they came into contact with the human skin. The savoury juice squeezed from leaves of the pigface was used to flavour cooked kangaroo and emu meat.[17] Subterranan fungi were sometimes described in the early records of Aboriginal food as 'native truffle' and 'blackfellow's bread'.[18] Surface fungi were also widely eaten, although a few varieties had to be avoided because they are poisonous.

Insects

Across temperate Australia, insects were a common Aboriginal food source.[19] White ants were a favourite food in the springtime.[20] Large egg-laying females were separated from the dirt by winnowing in a bark trough. In the Australian Alps, the arrival each summer of a population of bogong moths to aestivate (lie in a torpid state) provided an abundant food supply for many of the Aboriginal people who gathered there.[21] The moths were cooked on coals. Bees provided a source of sweetener and Aboriginal people collected it in a most resourceful way. The magistrate and Aboriginal Protector Edward J. Eyre provided an account of the gathering of honey from the Mid-Murray region:

> It is procured pure from the hives of the native bees, found in cavities of rocks and the hollow branches of trees. The method of discovering

the hive is ingenious. Having caught one of the honey bees, which in size exceeds very little the common house fly, the native sticks a piece of feather or white down to it with gum, and then letting it go, sets off after it as fast as he can: keeping his eye steadily fixed upon the insect, he rushes along like a mad-man, tumbling over trees and bushes that lie in his way, but rarely losing sight of his object, until conducted to its well-filled store, he is amply paid for all his trouble. The honey is not so firm as that of the English bee, but is of very fine flavour and quality.[22]

Shortly after first reading this account in the 1980s, I successfully used this technique to locate a European wasp nest around my home in the Adelaide Hills.

The leaves and stems of some eucalypts were sources of edible manna. Although this appears to be a plant food source, it is produced on the eucalypt by insect attack. Manna from the peppermint gum was infused in water and the resulting solution used as a drink.[23] Sugar lerp bugs are also an insect food which appears on eucalypt leaves. Their Australian English name is derived from the Western Victorian Wemba Wemba word *lerep*.[24] These minute sapsuckers produce a sweet white flaky substance as a small protective shelter. It can be scraped off, simply by running the leaf through the teeth. According to one nineteenth-century writer, Aboriginal people could collect 18 to 23 kilograms of lerp substance in a single day when in season.[25] The mallee trees that supported these insects were often many kilometres away from water.

Crustaceans and Shellfish

Crustaceans were another abundant food source available to Aboriginal people living in marine, estuarine and riverine environments. Along rivers and more permanent streams, Aboriginal women obtained freshwater crayfish from among underwater debris, sometimes using nets.[26] The species collected in this manner included the marron, yabby and the large freshwater lobster. Aboriginal men also gathered freshwater lobster using a large bow-net, which was dragged close to the bottom of the shallows by two or three people.[27] On Lake Alexandrina reed rafts were used to travel to mussel beds, where the women dived with net bags to gather the molluscs.[28] Observing this in the Mid Murray region, Edward Eyre wrote:

The women whose duty it is to collect these [mussels], go into the water with small nets (*lenko*) hung around their necks, and diving to the bottom pick up as many as they can, put them into their bags, and rise to the surface for fresh air, repeating the operation until their bags have been filled. They have the power of remaining for a long time under the water, and when they rise to the surface for air, the head and sometimes the mouth only is exposed.[29]

Aboriginal women kept mussel shells for use as spoons and cutting implements.[30]

The collecting of food such as crustaceans and shellfish has left an enduring pre-European relic in the form of middens upon the landscape of temperate mainland Australia.[31] Middens, comprised of cockles, mussels and other remains from cooking fires, were commonly found along the coast and on the banks of the Murray and Darling Rivers.

Fish

Fish were a favourite food item in southern Australia. Lower Murray people gave cultural significance to the fact that when their babies tried to speak, their first words were *mam*, which sounded like *mame*, being their word for fish.[32] Adults interpreted this as the infant's desire to eat fish. As with other aspects of their environment, Aboriginal people keenly watched for signs of fish activity. For example, cliff top lookouts were used as vantage points to see when fish schools arrived in coastal areas. When large numbers of fish died for natural reasons in the river or lake, often due to seasonal change of water conditions, these were quickly gathered.[33] Some of the seasonal changes were quite dramatic. Before the construction of the barrages across the Murray mouth separating the Coorong from Lake Alexandrina, the incoming salt water drove certain species, such as the Murray cod, upstream, suspending fishing in the lakes until it receded.[34]

Fishing techniques ranged from netting, spearfishing and trapping, to opportunistic harvesting and storage. Before the arrival of Europeans, Aboriginal people in southern Australia did not widely use the fishhook and line.[35] Nevertheless, the use of bone bi-points or fish gorges (*muduk*) and fishing lines has been recorded along the Murray River near the Victorian border.[36] Shell fishhooks have also been recovered from coastal shell middens in eastern Victoria.[37]

Marine net fishing often involved the coordination of a large number of people. The colonist Thomas Worsnop, whose study of Aboriginal people he encountered in South Australia has informed some of this book, provided a vivid account of Aboriginal people sea fishing in the nineteenth century:

> In Encounter Bay I have seen the natives fishing almost daily. Two parties of them, each provided with a large net, square in form, with a stick at either end, and rolled up, swam out a certain distance from the shore, and then spread themselves out into a semicircle. Every man would then give one of the sticks round which his piece of net was rolled to his right hand man, receiving another from his left hand neighbour, bringing the two nets together, thus making a great seine. They now swam in towards the shore, followed by others of their number, who were engaged in splashing the water and throwing stones, frightened the fish and prevented their escape from the nets.[38]

Nets were generally made from sedge or water-flag root fibre. If nets were not available, then branches could be used to drive fish upon the beach.[39]

Net fishing in freshwater creeks generally required fewer people than sea fishing, due to the more enclosed spaces. Sinkers and floats were never used in association with any type of net fishing in the south. Along the Murray and Darling Rivers people often fished from a bark canoe at night.[40] Contained by a clay hearth in the middle of the canoe, a fire served to attract the fish which would be struck by spear or club; the fire also served for cooking the catch. Rafts were made from reed stems and dried grasstree flower stalks, and the mobility across water they provided enabled the fisherman to reach areas favoured by particular species of fish.

During the day, it was common for men to stand motionless in the river and in shallow seawater, attracting fish such as mulloway and snapper with their shadows. When close, the fish were stabbed with large double-pronged spears.[41] David Unaipon, the Ngarrindjeri man from the Lower Murray who appears on the Australian $50 note, described how fishermen frightened fish from their hiding places with a loud noise, created by thrusting one of their large fishing spears into the water.[42] The compressed air caught between the prongs rose to the surface with a loud report.

The construction of long trenches by Aboriginal people to concentrate fish saved them much labour, as did the building of stone and wooden fish

Bark canoe from Avoca Station along the Darling River, which was pushed along with punting poles. PHOTO: D.H. CUDMORE, DARLING RIVER, NEW SOUTH WALES, 1904.

traps,[43] sometimes described as weirs in the literature. Some of the earth works involved were of a considerable scale, covering many hectares, such as those at Lake Condah in Western Victoria.[44] The use of fish traps and weirs enabled Aboriginal people to seasonally congregate in larger numbers than would otherwise have been possible. They also had spiritual significance. At Brewarrina along the Darling River in New South Wales, the male Dreaming Ancestor Baiame was acknowledged as the creator of a series of large fish traps, made from rocks, each of which were then maintained and used by a particular family group.[45]

Rules sometimes applied as to who could visit fishing sites. Daisy Bates, recorded that:

> When the Perth, Gingin and other district people visited Mandura[h] in the fishing season (autumn) they were forbidden to go near the weir but were given all the fish food they could eat. Two or three months might be spent at these fishing grounds by the visitors, who lived exclusively upon the fish.[46]

Not all Aboriginal groups in temperate Australia fished. The Tasmanians stopped eating fish some thousands of years ago. This dietary change is the likely result of a refinement in hunting and gathering strategies

Ngarrindjeri men, Harry Hewitt and Leonard Lovegrove, demonstrating river net-fishing. PHOTO: T. MCGANN, INMAN RIVER, ENCOUNTER BAY, SOUTH AUSTRALIA, ABOUT 1880.

that made fish redundant to the Tasmanian diet because other food was more easily gathered.[47]

Other Animals

Temperate Australia was a region rich in a variety of wild fowl, particularly waterbirds. The large expanses of lakes and lagoons enabled Aboriginal people in temperate Australia to exploit a resource and build up dependency much greater than in any of the arid regions. Aboriginal hunters had many methods for capturing the diverse species. Precise knowledge of the habits of hunted species was particularly important for techniques such as snaring, as often the hunter was not around to observe whether his snare had been placed in the correct position.[48] The use of snaring-rods, long poles with a noose attached to the end, was a variation of the snare technique common in South Australia and Victoria.[49] One method of catching swans involved the hunter, armed with a swan-wing decoy and snaring-rod, hiding among water-flags and reeds by the edge of a lagoon. The splashing of the wing, imitating a bird in distress, attracted distant swans. The loop of the snaring-rod was quickly extended over a curious

Natural rock formations upon which Aboriginal people maintained fish traps, made from loose boulders and wood. PHOTO: P.A. CLARKE, NOONAMENA, COORONG, SOUTH AUSTRALIA, 1986.

bird's head, the rod pulled in and the bird killed. Another strategy was to place upright sticks a short distance into a lake in areas where shags and cormorants were known to frequent.[50] The hunters would swim out with weed-covered heads, snaring the birds with rods as they landed to roost.

Catching birds settled on an open section of water often involved the hunter swimming. Wearing his hat made of rushes, reeds or bulrushes, he would swim out to the waterfowl and pull them under.[51] Another method was for a hidden hunter to entice teal ducks towards the bank by waving the flower tops of several reeds tied together.[52] When close enough, the hunter would stand up to throw clubs and spears at the curious birds as they took flight. In the 1980s I observed Aboriginal hunters in the Lower Murray use this luring technique, although the birds were dispatched with a shotgun.

Nets were widely used across temperate Australia to catch birds, particularly flocks of water species.[53] The nets were strung between two trees in the flight path of the birds. Ducks were flushed out of areas with thrown bark discs or boomerangs, while hunters imitated hawks or falcons with shrill whistles.[54] This kept the ducks flying low and into the outstretched nets, and often resulted in a large catch. Another method required two boomerangs, one which was thrown to make the birds stay low, and a second thrown much lower, which severed the head off any duck it hit. Large birds could also be taken by spear.[55]

Emus, being large flightless animals, were generally caught in the same way as kangaroos, by stalking with bough shields, or by trapping in concealed pits.[56] An alternative method was to lie in wait next to an emu pad leading to water. When the emu approached in late afternoon, the hunter would thrust out his hand, catching the bird by one of its legs while he clubbed it to death.

Southern Aboriginal people commonly ate reptiles, particularly larger species of skink and goanna. Snakes, however, were often avoided when encountered in the open, being too dangerous to catch. They were a particular hazard during bulrush-root collecting expeditions in the swamps.[57]

Aboriginal people tracked freshwater tortoises as they moved inland to lay their eggs.[58] The gathered tortoise eggs were kept covered with foliage before being fried in hot ashes. Along the river, men generally caught turtles by diving for them. Frogs were either dug out of the ground or caught in the swamps.[59] Tadpoles were also eaten.

Large-mammal meat was highly sought after by Aboriginal people across Australia, both as food and for its symbolic value. Whale and dolphin strandings occasionally occur along the Southern coast, and the Wanmaring clan at Head of Bight in western South Australia had 'occasional gorges in large fish food, dead whales and other large sea creatures being found after some great storm'.[60] Such events attracted many Aboriginal people for feasting. Indeed, Aboriginal people believed that they had an active role in some strandings. Songs were used by 'strong men' to 'cause' strandings.[61] For the lower southeast of South Australia, there is a transcription of a whale song in the Booandik language which translates: 'The whale is come, And thrown up on land.' These lines were repeated over and over, and understood as inducing a stranding.

The New Zealand fur seal and the Australian sea lion were also hunted.[62] So effective were Aboriginal hunting activities in the pre-European period, many of the main breeding grounds of seals were reduced to offshore islands, such as those in Bass Strait, largely beyond the range of Aboriginal hunters.

Kangaroos and wallabies were a major source of food. Hunters stalked kangaroos and wallabies just prior to dusk, a time when the animals became more active with feeding.[63] The hunter used a shield of branches to hide behind, allowing him to move within spear-throwing distance of the animal. A good hunter could strike the kangaroo or wallaby when its head was down feeding. In this way, there was a chance that the beast would die quickly and quietly, and not frighten away other animals.

In the southwest of Western Australia, Aboriginal people dug trenches in which to catch kangaroos. Worsnop described these traps: 'They were cut by the natives across the runs of the animals, and were covered with slight layers of brush or grass, being made narrow at the bottom, so that the kangaroos could not obtain a footing to bound out.'[64]

The large-scale hunting of big animals, such as kangaroos and emus, involved the cooperative efforts of groups of people. A large party of men would go out early in the morning, armed with barbed spears and position themselves in a large semicircle.[65] At this time many animals would be seeking cover. Women, children and other men would start driving game in the direction of the people lying in wait. Often this involved firing the countryside and using the topography of the landscape to the hunter's advantage. Gradually the space between driving party members was reduced, the game cornered and killed with clubs. If fewer people were available, then large nets could be placed across a well-worn animal pad, and game driven into it by hunters. Sometimes brush fences were used to drive kangaroos and wallabies towards a point or a concealed pit where they could be easily killed.[66] If pits were being used along kangaroo and wallaby pads, they were dug in the morning to allow the fresh earth scent to dissipate before the game came along during the night.[67]

Ivaritji wearing a wallaby skin cloak from the museum, similar to that she remembered as a child when her family lived on the outskirts of Adelaide. PHOTO: H.M. HALE, ADELAIDE, SOUTH AUSTRALIA, 1928.

Possums were another source of food. Aboriginal people located hollow trees where possums lived by examining tree trunks for fresh scratch marks and small pieces of fur.[68] When such a tree was located, someone would climb it with the aid of a pointed climbing-stick to chop toeholds into smooth and branchless trunks. To determine whether a possum was in a particular hollow, a stone was thrown in causing the animal to make rustling noises as it shifted. Another method involved inserting a stick with a roughened end into the hollow and twisting it. When this was withdrawn, the end was examined for fur. If within easy reach, the possum was pulled out of the hollow, and its head smashed on the tree trunk. If the animal retreated deeply into the tree, it was either chopped out or forced from the hollow with smoke. In Tasmania, Aboriginal women generally caught the possums, by climbing tall trees with no lower branches with the aid of a grass rope that was fastened around the trunk for sliding up.[69] On mainland Australia, possum-skin cloaks would have been traded into areas where the tree-climbing marsupials were not commonly found because of a lack of tall trees. In the temperate region the skins of possums were highly valued for use in the making of warm winter clothing.[70]

Burrowing mammals, particularly bandicoots and rats, were either dug up or smoked out of their holes.[71] In the Mid-Murray region, Edward Eyre recorded in 1845 that:

Rats are also dug out of the ground, but they are procured in the greatest numbers and with the utmost facility when the approach of the floods in the river flats compels them to evacuate their domiciles. A variety is procured among the scrubs under a singular pile or nest which they make of sticks, in the shape of a hay-cock, three or four feet [0.9 to 1.2 metres] high and many feet in circumference. A great many occupy the same pile and are killed with sticks as they run out.[72]

Eyre referred to a now extinct species of stick-nest rat and indicated the seasonal nature of some hunting practices. Wombats could also be dug up or smoked out of their burrows.[73] Another method of capturing wombats involved the hunter hiding in bushes during the late afternoon where he could observe from which hole a wombat emerged. When the animal moved on, the hole would be blocked about a metre in. The hunter would then frighten the wombat back to its hole, trapping him between the exit and the block.

Temperate Seasons

Aboriginal people could, at certain times, exercise a degree of choice in the food they ate. While animal foods, such as fish, emu and kangaroo meat, were highly favoured foods when available, vegetable foods, such as roots, were probably the mainstay when meat was not easily obtainable due to seasonal movement of animals and the difficulty in hunting in wet and cold weather. Operating around seasonal availability there were typical diets for different seasons. Taking the Adelaide Plains region, vegetables and grubs were mainly eaten during what we now call spring.[74] With the

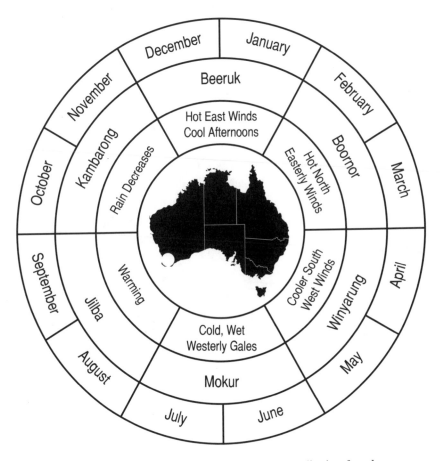

Aboriginal seasonal calendar for the Nyungar people, Swan district of southwest Western Australia. CHART: RAY MARCHANT, AFTER BATES (1901–14), BINDON & WHALLEY (1992) AND REID (1995).

commencement of summer, the eggs and young of birds were eagerly sought after, as were kangaroos, emus, fish and lizards, as these animals became more active for breeding. During the hottest part of the year, possums and wattle gum were procured, while in autumn, berries and nectar were available. In the winter, a variety of roots were consumed, as were possums and other animals.

Seasonal calendars in temperate Australia appear to have recognised at least the same number of seasons as the temperate region of the Northern Hemisphere, and often more. For example, in the Swan district of southwest Western Australia, the Aboriginal people recognised six seasons: *mokur*—winter, about June and July; *jilba*—spring, August and September; *kambarong*—late spring, October and November; *beeruk*—summer, December and January; *boornor*—early autumn, about February and March; and *winyarung*—mid to late autumn, April and May.[75] In the Murrumbidgee to Lower Darling region, four seasons were recorded for the Aboriginal calendar: *kurtie*—summer, distinguished by flowers and fruit; *weat*—autumn, known for the gossamer threads in the air and as the season that reptiles become inactive; *miangie*—winter, a hard time for Aboriginal people beginning with frosts; and *bakroothakootoo*—spring, a time of succulent herbs and the breeding of birds and kangaroos.[76] This similarity with European seasons may be due to the similarity between the Australian and Mediterranean climates. There may also have been smaller seasons that were not recorded. We also have a partial account of the seasonal calendar for the Bigambul people in the riverine district, on the eastern side of the shared Queensland and New South Wales border. Alfred W. Howitt reported:

> The seasons are reckoned by the Bigambul according to the time of the year in which the trees blossom. For instance, *Yerra* is the name of a tree which blossoms in September, hence that time is called *Yerrabinda*. The Apple-tree flowers about Christmas-time, which is *Nigabinda*. The Ironbark tree flowers about the end of January, which they call *Wo-binda*. They also call this time, which is in the height of summer, *Tinna-koge-alba*, that is to say, the time when the ground burns the feet.[77]

Presumably there were other seasons to mark the temperate autumn and winter months. The ebb and flow of floods may have been seasonal markers in some riverine districts. Europeans have imperfectly recorded the seasons for most other groups in temperate Australia. In particular what are generally not fully recorded are the seasons that do not correspond to the four seasons familiar to European colonists. The linking of seasons with the movements of celestial bodies is common across Australia.[78]

Enough of the early hunting and gathering traditions are recorded to show patterns predicated on the recognition of certain seasons. For example, to the Kaurna people of the Adelaide Plains the arrival of the 'autumn star', Parna, indicated a change of season and was a sign to leave the coast to make waterproof huts in the foothills.[79] Similarly, in the Yaraldi language of the Lower Murray in South Australia, the term recorded for autumn, *Marangalkadi*, was said to mean 'pertaining to the crow' (more properly a raven).[80] According to Aboriginal tradition, the autumn stars are low in the south-eastern sky because it was to the southeast of the Lower Murray that the 'Crow' Ancestor, Marangani, crossed into the Skyworld where he could be seen as a constellation. When he was at his zenith, both animals and humans were thought to enter the 'rutting season'.[81] In the Lower Murray, Yutang (winter) and Riwuri (spring) were symbolic of the male Dreaming Ancestors Ngurunderi and Waiyungari respectively.[82]

In the Mallee region of western Victoria, Aboriginal people believed that the star Arcturus was the Dreaming Ancestor Marpeankurrk, the mother of a son, Djuit (Antares) and a daughter, Weetkurrk (star in Bootis, west of Arcturus). Marpeankurrk was the:

> . . . discoverer of the Bittur [termite larvae], and the teacher of the Aborigines when and where to find it. When it is coming into season with them it is going out of season with her. The Bittur is the larvae of the wood ant, which is found in large communities, and of which the Aborigines are very fond. They subsist almost entirely upon it during part of the months of August and September. When she is in the north at evening, the Bittur are gone and (Cotchi) summer begins. [83]

By observing the position of Marpeankurrk in the night sky, Aboriginal people in the Mallee region knew when to collect termite larvae, which would have been one of their favoured sources of food.

Seasonal population movement occurred among most Aboriginal groups in the temperate regions, even if the distance was only a few kilometres. This was forced upon them by both the weather and local food and water shortages. Aboriginal people generally travelled more during the summer months to take advantage of a wide variety of foods across the landscape, frequently changing their camping places.[84]

The summer months were a mixed blessing for Aboriginal people. One nineteenth-century observer recorded that summer was a 'great festival time' for Aboriginal people, when food was plentiful and travelling was easy. Yet although southern Australia has a relatively high rainfall, there are areas where surface water suitable for drinking was scarce during the height of the summer months. The mallee vegetation, which spreads in large patches in a belt from southwest Western Australia across to the western Blue Mountains in New South Wales, occurs in areas where surface water is scarce in spite of relatively high rainfall. The word 'mallee' is probably derived from the Aboriginal term *mali*, formerly part of Aboriginal languages in western Victoria and central New South Wales.[85] As a result of water shortages, Aboriginal people in mallee areas were more thinly spread across the landscape than in coastal areas. During droughts, when the soaks and springs became unreliable, water was obtained from cut tree roots. The Ngarkat people of the Murray Mallee relied heavily on root water and only needed to travel to the Murray River at times of severe drought.[86] Many of the streams in southern Australia are intermittent, meaning that they cease to flow in the height of summer and become a series of brackish pools. The summer camping places in sand-dune areas were also often away from surface drinking water. Therefore, even in temperate Australia Aboriginal people needed to know where to obtain water from wells, springs and soaks.

In some areas, hunting and gathering activities, such as tracking animals, were difficult during the cold and rainy season, when Aboriginal people tended to stay around camp. While the coastal zones of temperate Australia were rich in natural resources, in particular, in food such as fish, molluscs and coastal berries as well as meat from occasional whale strandings—and many of these foods were available for the greater part of the year—the onset of winter winds and rains made the coast a harsh zone in which to live. 'Saltwater' Aboriginal groups then moved away from the coast and towards their inland retreats. For 'freshwater' people living along the edges of lakes and rivers, the yearly movement was between the lakeside and the forest. As winter approached, the Tangani people, for example, moved away from the coast to camp along the mainland side of the Coorong where firewood was plentiful, and shelter from weather available.[87]

There were also political reasons for some movements. The Tangani clans avoided camping on the mainland side of the Coorong at certain times because they were open to attack here from the Ngarkat people, who normally ranged in mallee areas away from the river. The Tangani considered that they were not likely to be attacked during the winter, as most Ngarkat incursions were during drier times of the year when water shortages forced inland people towards the lakes district.

In the south, Aboriginal people tended to live in higher density, but nevertheless still had a nomadic life that was organised according to their perception of the temperate seasonal calendar. Much of their hunting and gathering technology was based on maximising marine and riverine resources.

Nine

The Central Deserts

Much of Australia is desert, with up to two-thirds of the continent defined as arid. As ice ages have come and gone over the last two million years, there have only been brief wet periods in which the arid zone was confined to the centre of the continent. Presently, the vast Australian desert region spills as far as the Indian Ocean in Western Australia, but is elsewhere contained by coastal regions with higher rainfall. When the world sea levels fall as the polar ice caps grow, Australia becomes a larger, colder and drier place. Over the last 50,000 years or so, Aboriginal people have adapted to living in arid environments, to the extent that they have only avoided the worst of the deserts during rare times of extreme drought when rain does not fall for several years.

The Europeans who came to Central Australia from the late nineteenth century, saw endless sand hills and low desert ranges which were to them relatively featureless wastes. The only potential, apart from mining, they could see in them was for the grazing of robust and wide ranging animals such as cattle. To Aboriginal people living in the arid zone their country is not a desolate waste, but a landscape full of religious meaning, being the creation of many Ancestors. The desert dwellers possess an extended network of alliances. By the early twentieth century, anthropologists recognised that the whole of the Western Desert, spreading out west from Alice

Springs into Western Australia and South Australia, was essentially a single cultural bloc, with related dialects spoken throughout.[1] The material possessions of desert Aboriginal people were relatively slight, in contrast with coastal groups, due to the need to maintain maximum mobility. Nevertheless, the strategies for living in the desert were equally as sophisticated as those used by hunters and gatherers elsewhere on the continent. Aboriginal cultures flourished in arid Australia—albeit in less dense numbers, but in greater ranges.

Desert Range

Unlike the deserts of Northern Africa, Central Australia is not comprised of degraded rainless deserts. Here, even the driest sandy deserts, such as the Simpson which receives an average of only 100 millimetres of rainfall per year, have some vegetation between the dunes. During the dry part of the seasonal cycle, the Australian deserts look bleak, abandoned and hardly the place for a thriving Aboriginal population. And yet the transformation of the interior after rare bouts of prolonged rain is spectacular, with expanses, such as the normally dry Lake Eyre, filling with water and the surrounding countryside becoming a sea of flowers. As put by biologist Penny van Oosterzee, Central Australia is 'a land driven by extremes, not by averages'.[2] The Australian arid region, referred to as the 'outback' and 'never-never' by Europeans, is not ecologically bland, but has many different habitat zones: desert mountains, riverine woodlands, mulga woodlands, sand dunes, sand plains, chenopod (salt bush) shrublands and gibber plains. The flora and fauna varies accordingly, although many of the fauna have become extinct since European impact on the desert.[3]

The desert regions were among the last tracts of Australia to become part of a European-modified landscape[4] and therefore retained populations which lived traditional lifestyles which have interested scholars since the nineteenth century. The scholars who studied Australian desert dwellers have backgrounds as interesting as the people they studied. The groundbreaking anthropological work by W. Baldwin Spencer and Frank J. Gillen in the 1890s took place chiefly around Alice Springs, a region known by Europeans as the 'Centre'.[5] Their publications raised the profile of the study of Aboriginal cultures overseas. Spencer was the Oxford scholar, while Gillen was a telegraph operator living at the frontier, who had all the necessary connections with Aboriginal people. In the early twentieth century, the amateur anthropologist and humanitarian Daisy M. Bates worked with southern desert people from her bases at Eucla and Ooldea Siding along the East–West Railway Line.[6] This eccentric woman was famous for her Victorian-style clothing and for once being married to the infamous Boer War soldier Harry 'the Breaker' Morant.

From the mid-twentieth century, a generation of scientists and anthropologists who were investigating Aboriginal relationships with their land turned their interests towards the Western Desert. Museum researcher Norman Tindale, with his American fieldwork collaborator the geneticist Joseph B. Birdsell, contributed to these studies because: '... it is in the Western Desert, in the most challenging environment, that some of the most intriguing aspects of aboriginal geography and ecology survive and give us clues as to the ways of the southern peoples'.[7] During the twentieth century, the Australian deserts were where hunters and gatherers could still be observed living more or less as they had done for millennia. Many of the stereotypical views of Aboriginal cultures that are held by Europeans have been based on observations from this last frontier.

For thousands of years the Australian desert country has been home to Aboriginal groups that to varying degrees were related by marriage and who had shared Dreamings and material-culture traditions. A number of areas within the arid centre of Australia provided refuges for hunters and gatherers during times of hardship and drew groups together. For example, in terms of the movements of people, the Lake Eyre Basin region, covering the corners of the states of Queensland, South Australia and of the Northern Territory, was like a pulsating heart. Here, groups such as the Diyari and Wangkangurru people moved out into the desert in search of food after rains had fallen and retreated back to their camps along the Cooper and Diamantina Rivers in times of drought. Similarly, in the Macdonnell Ranges of Central Australia, Aboriginal people, such as the Arrernte and Luritja, had waterholes in the tributaries of the Finke River which served as bases. Other desert dwellers, such as the Warlpiri of the Tanami Desert and the Pitjantjatjara of the Western Desert, relied on series of rockholes of varying reliability for their main refuges.

The desert dweller's pattern of land use meant that people were mostly spread out, coming together in groups of a few hundred only during ceremonial occasions when the land could support extra from hunting and gathering. Yet in spite of the wide open spaces, Aboriginal people in the desert were neither alone nor subject to random movements. Anthropologist Robert Tonkinson described the security he observed in the Mardudjara people of the western Gibson Desert in Western Australia, 'security in knowing both what can be seen and what lies beyond, and in the certainty that other groups, of kin and friends, are out there, perhaps visibly manifested by their hunting or campfire smokes, which can often be seen from distances of up to 50 miles [80 kilometres]'.[8]

The desert dwellers, with outward looking social networks, were also predisposed for establishing relationships with new people and places. Aboriginal population movements, which were caused by a combination of social and environmental factors, were part of the constant process of redistributing people across the landscape. It is a popular assumption of many Europeans that Aboriginal movements were static, to the degree that each 'tribe' had 50,000 or so years of history on each piece of land. Nothing could be further from the truth. Aboriginal populations are constantly moving, expanding and contracting in response to the cultural and physical environments.

From the desert region in particular, Aboriginal people have been fanning out into the better watered surrounding areas since before Europeans arrived and have continued to do so since. And the desert produced people whose mobility and physical endurance meant that they were able to exert territorial pressure on their neighbours during times of hardship, brought on by population movements or drought. For example, in the 1830s the first European settlers observed the Kokatha people, who speak a Western Desert language, as far south as Port Lincoln in the temperate zone, having come down from the Gawler Ranges.[9] The missionary Clamour W. Schürmann recorded that the seasonal feast upon *nondo* 'beans' (*Acacia* pods) by the Nawu Banggarla people who lived around Port Lincoln was disrupted because 'the Kukata [Kokatha] tribe, notorious for ferocity and witchcraft, often threaten to burn or otherwise destroy the Nondo bushes in order to aggravate their adversaries.'[10] Northern desert neighbours had pushed the Kokatha south. The movement of one group often caused ripples across the political landscape. After European settlement, the movement of people increased, with many desert groups leaving the central areas to go west towards the desert fringe; south to live along the East–West Railway Line; or east towards the Overland Telegraph stations during the late nineteenth century.[11] During the mid-twentieth century, European patrol officers cleared out the Maralinga area for nuclear testing, sending further waves of Western Desert people towards the southern coast.[12] Since European settlement, desert dwellers, such as the Warlpiri, have also moved into the southern Kimberley and around Katherine on the edge of Arnhem Land.[13] Along with the movement of people comes the introduction of new cultural practices and languages.

Quest for Water and Food

Aboriginal people living in the Australian arid zone had to rely on a variety of water and food sources which, in contrast to the temperate and subtropical regions, are thinly spread over a wide area and are largely dependent on chance rainfalls and El Niño oscillations which have cycles longer than a year.

Prior to European intrusions, the type of water sources Aboriginal people used depended on the severity of the season. People living in some arid areas, such as the Flinders Ranges and Lake Eyre regions in South Australia, used skin bags to carry drinking water short distances. In the Western Desert, these bags were not generally used, possibly due to the scarcity of marsupial skins. For Aboriginal people, knowing your country meant having detailed knowledge of the different water sources, including where in the landscape they were located and the reliability of each in relation to the season. According to the anthropologist Ronald Berndt, the Western Desert people living around Balgo in the Great Sandy Desert in Western Australia distinguish eight different types of landscape features that produce drinking water. These are:

> Soak (*djunu*), subsurface water, for which they must dig; rockhole (*waniri*), some virtually permanent; spring (*windji*), fairly rare; creek or river (*giligi*), which flows only occasionally, but sometimes leaves waterholes which last for varying periods; billabong (*walgir*), which fills up after heavy rain; swamp (*baldju*), which results from rain and does not last long; claypan (*waran*), a temporary receptacle from rain water but usually a plain; and salt lake (*baragu*), which can be relied on to produce drinkable water, at least in parts and during good seasons.[14]

For desert Aboriginal people, the choice of water depended on the season and where they were hunting and gathering. The decline in animal and plant foods surrounding the permanent waterholes due to human pressure was a factor in pushing people towards areas with less reliable water.

The replenishment of desert water sources is extremely irregular. In some parts of the arid zone it is possible in one step to go from a dry barren patch of ground to one covered with ephemeral herbs that have sprung up from a recent localised shower. Summer rains refill the water table storage, replenish rockhole catchments and the reserves in the sandy creek beds. Most of the creeks only flow as continuous surface streams during floods, existing as a series of isolated waterholes at other times. When Aboriginal people are travelling, the choice of their route depends upon the season and weather conditions. At dusk, the movement of birds, in particular pardalotes and pigeons, may point to the direction of open waterholes in the desert.

Rock cavities that collect rainwater are known in Australian English as 'gnamma holes', based on an Aboriginal word for hole, *ngama*, from the Nyungar language of the southwest of Western Australia.[15] These are naturally occurring hollows in impervious rock, such as granite, with their necks widened to enable human arms to scoop up water. Some ngamma holes can only be accessed through a narrow gap, with the water level a metre or more below the opening. Aboriginal people formerly used a variety of improvised plungers, straws and sponges made from plant material to get at water held in deep recesses.[16] They also usually capped the entrance with stone slabs or covered them with bushes to prevent algal growth and animals fouling the water. Covering the opening also reduced evaporation. Some of the ngammas are very large, holding as much as 200,000 litres of water when full. Aboriginal people noted the location of these sources of water by the presence of insects, such as mud-daubing wasps and bees, or by ant trails.

While claypans are normally dry, after rain they fill with surface run-off and underground drainage. Described as 'soaks', they are valuable sources of water which allow hunters and gatherers to penetrate desert areas that are not usually accessible. The botanist and anthropologist John B. Cleland, writing in 1966, noted that soaks:

> . . . on the edge of the eastern side of the Simpson Desert, known as 'mikaris' have enabled natives in good seasons to penetrate far into this inhospitable region and even to cross it. Unfortunately, sand-drifts,

A Luritja man drinking water from a shallow wooden dish.
PHOTO: W.D. WALKER, WEST OF OODNADATTA, NORTH SOUTH AUSTRALIA, 1928.

the results of long droughts, are covering these over, for the natives no longer clear them and there is no one who now knows where they are.[17]

Not only did Aboriginal people maintain their soaks, they also modified them to improve their water-holding properties. In 1897, the explorer Richard Maurice described Aboriginal modifications to a water source at Boundary Dam, near the border between Western Australia and South Australia:

There is a little flat beneath a rain-washed side of a sandhill exposing clay with a little creek connecting it with the lake. This the natives have dammed up to about 5 ft [1.5 metres] high and 10 ft [3 metres] broad and thrown bushes in to prevent evaporation. On the NE side is another hole square in shape, but filled up with silt. This Injida [a local Aboriginal man] stated to be the work of whites and we afterwards proved that these same whites must have been Giles' party.[18]

Travelling through the deserts, Maurice came across other water places that were important to the Aboriginal groups. For instance, he described the permanent soak at Ooldea as a 'tribal meeting place', where trade, dispute resolutions, marriages and initiations would take place.[19] This place became a siding for the East–West Railway Line and was made famous for being the campsite of Daisy Bates.[20] It is also an important Dreaming site, as are many other desert water sources.

To this day Aboriginal people know how to dig wells in areas where water seeps up from deep subterranean sources, in some cases where fault lines cross aquifers and the underground water is forced upwards.[21] Ladders made of notched poles are used to get 6 metres or more below the surface. Mud scooped from the bottom of the well is packed along the walls to help reinforce the soil from collapse. Grass and sand is used to filter drinking water, which can be extremely toxic at the end of a drought if filled with dead animal and plant material. To avoid the water fouling because of dead animals, branches were sometimes leant against the wall to allow animals that had fallen in to escape.

In the same manner as rock cavities, water also collects in large hollow trees, and can be accessed by chopping into the trunk. Water could also be obtained from the roots of certain species of tree. Among the 'water trees' found in the arid zone are the needlewood (*Hakea leucoptera*), particular species of gum and mallee (*Eucalyptus* species) and some wattles (*Acacia* species). For water, Aboriginal people targeted the lateral roots that run just beneath the surface of the ground, their position marked by a slight rise or crack in the ground where its rapid growth after the last rains had displaced the hardened soil.[22] The size of the roots ranges from a centimetre in diameter to about the size of a man's wrist. Once located, the soil was scraped away from the whole length of the root with a wooden shovel. The lateral roots were prised off near the trunk of the tree with a digging-stick or spear-point, and then broken into sections between half a metre and a metre long. The water was drained from the roots by leaning the pieces vertically against a tree trunk with the dripping ends inside a container such as a wooden dish, wallaby skin bag, or a simple trough made from bark removed from the roots. One long mallee root was said to satisfy the wants of two or three thirsty adults. The ends of the roots could also be plugged up with clay for transporting the water over long distances. As only a few roots would be taken each time, the tree would generally survive.

Aboriginal people also used the stems of young gum trees, mallees and stringybarks for the purpose of extracting water to drink.[23] Breaking several saplings at their roots and removing the tops, the root end was then placed on top and the branch end set on end to drain into a container. Not all plants, even when they are the right species, produce water. Trees growing in hollows between long rolling ridges will have a greater abundance of water in their roots than those growing upon the crest of a ridge. Although the supply of water from roots and stems is not strictly seasonal, it is probably only a reliable water source in trees growing in favoured areas.

Animals were also sources of water. In the desert, Aboriginal people used at least two species of water-holding frog as a source of drinking water, as John Cleland recounted:

> The natives can detect by cracks on the surface of dry ground on claypans where these bloated-like creatures are hidden away awaiting the next rain-storm. By stamping on the ground the croaking of the frogs may be heard though only at the end of a long period of drought, when the frogs anticipate rain, will they respond to the artificial thundering overhead.[24]

Once caught, the clear water stored in the bladder of the frogs as a reserve for when the animals are less active between rains was extracted.

The desert is a notoriously unpredictable landscape and family groups coped with this by relying upon older members who had some memory of what had occurred previously. During the peak of the worst droughts, desert dwellers needed to know which of the rockholes, wells and soakages were still likely to contain some water when all the other sources had failed, and which of the neighbours' land was still likely to have some food and water left. This group memory is also encoded in Aboriginal Dreaming accounts, told in song. Aboriginal people believe that certain individuals are 'rain-makers', having the ritual power to alter the weather and bring water to their country.[25]

Plants

The desert contains a wide variety of plant foods, albeit thinly dispersed, which occur in particular habitat zones.[26] Fruits collected by desert people include desert raisin (*Solanum centrale*), bush tomato (*Solanum chippendalei*), mistletoe (*Amyema* and *Lysiana* species), wild currant (*Canthium attenuatum*), desert fig (*Ficus platypoda*), native orange (*Capparis mitchelli*), Australian plum (*Santalum lanceolatum*), quandong (*Santalum acuminatum*) and conkleberry (*Carissa lanceolata*). Seeds were obtained from various wattles (*Acacia* species), munyeroo (*Portulaca oleracea*), woollybutt grass (*Eragrostis eriopoda*), native millet grass (*Panicum decompositum*), coolabah (*Eucalyptus coolabah*) and kurrajong (*Brachychiton gregorii*). Nectar can be obtained from gum and mallee (*Eucalyptus* species), honey grevillea (*Grevillea*

A Wangkangurru woman grinding munyeru (Portulaca oleracea) *seed between grinding stones and into a wooden dish.* PHOTO: G. AISTON, NORTHEAST OF SOUTH AUSTRALIA, EARLY TWENTIETH CENTURY.

juncifolia) and corkwood (*Hakea divaricata*). The soft flowers and leaves of plants such as the bush banana (*Marsdenia australis*), parakeelya (*Calandrinia balonensis*) and munyeroo provide soft greens. Edible gum from various species of wattle are gathered. There are also tubers, such as from the mallee, desert yam (*Ipomoea costata*), onion grass (*Cyperus bulbosus*) and desert truffle fungi (*Choiromyces aboriginum*, *Elderia arenivagra* and other species).

In the last chapter I noted that southern groups on occasions collected nardoo (*Marsilea* species) a small fern with a clover-like leaf and an edible sporocarp (analogous to a seed). This is a widely recorded desert plant food, which lives in the mudflats between dunes, appearing soon after rain has dried up. The Australian English name is based on an Aboriginal term, *ngardu*, from the eastern Lake Eyre Basin languages.[27] The nardoo has had some bad press in European eyes, being the food that the explorers Burke and Wills attempted to live on before perishing from starvation at Cooper Creek in 1861. It is likely that they did not properly prepare it and probably required other food sources as well. Nevertheless, Aboriginal people in parts of the arid zone relied fairly heavily on this food source. Thomas Worsnop described the Aboriginal process of making nardoo damper as follows:

Linda Crombie, a Wangkangurru woman, collecting ngardu *sporocarps.*
PHOTO: P.A. CLARKE, PANDI PANDI, NORTHEAST SOUTH AUSTRALIA, 1986.

> They winnow and grind the seed [sporocarp], putting the flour into a
> cooliman or wooden trough, and mixing it thus—the lubra [Aboriginal
> woman] takes up a good mouthful of water and squirts it occasionally on
> the flour, kneading it meanwhile into a paste. When sufficiently kneaded
> it is not at all palatable to the European taste, as it leaves a hot astringent
> sensation in the throat, but it will sustain life for a long time.[28]

This plant often grows in thick mats, making it a simple task to quickly
collect an abundance of food. During dry periods, the sporocarps remain
caked in the hardened mud awaiting the next rains to germinate.

As noted earlier, the ability to use grass seed as food has allowed much
more occupation of Central Australia that would have been possible
otherwise. Desert dwellers stood apart from the coastal people through
their extensive use and reliance on grindstone technology.[29] The seed was
processed by grinding, then baked in the ashes of a fire to make a solid
bread loaf or cake. Groups that used grindstone technology extended from
the Kamilaroi in central eastern New South Wales across to the Alyawarra
and Warlpiri people of Central Australia and on to the Watjarri people in
the Murchison River region in the central coast of Western Australia. In
many areas the Aboriginal name of the grass food that is produced is

konakandi, which reputedly translates as 'dung food', a reference to the appearance of the wet meal before it is cooked in the ashes.[30] A set of wooden containers with an inner grooved surface is utilised in the gathering, winnowing, cleaning and holding of the grass seed through its processing.

The collecting of grass seed was similar to what we might expect of early grain growers at the beginning of agriculture in the northern hemisphere. The explorer Augustus C. Gregory described how in 1858 at Cooper Creek in north-eastern South Australia he observed Aboriginal people cutting grass down with stone knives, leaving enough stem for beating the heads off the straw, and the seed accumulating in heaps.[31] The collecting process could be as elaborate as the grinding itself. During a Central Australian expedition in August 1930, Norman Tindale filmed Alyawarra people processing *otteta* (native millet grass) seed. He described in detailed the process before milling commenced:

> This grass springs and flourishes after northwest monsoonal rains, growing luxuriantly on plains where the storm showers flood the soil temporarily to a depth of a few centimetres. The seed heads are ready by late autumn. At this time the country is dry and the ground sunbaked. It is possible to gather some grain in ear but the Aborigines tend to rely on the activities of a species of ant which has the habit of carrying the seeds to their nests where they arrange them in a ring around the entrances to their holes. Women take advantage of this to sweep the mixture of grit, chaff and seed into their wooden dishes. After preliminary cleaning by winnowing and rocking in the dishes to separate grain from other particles the ears are hulled [husk removed] by treading the seed in a circular hole in the ground, conveniently placed near a tree so that the woman operator can support herself as she rotates her feet, right and left over the grain. The husked grain is removed from the husking hole, is again winnowed to remove the bulk of the dross [refuse], and then subjected to further rockings in the dishes, some of which are furnished with longitudinal riffles which seem to expedite the separation of the grain from the rest of the contents. Following several stages of this preparation, the grain is milled.[32]

Pitjantjatjara women performed a similar technique involving *wanganu* (woollybutt grass).[33] In Central Australia, surplus grain was sometimes stored in caves, hollow trees and huts.[34] The use of grindstones increased during the last 1500 years, possibly due to the establishment of a large, more permanent population in the arid zone.[35]

Insects

Desert Aboriginal people eat many different types of insect, particularly when the amount of vertebrate meat they are able to include in their diet is limited.[36] The larvae of wood-boring beetles and cossid moths, commonly called 'witchetty grubs', are a major source of food, usually gathered by prising open timber or by using grub-hooks made from wood or grass. The Australian English term 'witchetty' was probably derived from the words *wityu* (grub hook) and *varti* (grub) from the Adnyamathanha language of the Flinders Ranges.[37] In the desert woodland regions of Central Australia, the roots and the trunks of trees contain a large number of edible grubs, which are generally collected by the women.[38]

The Dreamings of Central Australia have Grub, Honey Ant and White Ant Ancestors and associated Dreaming rites. The honey ant is a major source of sweetness. They are dug up from ground nests in mulga country. Aboriginal people's advice on eating them is: 'You don't swallow them, you put them on your tongue and bite on the abdomen and suck honey from it.'[39]

The Australian stingless bees are a sought after food, with the comb, honey, bees and larvae all eaten together. Writing in the 1960s, John Cleland observed:

> In searching for a bee's nest at Macdonald Downs in Central Australia, the natives, instead of looking up the trees for issuing bees, went down on their knees in a likely locality and searched for small particles carried away from their nests by the bees and dropped. These having been found, it meant that somewhere close at hand, there was a nest. Likely trees were tapped and any hollow ones climbed and the stick poked down until the one containing honey was found.[40]

A variety of other insects found in galls and with wax scales was also eaten, as was the flying stage of termites.

Fish

The Diyari and Wangkangurru people of the northeast of South Australia lived on the edge of one of the driest deserts in the world, and yet paradoxically they ate fish. The permanent waterholes of the Cooper and Diamantina River systems are fed with water from the channel country of southwest Queensland. Here Aboriginal people used several kinds of fishing nets.[41] Bag-nets were up to 4 metres long and were woven from vegetable-fibre string. This net was placed at a narrow opening in a dam or weir and across creeks in flood. Fish swept into the net were collected in large numbers. Nets like these would be repaired when damaged and stored when not in use. The fragile stake-net or gill-net type was woven from rush fibre and made up to 30 metres in length. It was placed across a waterhole in the evening, attached to stakes at intervals of 2 or 3 metres. During the night fish would become caught in the mesh by their gills. The fishermen would check the nets in the early morning, extracting the fish. Nets like this were easily torn and needed constant mending. Aboriginal people living along other inland river systems to the west, such as the Finke and Frew Rivers, used similar nets. Fish are absent from much of the Western Desert, where water sources from drainage systems are not permanent and the existing rock holes are not replenished by river floods.

Other Animals

The Western Desert people pride themselves on being skilful hunters. Norman Tindale has suggested this is evident in the language group names Kokatha and Kukatja, which are based upon the word *kuka*, meaning meat.[42] Nevertheless, large game, such as kangaroos and emus, are not found in the core desert areas unless there has been plenty of rain. When working with Pintupi people on the western edge of the Tanami Desert, Donald Thomson noted:

> The scarcity of large game was apparent from the fact that few of the spears that I saw in the desert were fitted with barbs of bone and that when wooden barbs were used they were seldom lashed with the sinews of animals; generally, plant fibres had to be used although the Bindibu [Pintupi] obviously preferred sinews and used these when they could get them.[43]

In the arid zone, kangaroos and wallabies are generally found on the grassy plains near the ranges, whereas euros and smaller wallabies inhabit the rocky hills. Game nets are extensively used in the arid zone to catch large marsupials and emus. As in temperate areas nets are stretched across the favourite routes or game pads. The nets collapse around the animals as they try to escape through them. Hunters using nets require intimate knowledge of the animal's behaviour in relation to the landscape. A net set either in the wrong place or at an inappropriate time of the year is obviously pointless.

Nets for catching emus were often very long and sometimes comprised of rope made from sinews. One net found in a cave near the Darling River during the 1850s and now in the South Australian Museum, is made from vegetable-fibre rope and measures 54 metres in length. It is the longest Aboriginal net known. Amateur anthropologist Charles P. Mountford described the method of using these large game nets in notes made during anthropological fieldwork in the Flinders Ranges during the 1940s.[44] According to him, the net was quickly erected on poles at one end of a waterhole while emus were drinking there. Aboriginal hunters would then frighten the emus, stampeding them into the net. The emus would become tangled in the mesh, allowing the hunters time to kill them with wooden clubs. In this part of the arid zone—around the Flinders Ranges and in northeast South Australia—spears were rarely used in hunting due to the reliance upon clubs.

The explorer William C. Gosse encountered low brush fences used by Aboriginal people to trap game on several occasions in 1872. He described one of these structures in the Musgrave Ranges in Central Australia and the way it was used to catch wallaby:

> They are long lines of sticks, boughs, bushes, &c., which, when laid down, are about a foot [31 cm] high and about a quarter of a mile [0.4 km] long, and in the form of two sides of a square, forming a corner. At this corner, for a few yards, the fences are about 4ft. [122 cm] or 5ft. [152 cm] high, made more substantial and laid with boughs. Over this point is thrown a net, or if a net is not obtainable it is covered with boughs. The natives hunt the wallaby by spreading themselves out, and by beating the bushes and making a great noise, when the animals are frightened into the lines, and then hop along until they reach the covered portion, where a native is hidden behind some bushes. As the wallaby reaches his den he is quietly knocked on the head by a waddy.[45]

In another version of this technique brush screens are set up along animal tracks leading to claypans filled with water.[46] In some cases, a group of water holes might have all their entrances blocked except one,[47] which is staked out by hunters waiting for emus to visit. The hunting of game with such practices could only occur seasonally, but it enabled the collecting of large quantities of food to support groups gathered for holding ceremonies.

Reptiles are a major meat source for Aboriginal people in the deserts, being the dominant vertebrate fauna in most arid regions. The larger lizards, such as perenties and goannas, are found in trees or in burrows.[48] They are traditionally killed with a blow to the back of the head, with the innards taken out through the mouth and anus. After it is killed the perentie is put on the fire to remove its skin. The legs are skewed together and the tail folded under for cooking in the hot soil from a fire. Reptile eggs are also eaten, as are many smaller lizard species. While collecting reptiles as biological specimens, Donald Thomson noted in 1975 that: 'The Bindibu people who accompanied us hunted relentlessly so that we in competition were handicapped. They consider almost all lizards as game including small and rough-skinned agamids. . . . The only agamid that enjoyed immunity from the Bindibu hunters was *Moloch horridus* [the thorny devil].'[49] Some snake species are also eaten, although snakes tend to be found near permanent sources of water and are not encountered as often in open areas of the desert country.

Desert Seasons

Seasonal cycles in the arid zone tend to be less regular than elsewhere due to the El Niño oscillation and are best measured over several years. Europeans have generally not recognised that deserts have seasons, other than hot and cold times.[50] The northwest monsoonal rains begin to influence Central Australia in December, several weeks after the northern coastal areas are affected, as the winds change to the south.[51] The air is largely emptied of water by the time it reaches inland Australia, producing irregular rainfall, both in quantity and distribution. Desert people recognise from three to five main seasons of the year. The Arrernte of the Macdonnell Ranges recognise three seasons. *Uterne* is a hot and wet season, from December to March.[52] When the sun is out, the ground becomes too hot to walk on. Nevertheless this is the time of the year to collect fruit such as wild passionfruit, wild oranges, wild bananas and wild tomatoes because,

Diyari man polishing a boomerang club with an upper grindstone. Alongside him are two adzes used for woodcarving. PHOTO: G. AISTON, NORTHEAST SOUTH AUSTRALIA, EARLY TWENTIETH CENTURY.

in the perception of Arrernte people, the sun has 'cooked them ripe'. It is also a good time to dry chewing tobacco.

Starting in April, the season of *alhwerrpe* makes the desert colder and drier, the equivalent to the southern temperate winter. The season of *ulpmulpme*, from October to November, is windy and brings some rain, although less than with *uterne*. It is a period when the land starts to become green with the growth of leaves, flowers and seeds.

There have been several studies of the seasonal calendars of the Aboriginal people of the southern Western Desert, living around Uluru (Ayers Rock), Kata Tjuta (the Olgas) and the mountains in the northwest of South Australia.[53] These people speak languages such as Pitjantjatjara and Yankunytjatjara. The biologist Lynn Baker describes how the seasons here 'are named after the way the weather is'[54] and this calendar underlies the following description which is widely used, with some local variation, across the Western Desert cultural region. *Kuli*, from December to March, is the hot and wet season produced by erratic north-west monsoonal rains. Paradoxically, these isolated rain bursts may bring a brief period of starvation to

Aboriginal people as the animal food sources disperse across the desert to access areas away from permanent water and the plant foods take time to respond to the moisture. It is the start of a 'green time' and on the whole a good period for desert dwellers, when almost anywhere is suitable to make a camp. Each shower wipes the ground clear of old tracks, with every fresh imprint potentially leading to food. Large moths fly into Aboriginal campfires, providing an easy source of nutrition.

Putu kalitja is the period from March to May. It too is a 'green time', with the claypans still containing water from the monsoonal rains that have just finished. There are numerous insects, birds and fruits to feed on. However, snakes and lizards become less active during this season. From April to October, the winds tend to blow from the southeast. Rain that occasionally comes with the southwest winds encourages Aboriginal people to visit the more remote parts of their territory. While rain spoils the dried wild figs lying on the ground around waterholes, it does wash the ripe kurrajong seeds free of crow dung, from having passed through crows' guts, and makes them available for food processing.[55]

In spite of the often cold conditions, in the past Desert Aboriginal people went without clothing, using two burning sticks to wave across their bodies while walking. Older children carried sticks and infants were kept warm by their carriers. When camped, fires were placed inside windbreaks made from branches and built near the mulga scrub where there is plenty of firewood. People sleep in scooped-out hollows and it was the task of women to maintain the fires during the night.

In May, the rising of the Kungkarungkara constellation in the dawn sky signals the beginning of the season of *nyinnga*. This star group, known in English as the Pleiades, was seen by many Aboriginal groups as a number of women fleeing from men. This is a frosty time of the year, from May to September. It is generally cold and dry, with occasional storms from the south which on even rarer occasions carry snow. Bushfires are deliberately lit at cooler times of the year such as this, rather than during summer, because they stay small. The women gather vegetable foods and witchetty grubs, and as the grass dries off, the seed becomes ripe for collecting. At this plentiful time, ceremonies are directed, among other things, towards encouraging the production of dingos. In June, family groups move away from the ceremonial meeting places to their hunting territories out in the sand country, where they hope to catch dingo pups for eating. Water is usually still widely available and in this season the country is burnt in the course of hunting small animals.

Lerp sugar and the dried figs that are picked up from under trees are some of the foods eaten on these trips. Hunting time in areas remote from water sources is extended through the collection of morning dew.

The coldest point of the year is *wari*, around July and August in the *nyinnga* season. The clear nights produce frost and dew, and food becomes scarce. In August, the family group visits its bases in the ranges, where it hopes to kill euros and wallabies through lighting fires or by stalking them. Aboriginal groups continue to disperse during this season, exploiting their territory to its limits by visiting remote areas along tracks travelled by their Dreaming Ancestors. Possible meetings with their neighbours may present an opportunity for trade.

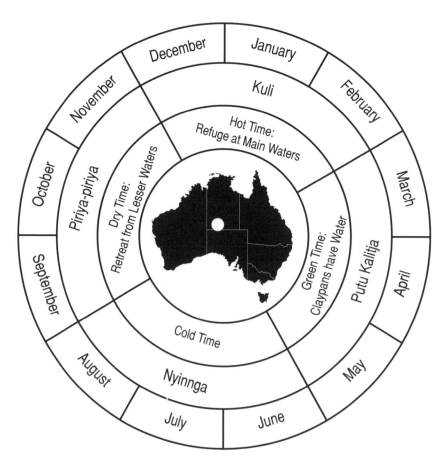

Aboriginal seasonal calendar for the Anangu Pitjantjatjara people, Western Desert.
CHART: RAY MARCHANT, AFTER MUTITJULU COMMUNITY & BAKER, 1996; TINDALE, 1972.

In September the hot and dry weather begins in the desert, with the arrival of the warm northwest winds. In spite of the cloud build up, there is usually not much rain but plenty of thunder and lightning strikes, which cause wildfires. This period is *piriya-piriya*, or *piriyakutu*, when many desert people retreat from the ephemeral waters to rely on more permanent sources. If it has rained, witchetty grubs and honey ants are easily found near the surface of the earth around the trunks of mulga trees. Large animals are killed in the vicinity of the waterholes they visit, along with birds that are knocked down with switches used by people hiding in the bushes. The women concentrate on gathering roots and other plant food.

The Walmadjeri people who live in the northern Western Desert cultural bloc, in the Great Sandy Desert of Western Australia, recognise four main seasons.[56] *Paranga* is the hottest season, from mid-October to February. Norman Tindale noted gravely that at this time, 'Planning one's movements from water to water was a vital mental activity in which there were no rewards for failure.'[57] Rain in this area mainly falls during *idilal*, from March to mid-May. This time is known as 'wet ground time', when there is plenty of green grass. People can cross their country with little thought as to their next watering point. Water can be obtained from shallow supplies lying in clay basins, although the inland 'salt water' country can only be visited during summer after the torrential rains. The coldest time of the year is in *makura*, from mid-May to mid-August. During *wilpuru*, from mid-August to mid-October, it is dry and cool.

Periods of drought were known to the Walmadjeri as *lalga*. At these times of hardship the Walmadjeri go to permanent waterholes and appeal to Wanambi, the giant Carpet Snake spirit, to release more water to them. Other strategies may involve travelling out of their country towards Fitzroy River in the southern Kimberley, possibly incurring the wrath of Aboriginal groups living there, who would be watching for their fires. Drought was a time when Western Desert people travelled far to find food and water. In the southern Western Desert it was called *ailuru*. Aboriginal people were keenly aware of the implications of the season on the potential movement patterns of their neighbours. In some cases their neighbours, if not closely linked, were like unwanted house guests. Norman Tindale observed that:

In the Western Desert a widespread term for strangers is *ngatari*, a word linked with the season of whirlwinds in hotter and drier months of the year, when drought could, in bad years make forced evacuations necessary by desperately water short 'foreigners', potential menaces to those more securely based.[58]

The Aboriginal groups who rely mainly on the small rock holes for water are the most likely people to raid the lands of their better watered neighbours during droughts.

During short-term droughts, people rely on foods such as the woodboring and root-feeding larvae of beetles and cossid moths, as their life cycles are generally two years or longer and are able to withstand periods of no rain. However, virtually all possible sources of food are utilised in times of desperation. Norman Tindale recorded an account from an elderly Western Desert man of how his group had once, many years ago, had to exist on hairy caterpillars from the large colonies living in bag-like nests in the branches of eucalypts.[59] Not all the stinging hairs could be removed by singeing with hot coals, making this the worst of all possible food sources. Yet in spite of the hardship, his group had survived.

As in all parts of Australia, Aboriginal hunting and gathering in the desert was based upon an intimate understanding of the environment. The knowledge possessed by Aboriginal people of the relationship between the seasonal cycles of the landscape and the impact of this upon the distribution of animal and plant foods was fundamental to their survival. In the fragile desert environments, Aboriginal movement patterns ensured that their impact on the landscape was minimised through the population being widely dispersed for as long as possible.

Ten

Beyond Capricorn

Northern Australia, situated beyond the Tropic of Capricorn, contains the greatest diversity of Aboriginal cultures compared with anywhere else in Australia. This is partly due to the rich variety in landscape forms, but also to the cultural diffusion from non-Aboriginal peoples to the immediate north. In some coastal northern areas, the population levels would have approached that of the densest areas in the temperate zone. As with Central Australia, Europeans were relatively late settling this part of the continent, preferring initially to concentrate on the more European-like regions in the temperate south. Northern Australia therefore retains a large and distinctive Aboriginal population today. Aboriginal groups in the higher rainfall areas of northern Australia see themselves primarily in terms of a relatively local set of social and cultural relationships, as distinct from the wider relations of the desert people. This is reflected in their relatively high diversity of languages, the comparative rigidity of clan boundaries, more restricted mobility and in their regionally distinct art styles.

Hunting and Gathering

The main geographical feature uniting northern Australia is its subtropical climate, under the influence of the northwest monsoon. In terms of landforms, the region is immensely diverse. The Kimberley is a rugged mountainous area located between a resource-rich sea and the inland deserts. The main river systems are the Fitzroy, King Edward, Drysdale, Berkeley, Chamberlain and Ord Rivers. There are many islands and reefs off the Kimberley coast that were seasonally visited by Aboriginal people, with Sunday Island being the home of an Aboriginal community. The people living in the Kimberley have varied lifestyles: the coastal groups maintain a maritime economy; inland people either exploit the resources of the plateau or live along river valleys; and southern groups living on the northern fringe of the Great Sandy Desert have some elements of an arid-zone lifestyle. In spite of the geographical differences, all the Kimberley people are linked through trade.

To the east of the Kimberley, in the Top End of the Northern Territory, is a region of many large river systems: the Victoria, Fitzmaurice and Daly Rivers in the west; the Adelaide, Mary and Alligator Rivers of the western plains of the Kakadu region; the Liverpool, Mann, Cadell, Blyth and Goyder Rivers in Arnhem Land. The environment of the Top End ranges from coastal zone, riverine areas of low-lying seasonal wetlands cut by river systems, and the Arnhem Land escarpment. There are many islands off the coast which support Aboriginal populations. To the north of Darwin live the Tiwi people on Melville and Bathurst Islands, which until recently were largely isolated from mainland Australia once the sea level rose and separated them about 4000 years ago. The rich carving and decoration traditions here are of a different style from the mainland. Further east off the northern coast are islands such as Croker, Goulburn, Milingimbi and Elcho Islands. The Aboriginal groups on these islands have strong links to mainland cultures.

East of the Top End is the Gulf of Carpentaria, which separates the Arnhem Land cultural groups from those of west Cape York. There are many river systems exiting into the Gulf: the Roper and McArthur Rivers in the west; the Nicholson and Flinders Rivers in the south; and the Gilbert, Mitchell, Edward and Archer Rivers into the eastern Gulf waters. There are several major island groups which are large enough to support Aboriginal populations: Groote Eylandt off the shore of eastern Arnhem Land; the Sir Edward Pellew group at the mouth of the McArthur River; and further east the Wellesley Island group which includes Mornington and Bentinck Islands. The use of ocean-going watercraft was fundamental to the hunting and gathering lifestyle of Aboriginal people living on these islands. The region provided plenty of food on a seasonal basis, with people hunting and gathering from the sea, tidal inlets and mangroves, sandy shores, dune thickets, rivers, swamps and inland bush. In contrast with dry parts of Australia, here Aboriginal people had a large set of tools to help them gather their wide variety of food. The people of west Cape York Peninsula were distinctive in their reliance on shell and bone for tool-making rather than stone.

The eastern coast of Cape York Peninsula was different culturally and physically from the western side. Today when travelling east to west across the Cape York Peninsula from Cairns by car or plane, you are struck by how quickly the coastal high-rainfall zone ends, becoming the seasonally dry inland region which covers much of the Cape to the Gulf. The larger river systems, the Normanby and Daintree are restricted to the southern end of eastern Cape York. Both the Pacific Ocean and the proximity of the Great

A Bardi man armed with spears and boomerangs. He is wearing a waist-belt with pearl shell ornaments hanging from it.
PHOTO: C.S. ASHLEY, SUNDAY ISLAND, KIMBERLEY, ABOUT 1900.

A Larrakia man, Mangminone, who was known by Europeans as Mr Knight. He is wearing head and neck ornaments, armlets and a bark waist band.
PHOTO: P. FOELSCHE, DARWIN, NORTHERN TERRITORY, 1879.

Dividing Range heavily influence the climate of eastern Cape York Peninsula, with dense rainforests in some areas. The influence of Papuan cultures upon Aboriginal people, through the Torres Strait Islanders, is more pronounced here than it is on the western side.

Plants

Rainforests are typically areas where a very large diversity of plant life occurs, and plant foods traditionally formed the backbone of the Aboriginal diet in the tropics. So varied is the flora that many of the plant foods used by Aboriginal people have no common English name. The following account, therefore, relates to only a small fraction of the food available across northern Australia, as an exhaustive list would be prohibitive.[1] Fruit was an important source of food, some of which was cooked, some eaten raw. The fruit of the nonda plum (*Parinari nonda*) are eaten raw, with the season of use extended by storing the dried fruits in sand. Burney vine (*Malaisia scandens*) berries ripen in February and are eaten cooked or raw. Various figs (*Ficus* species) produce edible fruit and are collected.

Tamarind (*Tamarindus indica*) pods, too, are collected for their pulp and the seeds discarded. Macassan visitors introduced this species to northern Australia over a century ago. Other foods may have come over with the ancestors of the Aboriginal people as they entered Greater Australia thousands of years ago. The Moreton Bay chestnut (*Castanospermum australe*) is normally available all year round, but it is generally avoided due to its long preparation time, which involves roasting, pounding and washing in running water. The candle nut (*Aleurites moluccana*) too is roasted before eating, and nuts of the screw palm (*Pandanus* species) eaten only after baking, as they are otherwise too spicy. Seeds of the matchbox bean (*Entada phaseoloides*) are baked, crushed and washed in running water before being consumed. Wild rice seeds (*Oryza* species) are eaten as damper. The hearts of fan palms (*Livistona* species) are baked in ashes, then beaten and mixed with water before eating. The embryo of a germinating mangrove fruit (*Avicennia marina*) is heavily relied upon as a food source, and eaten from March to August. The flowers, stalks and seeds of water lilies (*Nymphaea* species) are consumed raw, and the gum of the wild peach (*Terminalia* species) gathered from wounds made on the tree trunk. A large number of yams and other sources of edible plant roots, including taro (*Colocasia esculenta*), wild ginger (*Alpinia caerulea*) and various water lilies, are also utilised.

During the Kurlama initiations, the Tiwi people ritually eat the hairy yam (*Dioscorea bulbifera*) that they describe as 'cheeky' due to its poisonous state when uncooked.[2] This food is only collected and prepared by them for such ceremonies. At least one plant food was not grown locally, but came in on the tide. At particular times of the year, the sea currents bring coconuts (*Cocos nucifera*), called *kalukwa*, to the Arnhem Land coast in great numbers.[3] Aboriginal people keenly collected them for eating, even those that had germinated and had tender new shoots.

A special diet was prepared for northern babies, with particular foods that did not make the mouth sting. On Groote Eylandt, babies from six weeks of age on were given a mixture of honey and water.[4] When young enough to sit up, at about five or six months, babies were fed the cooked and hammered corms of the water ribbon (*Triglochin procerum*). Until the child's teeth had grown, the main meat eaten was cooked fish and crabs. Red meat was first chewed by adults and given to the infant. After baking to remove irritants and poisons, the kernels of screw pine nuts and mature cycad nuts (mainly *Cycas* species) were also given to children.

Indeed nuts from various species of cycad are among the most important plant foods in subtropical Australia.[5] These slow-growing plants occur in male and female forms, resembling small palm trees when fully grown. The nuts are yellow to orange when ripe, but in spite of their attractive colouring they are poisonous before they are processed for eating. In the Tiwi Islands, the cycad nuts become available in August and are collected in considerable quantities by the women for use in the Kurlama initiation rituals.[6] On Groote Eylandt, the cycad nuts come into season in September, at a time when Aboriginal people are holding ceremonies at their river camps.[7] Aboriginal people use several methods to prepare this food. Fresh nuts are roasted in hot ashes and the kernels mashed into flat cakes. These are then washed in cages made of burrawang fronds in running water overnight, before they are eaten the next day. Nuts that have fallen on the ground are processed by being cracked, left to dry in the sun for a day, then washed in running water for three nights before being made into cakes for baking. After this has been done, the cakes are ready for eating with honey. Mature nuts that have hard kernels are shelled and left to sun dry for a day, then are leached in fresh water for a further nine days. After this the kernels are ground, wrapped in bark and roasted. Older nuts are not as poisonous, and they are opened and the white powder from the kernels is made into a thick paste by adding water and mixing in a wooden container or baler shell. The paste is then wrapped in leaves and cooked. When a surplus of nuts is available, some are cracked and buried in damp sand for about a month. During this time the kernels start to rot, nevertheless they can be dug up, roasted into damper and eaten straight away.

As in southern areas of Australia plants are used to flavour food. The leaves of plants such as the peanut tree (*Sterculia quadrifida*), red jungle berry (*Drypetes lasiogyna*) and the wattle-flowered paperbark (*Melaleuca acacioides*) are used to cover shellfish, fish or meat that is being cooked in an earth oven, imparting a sweet taste to the food and a distinct tropical flavour.[8]

Fish

Subtropical Australia abounds with fish, but the presence of crocodiles makes fishing a risky business. Many of the more remote Aboriginal communities living along the northern coast, nevertheless, still heavily engage in fishing as a means of feeding themselves, although today this involves outboard motors and commercial nets.[9] From museum collections we know that in earlier times in Arnhem Land, Aboriginal people used a distinctive 'butterfly' or 'wing net', which is essentially two V-shaped wooden frames, covered with netting, that meet at the points. Several fishermen would work together, using open nets to drive the fish towards the shore. In northern Queensland, wooden-framed nets were similarly used.[10] The fish were finally caught as the net was closed, trapping them inside.

A number of fish poisons, made from plants, were used in small pools, such as those left by a receding tide.[11] These generally stunned the fish, forcing them to float to the surface. Hollow log traps were thrown into water holes to catch freshwater crayfish and some fish,[12] and even crocodiles were hunted with nooses on poles, or trapped behind screens erected in creeks at high tide.[13] Hunters probably avoided the larger crocodiles.

Other Animals

Although Aboriginal people across Australia hunted birds, in northern Australia the hunters had some unique practices. In 1895, a government geologist, Henry Y.L. Browne, observed hawk hunting hides between Big Gregory and Little Gregory Creeks in the Victoria River district:

> Some curious erections, made of flat stones, built up in the form of a horseshoe, were seen here, which are said to be erected by the blacks with a view to enabling them to catch hawks, which are plentiful in this region. Their modus operandi is as follows: The native covers one of these stone places with boughs, and ensconces himself inside, at the same time making a small fire, the smoke of which attracts the bird's notice. He is provided with a pigeon or other small bird which he exposes to view on the top of the stone 'trap', and the hawk, seeing this, swoops down upon it and is grabbed by the man beneath.[14]

The smoke lure works because birds of prey are attracted to bushfires for the feast of small animals that are exposed when fleeing the flames. Although the hawk flesh is edible, it appears the hawk feathers were the main attraction for hunting them. These were obtained for ceremonial decorations and the talons were made into ornaments by stringing them together. In Queensland, Aboriginal people also use smoke, killing Torres Strait pigeons by smoking them out of trees they had roosted in, as well as throwing sticks into flocks and striking them with switches.[15] Small birds are also caught in sticky fig tree sap smeared onto tree branches.[16]

Across northern Australian waters the main animals caught are dugongs and turtles. They are both hunted by harpoon from dugout canoes, with dugong usually caught on calm and moonless nights and turtles taken during the day.[17] This technique is similar to that used by some Melanesian groups, but is unknown in southern Australia. Dugongs are also caught by chasing them into mangrove-lined inlets that then have large nets placed across their exits which entangle the dugongs as they try to escape. Turtles are also sometimes caught as they lay eggs in the dunes behind a beach.[18]

One of the most bizarre hunting techniques recorded for Australia is the use of suckerfish to catch turtles. In the waters surrounding the Cape York Peninsula, when the suckerfish were caught:

> They were laid in the bottom of a canoe and covered with wet seaweed, a strong fishing line having been previously made fast to the tail of each . . . A small turtle was seen and the sucking fish was put

Net used to hunt dugongs feeding on sea grass in coastal mangrove inlets.
PHOTO: N.B. TINDALE, PORT ESSINGTON, NORTHERN TERRITORY, 1921–22.

A Wik man repairing spear points with hot gum as cement. Gum was essential for making many different artefacts and was traded.

PHOTO: U.H. MCCONNEL, ARCHER RIVER, NORTHERN QUEENSLAND, EARLY 1930S.

into the water. At first it swam lazily about, apparently recovering the strength which it had lost by removal from its native element; but presently it swam slowly in the direction of the turtle till out of sight. In a very short time the line was rapidly carried out, there was a jerk, and the turtle was fast. The line was handled gently for two or three minutes, the steersman causing the canoe to follow the course of the turtle with great dexterity. It was soon exhausted and hauled up to the canoe.[19]

Away from the coast, Aboriginal hunting techniques are similar to that of other regions further south. In the inland forests hunters stalked kangaroos, wallabies and other larger game and used large game nets and pits.[20] Men also killed flying foxes with switches, after concealing themselves along flight paths.

Monsoonal Cycles

Europeans living in subtropical northern Australia typically recognise just two seasons, the 'wet', which commences with the monsoonal rains in late December, and the 'dry', which commences around May. Most of the yearly rainfall occurs in the few months referred to as 'the wet'. During the height of 'the dry', much of northern Australia is shrouded in smoke from countless small fires.

Donald Thomson was one of the first researchers to accurately describe the system of seasonal behaviour for people anywhere in Aboriginal Australia. Due to the length of time he spent in the field moving about with hunters and gatherers, he had ample time to observe the cyclical changes. In 1949 he noted that Aboriginal people in Arnhem Land divide the year into six or more seasons and 'state without hesitation the appropriate occupational sites at each of them, and their activities and food supplies which depend upon the seasonal conditions, with an insight and a precision that no white man who is not a trained ecologist and well versed in botany and zoology, could approach'.[21]

The seasons recognised by Aboriginal people are determined by the temperature, rainfall and wind direction. While the seasons are determined by weather conditions, their character is based on hunting and gathering practices tied to the ripening of fruits, the appearance and disappearance of animal foods, and even opportunities for trade. Seasonal winds, for example, were particularly important in heralding the arrival of Macassan visitors, with whom some Aboriginal groups had strong economic and ceremonial bonds. Like elsewhere in Australia, phenomena such as plants flowering and the appearance of constellations in the heavens are seasonal indicators which help Aboriginal people to locate themselves at favoured places at different times of the year. In the Kimberley region of northern Western Australia, the Aboriginal inhabitants have a calendar with between five and nine seasons.[22] Six seasons are recognised by groups living in the Top End of the Northern Territory.[23] The Yanyuwa people who live in the McArthur River region in the southern end of the Gulf of Carpentaria recognise five seasons in their calendar. At the tip of western Cape York, the Wik people at Aurukun note seven seasons, while the Alngith at Weipa recognise five.[24] On the eastern side of Cape York, the Umpila-speaking people between Princess Charlotte Bay and Lockhart River have a calendar with six seasons.[25] The description of Aboriginal seasonality that follows is a sweep from west to east.

Far Western Kimberley

The Bardi people living on Dampierland Peninsula in the far western end of the Kimberley recognise six seasons in their calendar.[26] *Mangal* is the main monsoon season, with storms and strong winds blowing in from the ocean beginning in late December. At this time of the year, Aboriginal people move away from the coast to take shelter in paperbark-covered houses. The vegetable food gathering is restricted to a few roots and fruits, and turtle eggs are collected. When the 'wet' is over, towards the end of January, the period called *ngalandany* commences. The name of this season literally means 'no fruit', and the period is considered a 'rubbish time', with temperature and humidity both high, and little or no wind. Aboriginal people tend not to move around at this time, which lasts until about late February. In March, the *iralbu* season is marked by large tides. When the tide is out, the lower levels allow reef hunting and gathering. The accessibility of shellfish put the Bardi people in a favourable economic position, as they produce the pearl shell pendants that are traded into Central Australia.

This is also the time for collecting fruit. The weather is initially still hot and windless, but cooler winds start blowing from the southeast as April approaches. The appearance of the mangrove fruit indicates that it is time to shift the camp to beaches and tall dunes where mosquitoes are less of a problem. Animal food, such as goannas and kangaroos, are 'fat' and therefore good eating at this time.

For the Bardi people, *bargana* is a cold season, from about mid-May to late July, when people need night-time fires to keep warm. This is the time to hunt dugong and go fishing, as many of the marine creatures have become 'fat'. From the inland bush country, people gather fruits and honey, and hunt wallaby, lizards and snakes. When the west winds start in early August, a warmer season known as *djallalayi* begins. The low spring tides provide another opportunity to collect shellfish from the exposed reefs. *Lalin* is the build up to the main wet season, as the wind shifts from westerly to north-westerly in early October. This is the turtle hunting time, with the Bardi tending to camp close to the coast.

North-western Kimberley

The Aboriginal groups living around Kalumburu in the north-western part of the Kimberley observe a calendar with seven seasons.[27] Here most of the heavy rains fall during *wundju*, from January to mid-February. Due to the constant rain and the lack of plant-root foods, this is a hard time of the year. Most of the food is gained by hunting. Wet-season bark shelters are constructed on well-drained soils, usually up in the hills. In the past the reefs and islands in the Admiralty Gulf region of the Kimberley could only be visited during the wet season, due to the lack of fresh water at other times, and because once the southeast trade winds arrived, the waters were too dangerous for travel. During *maiaru*, from late February to March, the rain eases but there is still little plant food to eat. The new root foods become available in *bande manya*, April, which ends the lean times of the wet season, and people leave the hilly country and camp on the sandy banks of creeks and rivers.

At the end of April is the season of *goloruru*, when the southeast trade winds blow and more roots become available. *Yirma*, from May to August, is a cool and dry time of the year, when Aboriginal people with territories in the riverine areas are able to gather large amounts of swamp plant roots. Men burn the grass and spinifex country away from the rivers and hunt in organised groups. During the early to mid dry season around Kalumburu, people from inland regions move towards the coast to share in the food, hold joint ceremonies and for trade. At other times of the year, this area can only support the local population. *Yuwala*, from September to early November, is a hotter period when root foods become scarce. Pools are poisoned for fish before they dry up. *Djaward*, from mid-November to late December, is a hot season that has thunderstorms which mark the approach of the rainy season. Many edible fruits become ripe at this time. Throughout the year, a number of signals in the landscape are linked to seasonal activities—for example, the flowering of woollybutt tree (*Eucalyptus miniata*), which is a sign that crabs can be caught; the presence of march flies, which means that freshwater crocodile eggs are available; and fast-moving clouds, which signal that it is time to collect turtle eggs.

Kakadu

The Kakadu region is an area where Australian National Park authorities have tried to implement Aboriginal methods of land management, including burning the landscape.[28] The Gagudju people, after whom the national park was named, recognise six seasons in their yearly calendar. *Gudjewg*, from early January to late March, is the time of growth, brought on by heavy cyclonic rain with winds from the northwest. There are some fine, hot spells and the land is covered with tall spear grass at this time. Magpie goose eggs are available and yams are ready for digging. The beginning of April brings light easterly winds, freshening towards south-easterlies. This time is *bang-gerdeng*. The change in winds brings a stormy period, which flattens the grass. The inland plains fill with water and many Aboriginal people are pinned down by the weather in their coastal camps. The wild honeysuckle plants (*Banksia* species) commence flowering and wild rice is ready for collecting. This is a busy season for women, who harvest yams and roots. *Yegge* is a cooler period when the storms cease, and runs from early May until early June. It is the start of a long, dry period, with cool nights and misty mornings. Women collect water lily stems from the swamps and yams from the inland vine thickets, while the men commence burning the dry grass. The fires bring in many kites, which feed on the insects and other food forced out into the open, and the kites in turn are hunted by other animals.

By the time of *wurrgeng* in Kakadu, from mid-June to mid-August, many of the creeks have ceased to flow. This provides an opportunity for fish poisons to be used in the billabongs as an aid to fishing. Dry winds continue to blow in from the southeast. This is the coldest time of the year, especially at night on the Arnhem Land escarpment. Flowering trees produce nectar for 'sugarbag' (Australian bees) and for lorikeet parrots, hunted for their feathers which are made into ornaments. *Gurrung* is a hot and dry period, from late August to late September. Wildfires occur and new leaves appear on some of the trees. The hot winds ripen the screw pine fruit, which contains an edible nut. The foods taken in this season include file snakes, freshwater mussels and long-necked turtles. Magpie geese are hunted, as they arrive in thousands to feed on spike-rush (*Eleocharis dulcis*) tubers on the drying plains. In the era before shotguns became common-place, special wooden platforms were constructed in the swamps to hide hunters who speared the geese.

By October, the humidity resulting from the built-up rain clouds brings on more intensive plant growth. Winds are unsettled, blowing from any direction. A large number of fruits become available, including the billygoat plum (cocky apple, *Planchonia careya*). Nevertheless, most of the animals hunted are thin. The Gagudju people know this time of the year as *gunumeleng*.

North-eastern Arnhem Land

The Yolngu people in north-eastern Arnhem Land have a calendar related to that of the Gagudju. It is not so much the physical indicators of each season, such as temperature and winds, that vary across the Top End, but the landscape-based activities. The following description of seasons comes from the Gupapuyngu language of north-east Arnhem Land.[29] Their growth season is *barramirri*, from December to January, which occurs within the monsoon period. It is marked by high tides and heavy rain that falls on most days. Shellfish, magpie geese and a few types of fruit are some of the foods obtained in this season. Because of the weather, the Aboriginal people led a relatively sedentary existence at this time. Before the missionaries established settlements, Aboriginal people rested in wet-season bark huts, with a smoking fire placed under the houses to help drive away the now abundant mosquitoes. Much of the inland region is covered by freshwater swamps, which people cross in bark or dugout canoes. Most of the fishing at sea is done close to shore, because of the rough conditions.

The main flowering season, *mayaltha*, starts in February and goes through to early March. Light winds replace the stronger ones of the monsoon. There is little bush food, although cycad nuts become available for eating. By mid-March *midawarr* commences and the winds turn around to east-southeast. The fruiting season begins, and root crops and barramundi become available. This is a season that Yolngu people look forward to, as there is an abundance of food and the storms are largely over. The tree bark for paintings is collected now, while the sap is still rising in the trunk making removal easy. Men start to plan hunting trips involving travel over the calmer seas.

Dharratharramirri is the early part of the dry season, running from May to August. This period is noted for its cool nights and heavy dews, with the winds turning around to south-southeast. Aboriginal people become much more mobile at this time, hunting farther away from their main camp sites, setting up temporary overnight camps. The main dry season, *rarrandharr*, is from mid-August to mid-October, and the winds turn from southeast to northeast. Although introduced mango fruit is available, water becomes scarce. Small sharks and stingrays are caught and turtle eggs and honey are gathered. This is the season for holding ceremonies, when the cold weather has passed and there is still an abundance of food about.

Dhuludur is the pre-wet season, from late October to late November. This is a cloudy, humid period, with thunderstorms coming with the north and northwest winds. The main foods at this time are small sharks, stingrays, turtles and threadfin salmon, which are caught from dugouts and outriggers while the sea is still calm. Flood plains begin to fill with water and the bush begins to recover from the dry season fires, which have largely ceased.

Southern Gulf of Carpentaria

For the Yanyuwa people of the McArthur River area at the southern end of the Gulf of Carpentaria, the main wet season, *lhabayi*, runs from early January to about mid-March. The last few weeks of the season are noted for their cyclonic winds and fierce 'knock-him-down' rains.[30] *Rra-mardu* is a cool time of the year, with southerly winds. This season usually starts in early April and goes through to the end of July. There is little rain, but lots of dew and coastal fog. The major ceremonies are usually held in this season. By August to early October, as the weather warms, the season of *ngardara* begins. The winds shift to come from the north across the sea. *Na-yinarramba* is the build-up of rain cloud and humidity before the wet season, with winds becoming more westerly. The commencement of *wunthurru* in early December is marked by the first wet-season storm, followed by heavy showers. The initiation ceremonies are held at this time, and usually stretch into the *lhabayi* season.

Western Cape York

The Wik people living at the tip of western Cape York Peninsula know the build-up to the wet season as *um kaapak*. The cyclonic winds and heavy rains restrict human movement, with the high Gulf seas pushing seawater into low-lying inland areas.[31] Mud crabs are collected as they come up on the high tides. Freshwater shark, bream, turtles and swordfish are taken from the water. *Kaap* is the main wet season, starting in early February with northwest winds and almost continuous rain. A number of fruits and root foods are available then, and inland, hunters go looking for 'fat' kangaroos, goannas and bandicoots. The swamps abound with freshwater turtles and snakes. Birds, such as magpie geese, ducks and brolgas, are sitting on eggs.

When the bush hibiscus (*Hibiscus* species) begins to flower in late March, it is a sign that the wet season is ending. During *onchan wayath*, running through April, rain falls mostly during afternoon storms and the winds start shifting from west to east. Eggs buried in the mounds of the

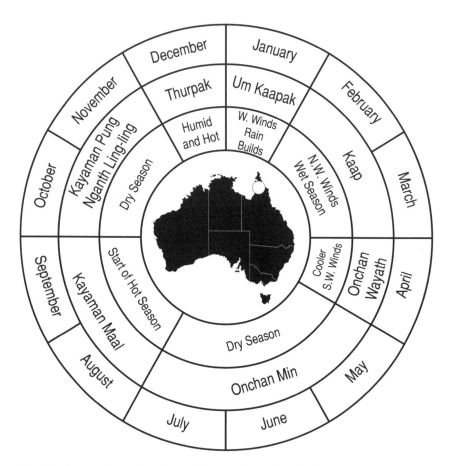

Aboriginal seasonal calendar for the Wik, northwest Cape York Peninsula.
CHART: RAY MARCHANT, AFTER AURUKUN SCHOOL & COMMUNITY CALENDAR (1985);
MCCONNEL (1930); REID (1995).

scrub fowl are ready for collecting. Freshwater prawns are caught with nets and the first of the hairy yam are ready for digging up. An abundance of dragonflies and the flattening of much of the grass through rain signal the end of the wet.

Onchan min is a cool and dry time of the year, usually commencing in early May and persisting until late July. This is a season with much bush food: the magpie geese eggs are hatching, the swamps are full of yams and 'sugarbag' (bee hive) is plentiful. People spread out across the country and hunters start burning the vegetation to allow for easier travel. The easterly winds start to dry out the wet inland regions. When the milkwood (*Alstonia actinophylla*) flowers, it is a sign that oysters and stingrays are ready for collecting.

Seasonal Calendar for Wik

By August to late September on western Cape York, it is getting warmer as the winds shift to around from the north. This time of the year is known as *kayaman maal*, when dugong and barramundi are caught, as well as stingrays which are now 'fat'. A variety of land reptiles are hunted, along with kangaroos and wallabies. Crabs and shellfish are collected during low tides. *Kayaman pung nganth ling-ling* is the really hot season, from early October to late November, with fresh water becoming scarce and grass drying out. The northwest winds blow 'stingers' (box jellyfish) on shore. It is often windy, thunderstorms loom and it sometimes rains. Women and children catch freshwater turtle in the low swamp water. The large 'king' tides signal the arrival of the season called *thurpak* in late November. This is the early build-up to the wet-season storms, when there is good fishing and many types of fruit available. Grass begins to spring up and the bush becomes green. In reality, all these seasons are fairly variable. *Thurpak* can actually start as early as October and as late as January, and is as variable as all the other seasons.

Eastern Cape York

The Umpila-speaking people live on the eastern side of northern Cape York.[32] As an Aboriginal group with a totally coastal-based economy, they formerly lived within a comparatively small foraging area and ranged only several kilometres between beachfront and the hinterland. Their beach-front camps allowed for a constant lookout into the sea and estuarine region to take advantage of schools of fish and calm weather to approach the reefs and offshore islands. The 'storm time' before the main rains come is *malan-tityi*, from December to February. When the climatic conditions became rough, the camps move to the narrow wooded sand ridges back from the shore. *Ngurkita* is the monsoonal period, when the winds come around from the northwest, from February to April and people move into wet-season huts with bark roofs. With the constant rain, this is a 'hard time' when food is difficult to collect.

During the season of *kuutulu*, beginning in April, the winds shift to southeast and the main rains end. From the end of the wet season, Aboriginal people visit the offshore islands to hunt the nesting nutmeg pigeons. The period from June to August is *kaawulu*, the early dry season. At this time of the year, camps are generally moved only a few hundred metres at a time. Water sources along the beach are plentiful and the relocations are only brought on by the need to avoid fouling the area, rather than exhausting local resources. Groups light fires to help in the hunting of inland wallabies and other small animals. Various species of yam provide important sources of plant food.

The proper dry season, from September to November, is *kayimun*, known for its hot sun. From October, shoals of mullet arrive and are speared in the estuaries, while the beaches are searched for turtle eggs. When the water in the creeks and rivers is at its lowest, hunters concentrate on cuscus, cassowary and echidna. Late in the dry season the fruit of the wongay plum (wongi tree, *Manilkara kauki*) was a major food source that enabled the population to concentrate along the coast. The cloud build-up season is *matpi painyan*, from November to December. As the seas become calmer with the end of the southeast winds, hunting trips in canoes are organised in search of mating green turtles and the dugong.

Part IV

CULTURAL
CHANGE

Eleven

Northern Contacts

Aboriginal cultures have never been static, but are vibrant and capable of changing in tune with the variable Australian landscape. From cultural contacts outside of Australia, Aboriginal people were able to selectively absorb new ideas and technologies. The region to the north of Australia has, in the past, served as both a bridge and as a barrier between Aboriginal Australia and the inhabitants of South East Asia and Papua New Guinea. During the peak of the ice ages, when sea levels were low, the island mass of Papua New Guinea was connected via a land bridge with mainland Australia. Nevertheless, for the last six thousand years the existence of the Timor and Arafura Seas has only allowed seafaring people to visit. For most of this time, the flow of people and cultures from Asia into Australia has been restricted and subject to the economies of countries to the north. From the 1700s there was a growth in trade centred on mainland China and spreading out across the Pacific Rim. As a result, Indonesians were seasonally visiting northern Australia as part of their trading cycle within the broader region. Over the last few hundred years, Torres Strait Islanders have also become involved in broader regional trade. Torres Strait Islanders are predominantly of Melanesian origin, but have maintained cultural contacts with both Australian Aboriginal people and Papuans. The legacy of all these pre-European relationships is reflected in the Aboriginal mythology, ceremony and the material culture of northern Australia.[1]

The 'Macassans'

To appreciate the depth of contact between Aboriginal people and the outside world, it is necessary to look closely at why visitors came here and how. The Indonesian and Malaysian seafaring people came to Australia from beyond the Arafura and Timor Seas in search of trepang, an edible 'sea-slug' also known as *bêche-de-mer* or the 'sea cucumber'.[2] It is actually not a slug at all, but a distant relative of the sea urchin. There are several varieties that are still commercially fished in northern Australia, most of which look like large slippers with prominent ribs after being caught. They have also been described as looking like withered penises when smoked and dried.[3] The thread-like filaments that protrude from the anus can be toxic if touched. The sun-dried trepang is highly prized in traditional Chinese cooking and is famous for its aphrodisiac properties. It was the basis of Australia's first known export industry and its value to the traders would have been counted in millions of dollars in today's money. While in Australian waters, the Indonesians also obtained items such as turtle shell, pearls, pearl shell, mother-of-pearl, sandalwood and cypress pinewood.[4] After Europeans introduced buffalo in the 1820s the visitors obtained horn here as well. From archaeological and historical evidence it appears that the Indonesians probably started visiting Australia in the seventeenth century, with a break around the eighteenth century. The nineteenth century was the trepang industry's heyday, but in 1906 the Australian Government banned visits by these traders in an effort to reduce foreign influence upon northern Australia.

Many of the Indonesians were Islamic traders from Ujung Pandang, situated to the northwest of Australia on the island of Sulawesi.[5] All of these Asian visitors are generally referred to in Australian history texts as 'Macassans'. Aboriginal people on Groote Eylandt in the Gulf of Carpentaria called them either 'Makasa' or 'Malayu'. The Macassans made regular voyages to 'the land of Marege', as they knew Arnhem Land, and to 'Kayu Jawa', which is the Kimberley coast. They came to Australia on large sailing boats known as *praus*. These vessels generally took about a fortnight for the 1600 kilometre voyage from Sulawesi. Timor was a key landfall for

'Macassan prau with crew and four dugout canoes' by Nakinyappa.
COLLECTED BY J. MULLOY AT YETIBA, GROOTE EYLANDT, GULF OF CARPENTARIA,
NORTHERN TERRITORY, LATE 1960S.

Macassan traders en route to and from northern Australia. It is estimated
that by 1800 some 1000 or more of these men were sailing annually to
Australia, where they would stay for the wet season (December to April)
to collect and process the trepang. They brought with them fowl and cats.
In their temporary settlements along the Australian coast, the Macassans
manufactured knives, cloth, sails and pottery made from termite mounds
for use during their trip. Food was grown in vegetable gardens established
in their Australian bases. These visits were not casual events, but well-
planned expeditions.

Macassans arrived with the onset of the monsoonal wet season and
sailed home when the dry season began. In Arnhem Land, their arrival
coincided with the seasonal movement of Aboriginal people away from the
coast, which reduced the risk of friction through competition for space and
resources. Once in Australian waters, the help of Aboriginal people was
sought as labourers, hunters and gatherers. Some of them became crew-
members on board the praus travelling on to Torres Strait or back to
Indonesia.[6] In the early twentieth century, at least some northern Aboriginal people knew that they had Macassan ancestry. From their likely
activities it is possible also that some slave-capturing parties from

Portuguese Timor visited northern Australia prior to 1818, taking northern Australian people and resulting in some Aboriginal people being spread across South East Asia.[7] Through contact with the Macassans, Aboriginal people became part of a much larger economic region, which linked China with Australia and the islands in between.

The Macassan expeditioners set up a number of trepang processing sites in Australia, including a large one at Raffles Bay on the Coburg Peninsula northeast of Darwin, and others at Arnhem Bay, Melville Bay, Port Bradshaw, Trial Bay, Caledon Bay and Groote Eylandt.[8] In the southern Gulf of Carpentaria, the Yanyuwa people interacted with Macassans on the Sir Edward Pellew Islands. In the 1980s, an elderly Aboriginal man remembered:

> West, north, south and east they [the Macassans] gathered the trepang and tipped them into canoes and then they carried them to the camp. There they boiled [in iron pots] the trepang; the hot water made the trepang increase in size. Then they gutted the trepang and again they were boiled, they were then dried over the top of a fire. The trepang were then placed on a beach in the sun, they were placed inside the prahus [praus] heaped up inside truly they were heaped up.[9]

The English explorer Matthew Flinders came across a Macassan fleet owned by the Rajah of Boni in the Gulf of Carpentaria in 1803 in the course of his circumnavigation around Australia.[10] Because his cook spoke Malay, he was able to converse with them. Flinders noted the bolder and more aggressive attitude of Yolngu people in northeast Arnhem Land—in contrast to Aboriginal groups encountered elsewhere, who were more timid—and blamed this on their previous contacts with Asian trepang fleets. He named the region 'Malay Road' in recognition of the Macassan's economic interests there. In the same year, the Frenchman Nicholas Baudin encountered praus of the 'Malays' off the Kimberley coast.[11] Visible traces of the Macassans' presence can still be found in many parts of coastal northern Australia. Tamarind trees and coconut palms, introduced for their fruits and nuts by the Macassans, often mark the location of old trepang-processing sites, where the remains of stone structures are sometimes also evident.[12] Their preferred bases were on small peninsulas or islands, from which it was easy to defend attacks from the land. The closeness of the relationship the

Macassans established with a few local Aboriginal people meant that the same places tended to be visited on each expedition.

In return for their labour and access to sites for setting up trepang-processing camps, Aboriginal people received a variety of goods, such as cloth, dugout canoes, knives, axes, glass, rice, sweetmeats, alcoholic liquor and tobacco.[13] The cloth they gained was made into strips which were used to make head and body ornaments and for incorporation into the decoration of ceremonial baskets. Aboriginal people were eager to obtain the metal tools brought by the Macassans for their woodcarving. The iron they obtained was made into broad blades for mounting onto the heads of fighting spears. Coastal Aboriginal people then traded some of these goods with inland groups.

The traders brought to north-western Australia and Arnhem Land the use of dugout canoes, consisting of a single hollowed-out log. Each prau carried at least several canoes when it arrived in Australian waters, which were essential for collecting trepang in the shallow waters. They were traded or lent to Aboriginal people, who also occasionally acquired them by theft.[14] After contact with the Macassans ceased in 1906, Aboriginal people manufactured all their canoes themselves from softwood logs. During the nineteenth century in the Kimberley coastal region, the practice of making dugouts was spreading south at the rate of 80 to 100 kilometres per generation of Aboriginal people, finally stopping around Broome where suitable softwood trees ran out.[15]

A Kimberley point made from bottle glass, probably gained from Macassans or Europeans.
PHOTO: C.P. CONIGRAVE, MOUNT CASUARINA, KIMBERLEY, WESTERN AUSTRALIA, 1912.

Aboriginal people in northern Australia used Macassan-style pipes for smoking.
PHOTO: N.B. TINDALE, GROOTE EYLANDT, GULF OF CARPENTARIA, NORTHERN
TERRITORY, 1922.

In the 1950s, the anthropologists Ronald and Catherine Berndt recorded Yolngu people singing about the visits of the Macassans, the whole cycle containing about 150 individual songs.[16] The songs included references to the cooking of rice in earthenware pots and the food being used to pay Aboriginal people who worked in the Macassan seasonal settlements. Over the centuries of visiting the northern Australian coasts, the Macassans came to be incorporated into the Aboriginal world view in two distinct but related senses. On the one hand, in Aboriginal eyes they shared a pre-existence with all things in creation as part of the Dreaming. At the same time, they were annual visitors who entered into direct economic relations with them. The seasonal nature of their associations may have prevented the spread of Islamic faith from Indonesia into Aboriginal Australia.

Although there were some isolated outbreaks of hostility, overall the relationships between the Macassans and Aboriginal people were amicable. The Yolngu people welcomed them with diplomacy ceremonies and reciprocal exchanges of gifts to ensure all-round success.[17] At the end of the trepang season, the raising of the mast on the prau was a sign that the Macassans were soon to depart. This was accompanied by ritual mourning by Aboriginal people expressing sadness at the departure of their Macassan friends. To the Yolngu the mast also symbolised the departure and journey of the spirits of their dead, a notion arising from the Macassans. Ceremonial masts became a feature of much of the Arnhem Land mortuary ritual.[18] The hollow log coffin used in Arnhem Land funeral rites is symbolic of a Macassan prau, a boat taking away the spirits of the dead. The orientation of ceremonial life in north-eastern Arnhem Land was influenced by Aboriginal contact with the Macassans.[19]

After the praus were prohibited from visiting Australia in 1906, Aboriginal people mostly remembered the Macassans with nostalgic affection, as recorded in their songs and art. The Macassans arrived in Australia on a seasonal basis as relatively small groups of people whose interests did not directly threaten Aboriginal custodianship to land. Unlike the British, the Macassans did not come to Australia to colonise it but to pursue trade links. While Japanese pearlers and traders, and a few Europeans, continued with some trepanging in northern Australia, the Macassans left a legacy. Aboriginal groups in the coastal region from the western Kimberley to the southern region of the Gulf of Carpentaria had incorporated a small part of the Macassan culture.

Torres Strait Islanders and Papuans

There is no clear cultural line that separates Melanesia from Australia— where the characteristics of Indigenous language, religion and material culture suddenly change.[20] Instead, there is a complex picture of cultural diffusion. The Western Torres Strait language is part of the Australian Aboriginal family of languages, although it is not spoken on mainland Australia. The Eastern Torres Strait language is distinctly of a Melanesian type. At first glance, people throughout the Strait have the physical appearance of Melanesians, while their religious practices and material culture have a strong Papuan flavour. Horticulture in the Straits was widely practised before Europeans arrived, although its importance relative to hunting and gathering varied. Groups living close to Papua regularly cultivated their land. The Islanders in the north-eastern Torres Strait area used their rich volcanic soils to grow yams, bananas, coconuts and various other fruits and vegetables. In contrast, the large rocky islands on the western and south-western sides have abundant sources all year round of wild food and here cultivation was marginal and the soil difficult. Torres Strait Islanders living on smaller islands in the central region in pre-European times were mainly fishermen and traders.

Outside the Torres Strait region, the language differences between Papua and Cape York Peninsula are marked—in spite of the existence of the former land bridge connecting Australia with New Guinea and their shared trade networks. Yet the influence of Torres Strait Islanders and Melanesians upon Aboriginal cultures was strong, particularly on Cape York Peninsula, the closet part of Australia to Papua New Guinea. A number of anthropologists have remarked on this including Donald Thomson, who recorded the use of snake-skin covered drums, bark-strip skirts, masks and dance enclosures in the cult of the Crocodile Ancestor among the Koko Yao people at Pascoe River, Princess Charlotte Bay, on the eastern side of the Peninsula.[21] From their similarity to Papuan artefacts, these artefacts are assumed to be of Papuan origin and a relatively recent inclusion in the Aboriginal material culture. Thomson also recorded the use of these items in the cult dances of the Sea Eagle, Sea Gull and Torres Strait Pigeon Ancestors on the western side of the Cape, among Aboriginal groups south of Batavia River. Similarly the Wik people on the Gulf side consider that their totemic Ancestors travelled north in the Dreaming period, as do migratory birds today, to Maubiag Island in the Torres Straits and on to Papua, before returning with new technologies.

Ceremonies related to that of the Sea Gull and Torres Strait Pigeon exist on both Maubiag Island and in Papua. The Sea Gull Ancestor, Shivirri, is said to have introduced into Wik culture two kinds of drum: one from hollow pandanus wood for soft sounds, and the other from messmate wood for loud sounds. Furthermore, this Ancestor is said to have brought in the bow and arrow, although only for ceremonial use. Interestingly, a set of Wik arrows acquired by the South Australian Museum in the 1930s from the anthropologist Ursula McConnel were made without points. The making of Papuan-style bows and arrows by western Cape York people is unique in Aboriginal Australia. A number of other Papuan-style objects are used in ceremonial dances on the Gulf side of the Cape, either traded through the Torres Strait or made locally, but based on the northern forms. These objects include plaited pandanus and palm-leaf armlets; pearl shell pendants; necklets and headbands made from cowrie and pearl shell; nautilus shell nose-pegs; wooden ear ornaments; and ornamented clubs.

In the case of pearl shell, it is the shape, not the making of the object itself, which shows the northern influence.[22]

As well as artefacts, Aboriginal people living on Cape York Peninsula have adopted various customs from the Torres Straits Islands and from Papua.[23] Examples of these include sleeping platforms (which can be two-storeyed) and the construction of round houses made from bark similar to those recorded on the Islands. Also used on the Cape is the Papuan communal pipe. Unlike the Macassan-type opium-based pipe, it is sealed at both ends with wax and has holes on the top at either end for holding a cigarette and for breathing in. Some of the string bag styles from western Cape York Peninsula are also like those of Papua. The mourning rituals of the Wik people, too, show a strong influence from Torres Strait Island and Papuan cultures. I witnessed the concluding phase of mourning with a Wik 'house opening ceremony' at Aurukun in 1999, when the relatives of the deceased returned to the building where the person had lived. 'Island-style' dance and song was interspersed with Aboriginal Dreaming performances. Ursula McConnel linked the use of the dugout to the spread of Papuan type cultures and claimed that on the eastern Cape the northern influence penetrated further south due to the greater accessibility of dugout canoes to the seas along this coast.[24]

This outrigger canoe is a type of watercraft that appears to have been introduced by Torres Strait Islanders. Outriggers and dugouts were used when harpooning large marine animals, such as this dugong. PHOTO: U.H. MCCONNEL, MORNINGTON ISLAND, GULF OF CARPENTARIA, QUEENSLAND, EARLY 1930S.

The influence of the Torres Strait Island and Papuan cultures in Cape York Peninsula was much stronger than for elsewhere in Australia. Nevertheless, Arnhem Land people also had contact with Torres Strait Islanders and Papuan people, whom they collectively called 'Badu' after the island (Mulgrave Island) of that Indigenous name adjacent to Banks Island in the Strait.[25] In the case of the Yolngu people, this contact appears to have been much less than their contact with the Macassans, although it would have increased when European pearl luggers and their Islander crews become more active in the region during the late nineteenth century. The association of Badu with the 'Home of the Dead', for the Yirritja moiety of the Yolngu, indicates how the Torres Strait region was placed on the extreme edge of the cultural landscape of the Arnhem Landers. Occasional canoes from Papua New Guinea washing up on the Arnhem Land coast were considered by the Arnhem Land people to be gifts from the Yirritja dead and other spirit beings.

As is quite clear Aboriginal Australia was not totally isolated from the rest of the world immediately prior to the arrival of Europeans. Aboriginal groups in northern Australia had contact with Asian and Melanesian cultures for at least several hundred years before the British permanently settled. Over that time the Macassans and Torres Strait Islanders were incorporated into Aboriginal ceremonial life. However, Aboriginal people met these visitors on their own terms, which did not involve loss of land, and they were selective in what they absorbed from other cultures. Cape York Peninsula people were in direct contact with the horticulturists of Torres Straits, and yet they did not take up their practice of growing crops, although they did take on other elements of Melanesian cultures. Contrary to what many people believe, it was the combination of the adaptability Aboriginal hunting and gathering lifestyle and the variable Australian climate, rather than lack of knowledge, that prohibited sedentary food-producing practices spreading south into mainland Australia.

Twelve

Arrival *of* Europeans

The first permanent European settlement in Australia began on 26 January 1788 when Governor Arthur Phillip arrived from England with the First Fleet at Sydney Cove in Port Jackson. On these shores Sydney was to become the capital of the Colony of New South Wales. Contact between these colonists and Australian Aboriginal people, who were referred to then as 'Indians', had first taken place a few days earlier on 20 January 1788 at Botany Bay. Here, by gesturing at each other, the Europeans and Aboriginal people appeared to have achieved some level of communication. The Captain of the Marines, Captain Watkin Tench, recorded the exchange:

> . . . a party of only six [Aboriginal] men was observed on the north shore, the Governor immediately proceeded to land on that side in order to take possession of his new territory and bring about an intercourse between its old and new masters. The boat in which His Excellency was, rowed up the harbour close to land for some distance, the Indians [Aborigines] keeping pace with her on the beach. At last an officer in the boat made signs of a want of water, which it was judged would indicate his wish of landing. The natives directly comprehended what he wanted and pointed to a spot where water could be procured, on which the boat was immediately pushed in and a landing took place.[1]

The Europeans in this meeting were in need of drinking water and were anxious for a peaceful reception from the Indigenous inhabitants. Three days after the First Fleet reached Sydney Cove, Tench was with some colonists on the south side of the harbour when they were met by a group of a dozen Aboriginal people, 'naked as the moment of their birth', who were walking along the beach. At first the two parties stayed apart, then Tench approached them with a small European child:

> . . . I advanced with him towards them, at the same time baring his [the child's] bosom and showing the whiteness of the skin. On the clothes being removed they gave a loud exclamation and one of the party, an old man with a long beard, hideously ugly, came close to us . . . The Indian [Aborigine], with great gentleness, laid his hand on the child's hat and afterwards felt his clothes, muttering to himself all the while.[2]

Aboriginal people were initially puzzled by the appearance of people looking pale and wearing clothes. After a few days of contact such as this, the Aboriginal people appeared to shun the British settlers. Later, as their land was taken from them they had no choice but to come into the 'settled' areas.

Ghosts as Kin

To Aboriginal people living around Sydney the appearance of non-Aboriginal strangers must have been an extraordinary event. The region of Australia south of the Tropic of Capricorn had probably never had Asian or Melanesian visitors, although rare Polynesian visits may have occurred on the eastern coast via New Zealand. As bizarre as the European arrival appeared to them, it was nevertheless something that had to be interpreted within the Aboriginal world view. In common with many other hunting and gathering societies around the world at that time which suddenly came into direct contact with colonising Europeans, the Aboriginal people at first thought that the white people were their own dead relatives returned from the spirit world.[3] Before the British settlers arrived, the Indigenous people of Australia had no concept that they were collectively 'Aborigines', but rather saw themselves as part of smaller local cultural identities. By their reckoning, the total landscape as they knew it extended not much further than their own country. It was not logical for them to assume that the Europeans had come from a vastly different place, on the other side of a planet of which they had no concept. Aboriginal people therefore concluded that Europeans were deceased relatives who had returned with new objects gained from the Skyworld and the Underworld. This association is evident in many of the recorded Aboriginal languages. For example, in the Ngarrindjeri language of the Lower Murray region of South Australia, missionaries Heinrich A.E. Meyer and George Taplin recorded the word *gringkari* to mean both 'dead' and 'Europeans (whom they imagine to have previously existed as black men)'.[4] Aboriginal people, therefore, treated many of the first Europeans, not as strangers, but as kin who were part of their moral order.

Some Europeans were able to take advantage of the Aboriginal belief that they were kinfolk. In 1803, Aboriginal people living near present-day Melbourne came across a recently escaped convict, William Buckley. Interviewed many years later, Buckley recalled that when he was first found:

> The women assisted me to walk, the men shouting hideous noises, and tearing hair . . . They called me Murrangurk, which I afterwards learnt, was the name of a man formerly belonging to their tribe, who had been buried at the spot where I had found the piece of spear I still carried with me . . . They think all the white people previous to death were belonging to their own tribes, thus returned to life in a different colour.[5]

With his new identity, Buckley lived among the Victorian Aboriginal people for 32 years. In 1835 he came across British colonists at the settlement at Port Phillip Bay. Buckley presented a fearsome sight, being 1.98 metres tall, wearing a kangaroo skin, armed with spears, shield and clubs, and with a crop of hair that had not seen scissors in over 30 years. At this stage he had been so effectively integrated into an Aboriginal society and culture, that he initially had difficulty speaking English.

If white people, such as Buckley, had not been assumed to be returned relatives, it is likely that they would have been completely avoided or perhaps killed through being mistaken as shape-shifting spirits. In order to explain what Aboriginal people thought of the Europeans when they first arrived, we must completely understand that there were no outsiders in the Aboriginal world—everyone had some place in the cultural landscape as they knew it. The incorporation of Europeans into Aboriginal tradition is well illustrated by the early Aboriginal concepts of the spirit held by the Kaurna people of the Adelaide Plains. In 1840 the German missionary, Christian G. Teichelmann, reported:

> One opinion of theirs is, that the soul or the spirit is living in Pin-de, that is either in a western country, or in the grave; (for this term is applied both to the Europeans and to every hole digged [sic.] in the ground, therefore grave; Pin-de Me-yu, is a stranger or European man;) and before the man is born, it is joined in the body. After the person is dead, the soul goes back to this place, and waits, as it appears to me, for another body.[6]

The Kaurna people therefore possessed the term *pinde* meaning 'to the west', 'a place to the west', 'foreign', 'European' and 'a pit' or 'a den'. Explaining these associations further the German missionaries Christian Teichelmann and Clamor Schürmann recorded:

> an explanation of the connection which exists between a den and the Europeans:—The natives believe in metemsychosis [sic.], and thought that the souls of their deceased ancestors were retained in a large den. When they at first saw the whites they took them to be the souls of their own forefathers, who, having changed their black colour into white, and having acquired all the knowledge they at present possess, had come back to see once more their native country.[7]

In this way, the first strangers were seen as a part of the Aboriginal world. By the Kaurna people assuming that the first Europeans came from the 'large den' in the west, they were simply making sense of the arrival of newcomers within the confines of their own views of the universe. The fact that the 'returning' relatives did not appear to recognise the people and places of their former lives did not pose a problem, as Aboriginal people believed that spirits had imperfect memories due to fragmentation of souls. Initially then, white people were treated as if they were part of the Aboriginal landscape.

Across Australia, Aboriginal people also referred to their beliefs concerning spirit beings and Dreaming Ancestors to explain the appearance of the first Europeans, their beasts and their means of travel. For example, the cattle stock that Aboriginal people observed was initially considered from a pre-European perspective. George Taplin recorded that before the establishment of cattle stations in the Lower Murray during the 1860s, two stray bullocks had travelled down river from runs in New South Wales and appeared in the Lake Albert region.[8] The strange beasts were considered by local Aboriginal people to be 'demons'. They were called *wunda-wityeri*, which apparently meant 'spirit beings with spears on their heads'.

Elsewhere, Europeans were sometimes mistaken for spirit beings. For instance, in south-western Victoria, the early colonist James Dawson, recorded from Aboriginal people that:

> The first white man who made his appearance at Port Fairy . . . was considered by the aborigines to be a supernatural being; and, as he was discovered in the act of smoking a pipe, they said that he must be made of fire, for they saw smoke coming out of his mouth. Though they were very ready to attack a stranger, they took good care not to go near this man of fire, who very probably owed the preservation of his life to his tobacco-pipe.[9]

Although Aboriginal people from the northern coastal regions used smoking pipes which were introduced by the Macassans, in the south the act of smoking was foreign when British colonisation took place.

European-style transport was equally disturbing the first time it was seen. The first ship that was seen by the Aboriginal people of south-western Victoria greatly puzzled them. According to Dawson, it was thought to be 'a huge bird, or a tree growing in the sea. It created such terror that a messenger was immediately sent to inform the chief of the tribe, who at once declared the man insane, and ordered him to be bled by the doctor.'[10] Another colonist, Christina Smith, recorded that when a European ship arrived at Rivoli Bay in the southeast of South Australia in about 1822 or 1823, local Aboriginal people thought it was a drifting island and became alarmed.[11]

In the 1930s, as the frontier of European expansion was reaching the last few untouched corners in Australia, Aboriginal people in remote desert regions had direct contact with outsiders for the first time. Historian, Richard Kimber, claimed that the Pintupi people, whose first encounter with aeroplanes were those used during the Mackay and Lasseter expeditions, interpreted them as Walawurru, the Giant Eaglehawk.[12] They also called the European and Afghan explorers, whom they had previously encountered, *mamu*, meaning devil spirits. By classifying foreign people and objects as deceased relatives and spirit beings, Aboriginal people brought them within the internal order of their own landscape.

The Isolation Ends

Around the world, relatively isolated communities have been prone to the diseases introduced by newcomers, which can decimate populations with no resistance to them. Infectious diseases generally spring from crowded environments, as can be found in villages and cities. Australia, with its relatively low Aboriginal population density over much of the landmass, was an unlikely incubator of virulent diseases. Nevertheless, once introduced into a population, a new disease can have a devastating impact. As the biologist Jared Diamond has pointed out, the spread of diseases among native populations has had a major role in European colonisation throughout the world.[13] For Aboriginal populations in temperate Australia, the first significant effect of European settlement was the outbreak and spread of a serious disease, presumed to be smallpox. One outbreak appears to have started in 1789 at Port Jackson in New South Wales. Watkin Tench was alarmed at the existence of an epidemic among the Aboriginal population, in the year after the British had arrived. He wrote:

> An extraordinary calamity was now observed among the natives.
> Repeated accounts, brought by our boats, of finding bodies of the
> Indians [Aborigines] in all the coves and inlets of the harbour, caused
> the gentlemen of our hospital to procure some of them for the
> purposes of examination and anatomy . . . Pustules, similar to those
> occasioned by the smallpox, were thickly spread on the bodies, but
> how a disease to which our former observations had led us to suppose
> them strangers could at once have introduced itself, and have spread
> so widely, seemed inexplicable.[14]

Since smallpox was not thought to be carried with the fleet, Tench did not ever solve the puzzle of how it was introduced, nor anyone since, although the fact that Europeans were the cause cannot be disputed. Nor the fact that the long isolation of the Aboriginal people, particularly in the south, left them open to such biological attack with catastrophic effects.

Within Australia, smallpox appears to have spread from eastern Australia along the Murray–Darling Rivers system in two waves. Based on the ages of Aboriginal people Europeans later observed to be pockmarked, the first wave to eventually reach the Murray mouth in South Australia is estimated to have occurred some time between 1814 and 1820, and the second between 1829 and 1831.[15] The 1789 outbreak at Port Jackson which was recorded by Tench does not appear to have passed quickly to the west over the Great Dividing Range, which provides an imposing natural block to the movements of people. The Indigenous people at the extreme north of Australia suffered from introduced diseases as well. The Macassans, for example, who were in direct contact with many other Asian people, could have brought smallpox there on several occasions during their annual trepang expeditions. Nevertheless, the relatively sparse population in the dry interior may have provided a barrier to it reaching the temperate regions, where the greatest concentration of Aboriginal people lived.[16]

From Aboriginal reminiscences, reproduced in many of the early historical sources, smallpox epidemics spread out in front of the wave of British settlement of south-eastern Australia, decimating southern Aboriginal populations in advance of many of their people ever seeing Europeans.[17] The impact of the disease was such that whole groups of people would have disappeared. The young people, the sick and the elderly relied heavily on the active hunters and gatherers in the family unit. The loss of the labour of these chief producers through sickness would have accelerated the death rate, through starvation, adding to the spectre of smallpox alone.

In the southeast of Australia, the effect of such a sudden decrease in local populations would have had an effect on social practices—for example, marriages and funerals—and possibly led to enforced movement among surviving groups. With such devastation preceding them, the observations by colonists about Aboriginal populations and cultural practices are limited. They could only observe the necessarily modified groups who survived. For this reason it is not possible to accurately map Aboriginal cultural distribution in south-eastern Australia as it would have been around 1788.

As with many changes the Aboriginal people experienced, directly or indirectly caused by the arrival of Europeans, their understanding of what was happening was initially informed by their own belief system. By the early 1800s, news reached Aboriginal groups in southern Victoria that Aboriginal life was collapsing along the eastern seaboard, due to illness and people being driven away from their traditional lands.[18] With the arrival of Europeans the landscape was being transformed, and the knowledge of this travelled in advance of actual settlement. According to early colonists, in Victoria people believed that in the farthest reaches of their known landscape there were wooden props which held up the Skyworld. Apparently the eastern prop, where British expansion was gaining, had rotted and unless gifts of possum skins and stone hatchet heads were sent straight away to the old man who looked after it, everyone would be crushed by the falling vault of the heavens. As historian Keith Willey put it, when this occurred it would be as if 'the ghosts or reincarnations of all the black-fellows who ever lived had broken through from the spirit world to swarm over the land'.[19] There was fear that the divide between the lands of the living and the dead would be permanently ruptured.

The healing practices and medicines of the Aboriginal people would have been of little use against many of the new diseases. Young shoots of a common reed were one of the medicines tried unsuccessfully by Lower Murray people as a cure for smallpox.[20] The shoots were pounded and administered with a river mussel shell used as a spoon.

While trying to deal physically with the arrival of such a disease the Aboriginal people also responded spiritually. The Tangani people of the Coorong had a death fear song concerning the arrival of a smallpox epidemic.[21] In the Dreaming for this song, a 'dream man', Kulda, came down to earth from Yuki, the Southern Cross, in the Skyworld. He foretold the coming of death and with his 'pointing bone' he took the spirits of the dead back with him via Kangaroo Island. When the South Australian Museum's ethnologist Norman Tindale was doing fieldwork in the 1930s, the Aboriginal people he spoke to still remembered the accounts that their grandparent's generation had given to them of the impact that the disease had had upon the local Aboriginal population. Tindale recorded that:

> The natives saw a man (meteor) come out of Yuuki [Yuki], the Southern Cross; they heard a noise and looked up (*meinyanga nampi*). They saw him move his hands and said '*Ha! peika bakki*' ('Ah! death coming'; '*peik*' = 'die'). The natives could not stand the *murki* [smallpox] and a great many died. The meteor was a *maldawuli* man [spirit man] whose name was Kuldalai [Kulda], he travelled westward through the sky and beckoned to indicate that all the people should

follow him. Then the smallpox came and many people followed him (literally went west) across to Kangaroo Island and beyond.[22]

Kulda was said to have appeared 'like a bright flash, too bright to look', which was presumably a large meteor. The method he used to attract people was first by smoke signals, then by waving his hands. Tindale's informants believed that many of the bones in the sand hills of the Lower Murray belonged to people that Kulda had beckoned to follow him.

In the first few decades after Europeans arrived, Aboriginal people suffered from many introduced diseases in addition to smallpox, including pulmonary tuberculosis, gastric and intestinal diseases, venereal diseases and Spanish influenza. On a frontier dominated by white men, Indigenous women were sought for wives and as servants. The removal of women from the Tasmanian community by sealers exacerbated a population decline, primarily caused through disease and conflict with Europeans.[23]

As the frontier of European contact with Aboriginal people moved across Australia, so too did this pattern. For example, it was estimated that between the 1870s and the 1940s, Aboriginal populations in the eastern Lake Eyre Basin region of the northeast of South Australia had

Tasmanian women and European settlers on Kangaroo Island, resting behind a windbreak. European sealers took many Indigenous women away from their country to become workers and wives. DRAWING: W.H. LEIGH, KANGAROO ISLAND, SOUTH AUSTRALIA, 1839.

plummeted to less than 10 per cent of their pre-European level due to the establishment of cattle stations.[24] In many regions a recent recovery in the Indigenous population has only occurred through a growth in the numbers of people of mixed European and Aboriginal descent.[25]

Aboriginal people had logical expectations that the British settlers would suffer from the same calamities as them. Some years after the British arrived in Australia, Aboriginal people still expected that Spirit Beings would punish the Europeans. For instance, in March 1843, a comet visible to Aboriginal people from along the Murray River was taken as a 'harbinger of all kinds of calamities, and more especially to the white people. It was considered that the comet would overthrow Adelaide, destroying all Europeans and their houses, and then to take a course up the Murray and past the Rufus River causing havoc in its path'.[26] The inclusion of the Rufus River in this explanation was probably due to it being the site of an earlier massacre of Aboriginal people by overlanders.

These doomsday beliefs occurred at a time when Aboriginal people were contemplating whether the conditions of their pre-European past were ever going to return to them. In this respect they were similar to the 'ghost dances' by Native Americans of the Plains during the 1890s, which were held to help the removal of Europeans from their lands.[27] The religious historian Tony Swain argued that British settlement and the subsequent high Aboriginal death rate caused a major alteration in the Aboriginal religions of south-eastern Australia, resulting in more emphasis in 'high gods' perhaps to help them survive the new calamities of disease and land alienation.[28] In northern and Central Australia, Aboriginal people incorporated into their ceremonial life elements of European colonial culture, such as the notion of a great flood and the salvation of adherents to the 'Old Law'.[29] This was an attempt to gain more power towards adjusting to the changes they were observing around them, with landscape being altered and the newcomers arriving in increasing numbers. Here, some aspects of Aboriginal secret religious life also changed, in line with the broadening of the Aboriginal worldview.[30]

Thirteen

Aboriginal Australia Transformed

The spread of European influences across Aboriginal Australia did not always begin with 'face to face' contact. Aboriginal people living in regions beyond the frontier of British settlement gained knowledge of strangers through talking to neighbouring peoples. European items, such as glass and metal, also penetrated into remote regions through an extensive trade system. The diseases brought to Australia from the late eighteenth century devastated Aboriginal populations ahead of European settlement. When more direct contact eventually occurred, the nature of the resulting relationship varied from place to place and across time.

Outbreaks of violence between European colonists and the Aboriginal inhabitants tended to occur in the frontier areas shortly after the initial wave of Europeans arrived. Aboriginal people refer to this period of colonialism as the 'killing times'.[1] Prolonged conflict was generally restricted to areas where the colonial control was stretched thin, such as the southern islands occupied by sealers and on outback stations. The general pattern was that in regions where the number of Europeans was high in relation to the Aboriginal people, and where the whole landscape was easily accessible to men on horseback, the settlement frontier period lasted only a few years. Where Europeans were low in number and the terrain was able to hide Aboriginal people who could maintain their traditional independence, the frontier period was much longer. In the southeast of Australia Aboriginal people became dependent upon the British settlers, as access to their lands and its resources was being rapidly removed. Unlike in the Americas, where tribal bands on horseback retreated from the advance of Europeans, in Australia the Aboriginal people would not have been able to migrate en masse away from the British settlers. The hunting and gathering lifestyle in Australia did not support this degree of movement in the long term.

European 'Discovery'

The European men that have been immortalised in the Australian history textbooks as the 'explorers' knew well that the key to their success was their ability to read the land for its Aboriginal occupation. European explorers relied on Aboriginal guides who had at least some experience of the landscape being negotiated. For instance, on his circumnavigation of Australia (1801–02), Matthew Flinders took with him Bongaree, an Eora Aboriginal man from the Sydney region.[2] Bongaree was the first Aboriginal person known to have sailed around Australia. Similarly, on Charles Sturt's Central Australian expedition (1844–45) two Aboriginal guides, Nadbuck and Jackey (Camboli), accompanied him from the Lake Victoria–Murray River region.[3] They had crucial roles in providing Sturt with intelligence on the land and its inhabitants, and established relations with local people as the expedition passed through their territories.

Encountering local Aboriginal people was generally a blessing to the explorers. Although large numbers of Aboriginal people posed a physical threat, the presence of numerous Aboriginal people was a sign that the country was fertile and well watered. For example, Prussian-born scientist and explorer Ludwig Leichhardt whose overland expedition in 1844–45 crossed Queensland to the Top End, took with him an Aboriginal guide from Bathurst in New South Wales, named Charley. After Charley had observed numerous campfires along the ranges, Leichhardt noted in his journal that 'this was welcome intelligence; for we knew that their presence indicated the existence of a good country'.[4]

There were occasions when Aboriginal assistance was taken by force. For instance, in 1839 John Bull found himself low on water when looking for land suitable for agriculture around Port Lincoln. His party was in dire straits 'until a black was caught, who was induced to point out some of their watering places in the direction of the new settlement'.[5]

European explorers often followed Aboriginal routes from waterhole to waterhole. Even when Aboriginal guides were not present, Aboriginal occupation of the region left clearly defined tracks that needy Europeans could use to their advantage. In 1838 in north-western Australia, English explorer George Grey, who later became Governor of South Australia, came across 'pathways as those we find in England, leading from a village to a farm house'.[6] In the same year, Aboriginal tracks helped the overlander Charles Bonney open up a stock route from New South Wales to South Australia. Bonney reported that the Aboriginal people, particularly along the Murray River, were very helpful to him. He claimed that 'the paths which they [the Aboriginal people] had made in travelling up and down the river afforded an unfailing guide as to the direction we ought to take in order to cross the great bends it frequently makes'.[7]

Dramatically in 1861 the famous trans-Australian explorers Robert O'Hara Burke and William J. Wills became lost on their return from the Gulf of Carpentaria. They were saved on this occasion when they came across an Aboriginal pathway that took them to a source of drinking water and a place where they found yams that had been dug up and left by Aboriginal people.[8]

The European settlers who followed the explorers also frequently appropriated the Aboriginal tracks they found in the landscape they had taken over. For instance, in 1846 a lost and sick European was found in the lower southeast of South Australia by a local Aboriginal man, who fed him and then took him 'to the native's track, which was easier walking than through the scrub'.[9] Aboriginal pathways would have provided a useful existing network for Europeans settlers who were establishing their own order upon the landscape. The South Australian geographer Charles A.E. Fenner acknowledged the influence of the Aboriginal people on European communication routes, citing R.A. Gibbins of the State Highways Department, who said:

> The aborigines showed a considerable amount of cleverness in selecting the best country to travel over in central Australia, and in that locality many of the roads and cattle tracks used today were at one time native pads. The Great Northern Railway, in many places, follows parallel with an old red ochre track used by the aborigines for

unknown years. When Europeans made their way into the interior, they soon realized the advantage of utilizing the aborigines' knowledge of bushcraft. River crossings, bogs, quicksands, and flooded plains were found to offer no great difficulty to the white man when he called in the aid of the aborigines, who had made pads through these swamps and morasses for ages before Europeans came. From each waterhole to the next the blackfellows had their pad, and this was invariably found to be the easiest way.[10]

The incorporation of Aboriginal tracks into stock routes and even parts of modern road systems has been recorded across Australia particularly from Central and Northern Australia.[11] However, the details of most Aboriginal routes in south-eastern Australia, both major and minor, are poorly known. Colonists of all lands generally do not fully acknowledge their debt to the landowners they have usurped and the first Europeans to settle in Australia rarely considered recording its Indigenous history as important.

Life on the Edge

Over much of Australia, but particularly the temperate regions which the British found more appealing, the 'discovery' of new lands by the explorers was quickly followed by distinct waves of European settlement. The first wave was represented by the establishment of sheep and cattle stations, which 'opened up' the country; this was followed by phases of more intensive farming, and the establishment of towns and railway systems, eventually leading to urban development in some cases. The settlers often absorbed Aboriginal landscape features besides tracks, such as camping places and water sources, and transformed them into a rural landscape. Each cultural group creates its own cultural landscape, layering it upon previous forms. The Australian 'pioneer' was not a European settler who became 'Aboriginal', but an individual who transformed the Australian wilderness into a model of Europe by clearing scrub, making dams, building fences and introducing foreign plants and animals.[12] In regions that were unfavourable to initial British settlement, such as the arid and sub-tropical areas, it was often the establishment of communication systems or mining that brought in large numbers of Europeans. Only the harshest deserts were left largely untouched. One of the Australian English terms for this country, the 'never-never', was derived from the 'never-never blacks', who for a long time were able to avoid all contact with Europeans.[13] In general Aboriginal people were treated as having an existence on the edge of the developing Australian society. Missions were established with the aim of saving heathen souls. They also alleviated the stress on the dispossessed Aboriginal inhabitants by providing a physical refuge, as well as distributed rations in areas where European settlement had forced the Indigenous people into considerable hardship by removing access to their land.[14] Missions were usually run by church groups or private humanitarian organisations. During the nineteenth century most governments left such establishments to run largely by themselves.

The British colonists brought with them their own images of the land and its people for imposition upon the Australian landscape. European missionaries and other officials attempted to mould Aboriginal people into an image of the European working class, by changing their appearance, restricting their movements, making them live in permanent houses, and by generally suppressing all forms of Indigenous cultures. The use of clothing by Aboriginal people increased greatly due to the local people learning what is described in Aboriginal English as 'shame', which is used to mean embarrassment. In the late nineteenth century at Port Essington northeast of Darwin, the Aboriginal inhabitants normally went without any form of clothing, although they did choose, or were encouraged by Europeans, to wear bunches of green leaves when entering the local town.[15] Eventually, Aboriginal people were encouraged to look and live like Europeans. Some Aboriginal people in Central Australia today still refer to the pre-European times as 'before trousers'. Although familiarity with the landscape was of value to Aboriginal people working as stockmen on cattle stations, much of their hunting and gathering knowledge was considered by the Europeans to be of little value to the 'civilising' process.

Throughout the nineteenth century, when the majority of British expansion in Australia occurred, the prevailing opinion was that the Aboriginal 'race' was doomed to annihilation in the face of European settlement. In spite of the good intentions of the powers in Britain, the sale and development of agricultural land was a greater concern to the Australian colonial authorities than Indigenous affairs. Left to their own the Aboriginal missions went about their business of saving souls, usually after destroying the 'primitive' customs of the local people. The numbers of people with 'full' Aboriginal descent were rapidly declining in the newly made rural and urban landscapes. The growing population of individuals with 'mixed' descent was seen as transitory, making way for the eventual absorption of the Indigenous population into the working classes. As long as missionaries were 'smoothing the dying pillow', the government authorities could largely ignore Indigenous issues while they concerned themselves with building a modern European-styled country.

As British crown land became alienated for sale in the newly proclaimed Australian colonies, the Aboriginal inhabitants became trespassers in their own clan territories as noticed by some European observers. For instance, by 1840 an early colonial doctor in South Australia, Richard Penney, claimed that in the Lower Murray region:

> The Lesser Murray, Currency Creek, and Encounter and Rapid Bay tribes are, for the most part, residing upon land that is actually sold, although not settled. The favorite resorts of the tribe for a series of generations will, in the course of time, be enclosed, and themselves excluded from all right to resort there.[16]

Setting up Aboriginal reserves on land that was marginal to both Europeans and Aboriginal people was not the answer. The concerned doctor added that 'all places are not the same to them; and though individuals are constantly moving from one station to another, yet there are particular locations always inhabited by some of the tribe'. Many of the places Europeans liked to settle and build upon, such as high ground near water sources, had been the favoured camping grounds for Aboriginal people for hundreds of years. The middens built up by Aboriginal cooking fires form excellent foundations for building houses, and Europeans were drawn to many of the same places in the landscape that were held special by Aboriginal people.

The seasonal movement patterns of Aboriginal people before Europeans arrived were such that people were generally thinly spread out across the landscape when there was plenty of food and water, but converged on particular safe areas during times of hardship. When Europeans took over refuge places of local Aboriginal groups, conflict or catastrophe was inevitable. European settlement at the fringe of the Simpson Desert in the northeast of South Australia was in a zone that was crucial for the survival of Aboriginal people. The establishment of cattle

Europeans often established their settlements in the same places that Aboriginal people had been camping at for generations. PHOTO: P. FOELSCHE, PORT ESSINGTON, NORTHERN TERRITORY, 1877.

stations here effectively brought about the total Aboriginal depopulation of much of the region, including areas beyond the boundaries of European settlement.[17] Similarly where there is irregular rainfall, large areas of land with variable habitat are needed to support the Aboriginal population in the long term. Few Europeans during the establishment phase of the Australian colonies understood the long-term climate pattern. This was particularly so for arid inland regions, which may have a series of mild seasons in good years, but in bad years suffer from droughts and on rare occasions from extensive flooding. It is a sobering realisation that for arid regions like the Simpson Desert, Aboriginal land-use patterns would have previously supported a greater resident population than is currently possible with the land dominated by sheep runs and cattle stations.[18] A closer examination of Aboriginal land-use by the first European settlers would have provided them with a warning about the highly irregular seasonal nature of the arid zone. This did not occur, with many overly optimistic station owners being forced off the land when the favourable times were followed by severe hardship.

Aboriginal Knowledge

In spite of the apparent antagonism between British and Aboriginal interests, the knowledge possessed by Aboriginal people was crucial for unlocking the landscape to Europeans. Aboriginal people acted as guides for explorers and colonists who were looking for water sources and open country for pasture. They helped track and recover lost stock before fences were made. Aboriginal collectors also gathered plant and animal specimens for early biologists, such as George Caley and Wilhelm Blandowski.[19] And Aboriginal people have continued to serve as 'trackers' up until the present—looking for people lost in the bush or searching for criminals eluding the police.

The craft of the tracker has attracted an aura of mysticism and respect by Europeans. In 1899 it was described admiringly as follows:

> When engaged in tracking upon anything like a clear trail ('clear' to his eye, not so to ours) the native expert scans the surroundings, not down on the ground close to him, as a white man would do, but casts his glance ten or twenty feet [three or six metres], or more, away to the front. Where trodden grass, or twig, or imprint in the sand, shows by the sheen of successive prints the trail he so eagerly seeks to keep in view. Viewing the track in this way the mounted native tracker will go confidently forward at a hand-gallop, with head leaning now to one side, now to the other, of his horse's neck, keeping this up for long distances, or until more difficult country is reached, when the pace slackens.[20]

Since the colonising period, Aboriginal trackers from the frontiers with hunting and gathering skills as well as familiarity with European ways have been the most attractive to the authorities. For instance, in the early part of this century the main police tracker in the southeast of South Australia was Alf Ryan, who originally came from the northern Flinders Ranges region.[21] In more recent times, Jimmy James was the main police tracker in South Australia.[22] He originated from the desert region of Western Australia, coming to the Riverland via Ooldea. Aboriginal people growing up after European settlement, when hunting and gathering was no longer practised, did not develop these skills. The use by the police forces of 'traditional' Aboriginal landscape-based knowledge to track criminals and lost people is consistent with the earlier use of Aboriginal skills by explorers, and amounts to official recognition of the unique view of the Australian landscape held by Aboriginal people.

The European settlers were not like any of the other foreign visitors to Australia. Although in many regions they arrived in a trickle, they soon came in such overwhelming numbers that they dominated the Indigenous people. The places they took over were often important to local Aboriginal groups, putting enormous stress on ceremonial and hunting and gathering activities. Aboriginal people could see the difference too. For instance, in north-eastern Arnhem Land the Yolngu people made a sharp distinction between Macassans and Europeans.[23] To them, the Macassans were welcome annual visitors, but the Europeans were like flying foxes: they arrived in hordes apparently randomly and invaded certain places. Some of the Yolngu names for Europeans are the same as for the flying foxes. Similarly, in the southeast region of South Australia, a Moandik man, Alf Watson, claimed in 1934 that their supreme Ancestor, Ngurunderi, had warned the Aboriginal people about the coming of Europeans and their

Aboriginal people often worked as labourers, whalers and spotters at the whaling stations during the nineteenth century. At Encounter Bay, discarded whale rib bones were used to provide the structure of Aboriginal shelters. WATERCOLOUR: G. FRENCH ANGAS, ENCOUNTER BAY, SOUTH AUSTRALIA, 1844.

Girls living on missions were encouraged to develop and use traditional Aboriginal techniques to make baskets for sale to Europeans. UNKNOWN PHOTOGRAPHER, POINT MCLEAY (RAUKKAN), SOUTH AUSTRALIA, ABOUT 1900.

destruction of the environment. Ngurunderi is reputed to have said 'Beware of *puruki* (ants)', who were the white people who swarm over the land.[24] The initial cultural impact of Europeans Australia-wide was also greater than that of any other foreign group because they arrived in regions, such as the southern coasts, which had probably never seen visitors directly from Asia or Melanesia.

While Aboriginal familiarity with local resources and their use was crucial to the establishment of European settlements, the history of Aboriginal relations with the European invaders is nonetheless essentially one of conflicting demand for, and attitudes to, land and water. The Aboriginal population was gradually marginalised with respect to the landscape and did not directly benefit from the nation-building activities taking place upon it. At certain times, such as during the Victorian gold rushes of the 1850s and the early twentieth-century heydays of the outback cattle industry, Aboriginal labour propped up the ailing farm and pastoral enterprises. Nevertheless, the welfare of the Aboriginal population sank increasingly into the background of colonial development. European transformation of the Australian landscape, through land clearance, fencing, irrigation, road and railway building, and the establishment of towns, removed forever the possibility of a society of hunters and gatherers existing in all but the most remote areas. Missions, and particular reserve areas around them, became central to some Aboriginal people as the physical landscape, and European perceptions of it, were no longer able to support a widely dispersed Indigenous population.

The initial contact between Europeans and Aboriginal people was one of immense misunderstanding. To the British settlers, Aboriginal people were first thought to be 'Indians', then unsophisticated wanderers who did not own or use land in any sense recognised by Europeans. This land was therefore 'terra nullius', unoccupied and waiting for colonial exploitation. To Aboriginal people, the white people were either their own dead kin returning with some memory loss from the 'Land of the Dead', or were potentially malevolent spirit beings. As anthropologist Les Hiatt noted, European and Aboriginal people had fundamental attitudinal differences in the manner in which they 'owned' land, commenting on the 'Aboriginal ethic of generosity that regarded exclusive use and enjoyment [of land] as indecent . . .'.[25] The continued poor understanding of Aboriginal cultures by the Europeans and their Australian descendants has marred relations between the colonisers and the colonised for over 200 years. For much of this time, Aboriginal people have been the primary interest of anthropologists and missionaries. Official histories written in textbooks celebrate the feats of explorers and pioneers who, as the orthodox versions go, entered a great 'unknown' land to pave the way for establishing another outpost for the British Empire. Nevertheless, to Aboriginal people their land was no wilderness; to them it was known in intimate detail. Aboriginal people played an important role on the frontier of European exploration of Australia, although this is rarely acknowledged.

Fourteen

Changing Cultural Landscapes

Change occurs in all cultures through time. For the world's Indigenous communities who have withstood colonisation from other peoples, it is generally accompanied by language loss, cessation of religious practices, decline in artefact and art traditions, movement away from key places in the landscape, disease and population decline. And yet, in Australia many distinctive Aboriginal cultures survive to the present. Even in parts of Australia where cultural changes have been felt most keenly—in south-eastern Australia—the descendants of pre-European Aboriginal groups maintain an identity. This is in spite of twentieth-century government policies of Indigenous assimilation into the predominantly European community, and discouragement of Aboriginal lifestyles, customs and traditions. More socially remote Aboriginal communities, such as some of those in northern and Central Australia, have been able to maintain strong links to the pre-European phase of their culture. Even here, however, there have been significant cultural changes since European intrusion into their country. The land has, too, experienced many changes. Over most of Australia, the widespread cessation of Aboriginal hunting and gathering practices, such as firestick farming, has forever changed the nature of the flora and fauna. Europeans have caused the extinction of some uniquely Australian animals, while introducing many foreign species of animals and plants.

Starting in the early 1980s, many Indigenous Australians have followed other Indigenous peoples worldwide in reasserting, or in some cases reclaiming, their identity.[1] In her autobiographical book *My Place*, Aboriginal author Sally Morgan described the discovery of her Aboriginality and how senior family members had hidden this from her as a child by always claiming that they were 'Indian'.[2] Rather than continuing in the shame of Aboriginality, Morgan celebrated it. In the same spirit other people who had grown up as Aboriginal people gained deeper insights into their past 'tribal' connections to the landscape by studying records derived from European sources, including reminiscences of colonists and anthropological journals. Therefore, a wider range of cultural influences shapes modern Aboriginality. This final chapter considers the nature of the cultural interaction between Aboriginal and European people in relation to the landscape and modern identity.

Absorption of European Culture

The circumstances of two cultures coming into contact never results in the instantaneous absorption of one by the other. At some stage there is a period of accommodation resulting in a blending of ideas and practices, even if one culture over time gains the upper hand and becomes the dominant force. However, this process does not exclude subjected peoples reviving and inventing cultural practices in the future.[3] In Australia, the investigation of how much cultural interchange took place is difficult because early written records on Aboriginal culture are generally patchy in coverage and usually commence at least several years after the first waves of European settlement. We must also take into account the inherent biases of such sources and be cautious about using accounts that relate to a period when the Indigenous population was recovering from the impact of foreigners who not only introduced different ideas and technologies but also brought along with them diseases and increased violence.

The makeup of all contemporary Aboriginal cultures is a complex mix of pre-European and post-European elements in varying degrees across Australia. This should not be surprising, as it is the nature of all cultures to be influenced by others. Indigenous peoples in the twenty-first century are as much products of Australian history since 1788 as are the Australians with predominantly European or Asian family backgrounds.

It is not possible to generalise about the 'contact' between Indigenous Australians and Europeans without sacrificing regional variations across Australia. For instance, Aboriginal groups along the northern coast were possibly better equipped to deal with the arrival of the British, because of their long history of visits from Melanesian and Asian peoples, than were Aboriginal communities living in the south. Furthermore, the social and political environment of each period needs to be taken into account. The government policies that dictated the nature of the first European–Indigenous relations at Sydney in the late eighteenth century were different from those relating to the 'contact' situation in the Western Desert during the 1960s. Since it is the essential nature of all cultures to absorb change and to reform, it is often difficult to distinguish 'traditional' (pre-European) elements of Aboriginal cultures from recently developed parts with at least some alien influence. This is apparent in some of the ceremonies of northern Australia that incorporated the seasonal arrival of the Macassans. Individuals react to new cultural experiences in a variety of ways: sometimes embracing change and at other times rejecting it, either wholly or in part. While some Indigenous people have fiercely resisted the adoption of new ideas, others accepted the intrusion of foreigners and their culture. A few individuals have become agents of change and are actively involved as cultural brokers between local people and the newcomers. Hunters and gatherers are not entirely passive agents in the transformation of their culture. All cultures undergo change through time.

Language Change

One way of mapping cultural adaptation is to investigate change in language. All languages are richly embedded with information about their culture and their cultural landscapes. Words and meanings are not clearly interchangeable, despite well-meaning assumptions. For example, in 1788 the first British settlers to Australia who arrived in New South Wales brought with them a small vocabulary of Aboriginal words that had been collected by Captain James Cook in 1770.[4] The aim was to establish a common means of communication with local Aboriginal people. Nevertheless, use of this vocabulary failed dismally, as the original list turned out to be from the Guugu Yimidhirr language of Cooktown in northern Queensland, and had no direct relationship with the languages around Sydney. The new settlers perceived a need to gain an interpreter, which led to the forced abduction of the Sydney Aboriginal man Arabanoo, who was then taught English. With some form of communication possible between the two groups, the Europeans had a better means of learning about the local Indigenous people and important geographical information, such as the location of pathways and water sources, in what was to them a 'new' landscape. Yet the capacity for Europeans to absorb Aboriginal environmental knowledge was limited and error ridden. Aboriginal people knew a lot about the plants and animals of Australia that would have been useful to the colonists. Ironically, Aboriginal people living around Sydney ended up learning the word 'kangaroo' from British settlers who were using the word list from northern Queensland, and they took it as a European word to mean all large animals. Europeans had grossly underestimated language and cultural diversity in Aboriginal Australia.

On the frontier Europeans used a basic set of Indigenous words to such an extent that it led to a few Aboriginal terms entering the emerging Australian variety of English. These were generally applied to what, to Europeans, were new elements of the landscape, particularly plants and animals. Words such as dingo (*dinggu*—dog), boobook (*bug bug*—owl species), gibber (*giba*—stone) and kurrajong tree (*garrajung*—fishing line, which is made from the bark of this plant) are all originally from Sydney languages.[5] Later, as the European frontier expanded, terms from other Aboriginal languages came into use by British settlers. From Western Victoria we can trace the introduction into Australian English of such words as bunyip (*banib*—amphibious spirit), yabby or yabbies (*yabij*—freshwater crustacean species) and lerp (*lerep*—leaf scale), all from the Wemba Wemba language.[6] By the late nineteenth century, when the establishment of the Australian colonies was well advanced, the capacity for European settlers to absorb Aboriginal words into English decreased, as they progressively became more dominant in the colonising of the land. Given the hundreds of thousands of words in the vocabularies of Aboriginal languages across Australia, the borrowings by Australian English are very few. The inequality in the social environment created by European settlement was such that local Aboriginal people were made to learn English. Rarely was it acknowledged as necessary for the colonisers to become fluent in the local Indigenous languages. This fact hampered the recording of Aboriginal cultures by early settlers. It has also contributed to the extinction of many pre-European forms of language in Australia.

When different people with different languages initially mix a pidgin language code often develops. In outlying regions of Australia, the growth in pidgin English led to it becoming a language in its own right, being a primary means of communication between many Aboriginal people. When children learn pidgin as their first language, the resulting language is called a 'creole'. On the European frontier, Aboriginal people learned to speak a creole, not from Europeans, but from other Aboriginal speakers. For example, by the early twentieth century there was an influx of Europeans into the northern and central regions of Australia to work on the Overland Telegraph Line and to set up cattle stations. The conflict over land led to the killing of Aboriginal people and the collapse of cultural life in many areas, particularly in the region between Roper River and Arnhem Land. In the missions set up to protect Aboriginal people, the new communities that emerged were based on survivors from many different language groups, who used pidgin English to communicate among themselves.[7] This social disruption in northern Australia provided the background for the development of several creole languages, some referred to as Kriol. These forms of language continue to grow in the face of the extinction of most of the more than two hundred distinct Aboriginal languages spoken on this continent in 1788.[8] With every language in the world that is lost, important sources of information about the land and other things disappear too.

In some parts of Australia, in particular the temperate regions where British settlement was most concentrated, the forms of speech used by Aboriginal people today range from standard Australian English to approaching non-standard Australian English, to creoles that incorporate many features of rural English. In the case of the Lower Murray region, the form of language spoken by Aboriginal people uses English words, such as *gammon* 'false' and *flog* 'beat', as well as a few terms from the local Indigenous languages, such as *nakin* 'see' and *korni* 'man'. This style of speaking is generally referred to as Aboriginal English rather than as a creole, due to its heavy reliance upon English for its grammar and many of its source words. When I first began fieldwork in southern Australia, I had to come to terms with a particular variety of Aboriginal English known as 'Nunga lingo' which was widely spoken by local Aboriginal people. Being married to an Aboriginal person from the Ngarrindjeri community of the Lower Murray, it also became the main form of English spoken in my home. To many speakers of conventional Australian English, Nunga lingo at first sounds like a totally foreign language. For example, words like *giyin* and *tjittin* have the respective English root words of 'going' and 'sitting'. Such transformation of words occurs within a predictable set of phonetic and syntactic language rules.[9] Nunga lingo and other post-European forms of speaking being developed by Aboriginal people are becoming Indigenous languages in their own right.

Artefacts

As the strategies for extracting a living from the land change, so too do the practices relating to artefact making. Many of the pre-European Aboriginal technologies have been lost or heavily modified in the face of European settlement, due to factors such as European control, changing economies and restrictions upon Aboriginal people in accessing parts of the landscape. As a partial halt to this decline, the relatively recent interest by outsiders in Aboriginal cultures has created an economic environment in which some Aboriginal art and craft styles flourish beyond their internal community use. There is a broad range of material now being produced by Aboriginal people for sale through art and souvenir outlets. Today, because of the importance of artefact sales to their local economy, some Aboriginal communities employ European art and craft advisers to help organise their end of the market. Such artefacts are not confined to dot paintings or traditional representations. In southern and eastern Australia there are basket- and mat-making practices that have persisted since pre-European times, largely through having become 'mission crafts'. Today, many of these early traditions of basketry are undergoing a revival. In Tasmania, too, Aboriginal people have maintained a tradition of collecting kelp shells for stringing into necklaces. The shells are cleaned of their outer dark matt coating, which reveals the translucent inner layers. The necklaces have a long loop, which is wound around the neck several times.

To many present-day Aboriginal people, their knowledge and practice of making pre-European style artefacts, such as basketry and necklace making, are important elements in the maintenance of their regional Aboriginal identity. The making of many other objects, particularly weapons, such as clubs, shields and spears, ceased in regions where adherence to hunting and gathering practices, and to fighting customs, was no longer possible after Europeans gained control over the country. A recovery of some artefact-making traditions has occurred by Aboriginal people basing new pieces on old examples held in museum collections and

Three 'mission style' baskets with flat bases, suitable for European domestic use, and a pre-European-style carry bag in the back centre. These are made with plant fibres, such as pandanus leaf, and vegetable dyes. The basket makers, Daisy Nadjungdarna and Reba, are women from Maningrida, central Arnhem Land, Northern Territory.
COLLECTED AT A BASKETRY WORKSHOP, TANDANYA, ADELAIDE, SOUTH AUSTRALIA, 1992.

on recorded images of objects in early European paintings. The artefacts and artworks they produce which incorporate the early designs are important points of connection to their particular Aboriginal culture. There are also Aboriginal artists who are involved in exploring, through modern 'fine art', contemporary Indigenous issues. The production of art has become an important means by which many Indigenous people express their identity.[10]

Religion

Across the world, the result of European missionaries' attempts to convert Indigenous people to Christianity has been the blending of 'old' and 'new' beliefs.[11] Where imposition by the coloniser ends and appropriation by the colonised begins is hard to define. Some missionaries, for example Teichelmann and Schürmann, have actively recorded Indigenous cultures, becoming scholars in their own right. Nevertheless, in the early nineteenth century the impetus for their study primarily revolved around the investigation of whether or not Aboriginal people believed in a supreme being.

This was an important issue for the purposes of eventual Christian conver-
sion and for determining whether Indigenous people could swear an oath
in a court of law. Indeed, the early interest in language and culture by
Europeans was mainly based on practical concerns, not upon any notions
of cultural preservation. It was not until the late nineteenth century that
this began to change with the growth of anthropological interest in what
were considered to be 'primitive' hunting and gathering cultures.[12]

It was an early missionary strategy to superimpose European notions of
God upon the Indigenous belief system. For example, while working with
Kaurna people of the Adelaide Plains during the 1830s the German
missionary Clamour W. Schürmann was frustrated in his attempts to
identify a suitable Aboriginal concept onto which he could graft Christianity. Eventually, Schürmann settled on the spirit Monaincherloo for use
as 'God' in the Christianising process. Concerning him, Schürmann said:

> As soon as I got this name, I substituted it for the hitherto used
> Jehovah, which they could scarcely pronounce; I told them of
> creation; of the incarnation, sufferings, death, resurrection, and
> ascension, of the Son of God; and I had the satisfaction of seeing, not
> only that I was perfectly understood, but also that I created a deep
> interest. If further discoveries do not show, that they combine ideas
> too pagan and absurd with the name Munaintjerlo [Monaincherloo],
> I mean to retain it for the name of God.[13]

He was disappointed and later wrote, 'The hope to have discovered a kind
of almighty creature among the natives again went to water.'[14]

The missionary's strategy was to initially incorporate some elements of
the Aboriginal religion into the Christian teachings, but to gradually strive
to make these subservient, and finally to eliminate them altogether. Tactics
such as undermining the authority of the religious leaders, disrupting
marriage practices, discouraging movement patterns, and the restrictive
spatial organisation of the mission itself, were all intended to contribute to
this transformation.[15]

The introduction of ideas by missionaries sometimes had unintended
consequences. For instance, in the Lower Murray region, Ngarrindjeri
people modified their Dreaming mythology as they came to embrace
Christianity. They took the supreme male Ancestor, Ngurunderi, as a
suitable interpretation of the concept of 'God'. The missionary George

Taplin came to the opinion that Ngurunderi was a 'vile character . . . in vice and everything bad', but was unsuccessful in stopping the Ngarrindjeri from using this name for God.[16] As the opportunity presents itself, Aboriginal people often explore ways in which their Dreaming Ancestors entered the cultural landscapes of their neighbours and of newcomers. In a religious system where revelations about the creation come from the ceremonial transfer of knowledge between senior members and in some places occasionally through dreams, the identity available for an incoming deity, in this case the Christian God, was likely to be similar to that of an Aboriginal Ancestor.[17]

History

Aboriginal people have developed their own accounts of European colonisation which have been incorporated into their cultures as myths or Dreaming stories. Rather than being strict accounts of their contact history, they tell how their lives were changed by European intrusion, without necessarily explaining why. For example, across northern Australia there are many Aboriginal accounts of the famous eighteenth-century British naval explorer Captain James Cook. In these local versions, which were recorded in the 1980s, he is believed to be among the first European settlers who came into the area, presumably in the late nineteenth century. In eastern Arnhem Land the following account was recorded in 1987 from Aboriginal people:

> Captain Cook and his wives—he only had two wives—he was born many years ago. That was from a long long time ago . . . Captain Cook was there first, before Adam and Eve. The birds, the trees, developed at the same time. Captain Cook was a yirritja man, from the yirritja group. Captain Cook was really a business [ceremonial] man . . .[18]

The locations linked with Cook in Aboriginal accounts include the Kimberley in Western Australia, Victoria River district in north-western Northern Territory, Cardwell in northern Queensland and Batemans Bay in southern New South Wales. In European history, Captain Cook is generally regarded as a national hero and the founder of Australia, being the first person to formally take possession of the land for the British

Crown and to start systemically mapping large sections of its coastlines. In the majority of these Aboriginal stories, which have a myth-like quality, Cook has the role of invader and is symbolic of all the negative things that Aboriginal people experienced on the frontier.[19]

In some northern regions, Aboriginal people also believe that the infamous Victorian bushranger Ned Kelly and the Christian Jesus visited them and took the side of the Aboriginal people in opposing Cook. In New South Wales there are Aboriginal folk stories that have 'Queen Victoria' giving local people reserves as compensation for their lands being taken away by the British settlers.[20] In Melanesia, such stories are related to 'cargo cults', and they provide a rationale of the unequal relations between Europeans and Indigenous people. In Aboriginal Australia they are important records of how Aboriginal people have experienced British colonisation.

Folk tales about early contact between the colonised and the colonisers have had willing European and Aboriginal ears. These accounts spring from the early frontier period and some of them are referred to by historians as 'captivity narratives'.[21] They include such examples as the stranding of Eliza Fraser among Aboriginal people in northern Queensland, the white woman held captive by Gippsland Aboriginal people in Victoria, and the escape of Aboriginal women from white sealers by swimming the Backstairs Passage in South Australia. Although from different parts of Australia, in various ways they all explore the brutality of the early frontier between Indigenous and European peoples. The facts behind these stories are elusive to historians, with the 'truth' existing in the message as interpreted by Aboriginal people and not necessarily in the historical events. In these cases, Europeans and Aboriginal people have both been actively involved in the creation of folklore.

Aboriginal people who survived the first wave of British colonisation tended to interpret the world according to their original cultural knowledge for many decades afterwards. For example, as discussed in the last chapter, increasing death rates in the Aboriginal population was due to the introduction of diseases from Europeans, such as smallpox and influenza. Nevertheless, this was sometimes explained by the people concerned as the result of power struggles between sorcerers within their communities. In 1859 the Port Elliot Aboriginal people, living south of Adelaide where there were many European settlers, attributed their rapidly decreasing numbers to the sorcery of neighbouring Aboriginal groups.[22] They would not believe otherwise when spoken to by a missionary. This has also been the pattern elsewhere in Australia.[23] In another example from the Kimberley, an Aboriginal 'bushranger' (outlaw) named Pigeon (Tjandawara) died in 1897 after being shot by police; local Aboriginal people, however, claimed that an Aboriginal tracker killed him by magical means.[24] Here the colonists and the colonised have possessed different models of what was happening and why.

Missionaries inadvertently encouraged Aboriginal people to blame themselves for their misfortune by introducing Christian notions of the struggle between good and bad and treating many of the pre-European Indigenous customs and practices as inherently evil. George Taplin's ethnographic description of Aboriginal sorcery practices as 'invented by some emissaries of Satan' is an illustration of this.[25]

Aboriginal people also explained environmental changes in the landscape brought on by European settlement in terms of their own cultural world view. For example, Central Australian Aboriginal people blamed the local extinction of marsupial species that were culturally and economically important—such as bandicoots—on the failure of their associated increase ceremonies.[26] In contrast, ecologists and biologists primarily blame European settlers for introducing foreign animals, such as foxes and rabbits. In the above cases, crises with external origins were being translated into a form that could be readily understood in terms of an Aboriginal view of their world.

Making the Land Human

In the pre-European period, Aboriginal people perceived the social and physical aspects of the world as closely linked. Culture and landscape existed together, with no true separation in Aboriginal thought. To them, the Ancestors made the land, imbuing it with their spirit and giving it meaning. Aboriginal people derived religious power from the landscape by acknowledging the deeds of the Ancestors. This contrasts with prevailing Western European belief leading up to the Industrial Revolution, which was that the whole physical world was subordinate to human purpose.[27] Aboriginal people were and are continually 'rediscovering' aspects of their own origin in myth, incorporating a continual series of modifications portraying the political and social shifts in the community. This process continues today, with Aboriginal beliefs and traditions adjusting in line with new cultural landscapes. How culture orders space is indicated in Aboriginal beliefs in the Skyworld and Underworld. The cultural landscape is therefore simultaneously both the perceived and the physical aspects of the land and its resources as altered by human activity.

The land as the British settlers first encountered it was essentially an Aboriginal cultural artefact. It was in turn mostly absorbed, radically changed, but not completely obliterated by waves of European colonisation. As we have seen, Europeans initially took advantage of selective Indigenous perceptions and uses of the landscape. Aboriginal hunter and gatherer knowledge was crucial during the early phases of British exploration and settlement in Australia. And while Indigenous knowledge was gradually overlayed by new perceptions of the increasingly rural landscape, the early Aboriginal inhabitants of the pre-European period had left lasting legacies on the landscape. The Aboriginal mode of subsistence was previously a major factor in the balance of the Australian ecosystem as it was in 1788, and Aboriginal burning practices had maintained a pattern of open woodlands in many parts of temperate Australia, and it was these areas which attracted European farmers. The takeover by Europeans of Aboriginal tracks and waterholes would have had a major role in determining the early British settlement patterns throughout Australia. European settlement would have been much different if Australia had been totally uninhabited by Indigenous people upon their arrival.

Captain James Cook arrived in Australia at Botany Bay, south of Sydney, in April 1770. He landed along the eastern coast several more times before taking formal possession of Australia for King George III of Britain at Possession Island in Queensland. Cook declared this continent 'terra nullius', without legal owners, and Australia accordingly was seen then, and for a long time afterwards, as devoid of legitimate Indigenous owners—an untilled and unkempt 'wild' land.[28] Particularly given our greater understanding of Aboriginal relationships to land, and given simple justice even without that understanding, this assumption must be considered flawed. Wilderness has classically been defined as an area of free-ranging beasts, beyond a frontier of civilised development.[29] And yet the evidence, some of it given in this book, suggests that, apart from a few isolated islands off the Australian coast and parts of the high country, 'wilderness' as a natural system did not exist when Europeans first settled here.

A coastal midden eroded and exposing shells and ash from Aboriginal cooking fires made in the pre-European period. PHOTO: P.A. CLARKE, ENCOUNTER BAY, SOUTH AUSTRALIA, 1986.

The land was humanised by Aboriginal people both culturally and physically, even if that was not at all obvious to the newcomers. Dreaming stories generally account for both the formation of the landscape and the creation of Aboriginal custom. Aboriginal people also had formal rights and responsibilities over specific tracts of land. Today, the landscape records past Aboriginal occupation in the form of place names derived from Aboriginal languages and with archaeological remains such as middens, burial grounds, scarred trees, rock art and stone artefact scatters. Aboriginal people have also permanently altered the structure of the Australian fauna and flora over the millennia of their occupation. And they have directed the patterns of settlement and movement of the people that followed them.

In spite of the available evidence pointing to Aboriginal people actively managing the environment through firing, there was only sporadic recognition by European colonisers of Aboriginal involvement in building the landscape. Early historical sources also tended to ignore or understate the contribution of Aboriginal geographic knowledge to the process of European settlement. [30] The British history of Australia in general writes off the positive and active roles of Aboriginal people. The processes of British colonisation in Australia gave primacy in its official records to its

The scars on red gums (Eucalyptus camaldulensis), *left by removal of bark for canoes, last many years.* PHOTO: W. RAMSAY SMITH, FLEURIEU PENINSULA, SOUTH AUSTRALIA, ABOUT 1920.

own conquering and modification of the environment. In most historical texts, explorers were generally cast as men on special expeditions funded by the establishment, not people who acted largely on their own through opportunism. Even the sealers, who were among the first Europeans to unofficially settle in many southern coastal regions, are hardly mentioned.

Until very recently, many scholars have also assumed that the first Europeans in Australia had occupied a 'wild' and 'untamed' landscape. Aboriginal people have for a long time been elusive to scholars of Australian history, and as a result, have largely been denied a major role in the story of the development of the Australian nation and unfairly relegated to the periphery. Apart from a few lines in an introductory chapter of a textbook, most local and official histories have treated Indigenous people only as part of the background of the Australian wilderness as the first European settlers experienced it. For individual anthropologists and historians, their scholarly interest in particular Indigenous cultures waned as members drifted into the new situations of fringe camps, cattle station camps, missions and town life. One anthropologist has described the lack of knowledge about Aboriginal involvement in the national history as the 'great Australian silence'.[31]

In the nineteenth century, the general decline in numbers of people of 'full' Aboriginal descent was taken as a sign that the population would soon diminish to the point of vanishing, as a wave of 'Europeanisation' swept northwards, commencing with Tasmania. And yet Indigenous Australia has not disappeared. While there is some published work since the 1970s that partly fills the vacuum of knowledge concerning Aboriginal history since European settlement, the subject deserves greater attention from historians.[32] Sadly, in comparison to British explorers, pastoral pioneers and miners, we know little of the backgrounds of the Aboriginal participants at significant historical events; often we don't even know their individual names or their cultural backgrounds. In the second half of the twentieth century Aboriginal people started 'coming in' to the central concerns of Australia. Issues such as Aboriginal land rights and Native Title have drawn attention to Aboriginal relationships to land and the colonising processes that alienated them from parts of the landscape.[33] Demographically, people of Aboriginal descent are growing rapidly in most regions.[34] Australian history is maturing, with greater recognition by scholars of the continual Aboriginal presence since before the commencement of European settlement and of how this has added, whether intentionally or not, to the processes that have transformed the Aboriginal landscape into its present cultural form.

Modern Identity

Since British settlement began, the manner in which Europeans have defined Aboriginal identity has changed. The first British settlers had wrongly assumed that they were one homogeneous cultural group. Developments in anthropological theory through the twentieth century brought about recognition of the internal diversity of Aboriginal cultures. Scholars and Aboriginal people themselves have revealed that Aboriginal society has many layers with complex interrelationships with the land. Finally, the false assumption of Aboriginal culture being 'primitive' has been rejected.

In Aboriginal society today, a level of common identity exists among those people who have shared histories and common life experiences through working on particular cattle stations or who are members of families that have lived on certain mission settlements. People take on some aspects of their identity through the residence, past and present, of their family group. The struggles of Indigenous people in the political sphere of the twentieth century over land rights and social justice has given some degree of common identity to many diverse people.[35] Aboriginal people from different regions across Australia are all related by their shared history and by contemporary Indigenous issues, if not through pre-European cultural links. The cultural landscape of contemporary Australian Indigenous people, as reflected in their oral traditions, gives prominence to massacre sites, former mission places, old ration depot sites, and pastoral stations and farms where Aboriginal people lived and worked.

Through the nineteenth century, the processes that transformed many local Aboriginal communities into missionised cultural groups were gradual. Nevertheless, in the twentieth century virtually all of Australia's Indigenous people were incorporated into a system of government control through the passing of various pieces of Aboriginal legislation.[36] In rural and 'outback' regions, many of those Aboriginal people who did not already live in remote regions were progressively forced into areas that were marginal to European land use. This changed the relationship that the population had with the landscape. The mission and the fringe camp became the partly sheltered environment for both Aboriginal cultural survival and change. Although many of these places were close to European settlements, they remained socially removed from them. Modern Aboriginal identity has its roots in such situations. The early establishment of ration depots and missions was the beginning of dependence, initially encouraged and then enforced, that the Aboriginal inhabitants had upon a welfare system progressively set up by Europeans.[37]

Today, the number of people who define themselves as part of the Aboriginal community is large and growing in size, as seen in the national Census figures. Although the Aboriginal population of southern Australia essentially exists today as a subculture of broader Australia, it has retained and developed many characteristics that make it stand apart from most non-Aboriginal cultural forms.

In what Europeans have described as 'settled Australia', where the impact of their colonisation has been most extreme, the descendants of the original Aboriginal population are revitalising their connections to the cultures that existed when the British arrived. The Indigenous Tasmanians for example were considered 'extinct' by the late nineteenth century, but their descendants have reasserted their Indigenous status in contemporary Australian society. Many of these people belong to families centred on the former sealing settlements of Bass Strait.[38] In northern Australia, the outstation movement from the 1970s saw many Aboriginal people return to the remote parts of the country that they were forced to leave in their youth.[39] In cases such as these, where the Aboriginal descendants have maintained a close historical relationship with the land, albeit while living on mission settlements or cattle stations, the relationship between them and their parent Indigenous culture is strong and tangible. The cultural landscape provides new places, such as Aboriginal settlements originally established by European authorities, around which Indigenous cultures have re-emerged and grown.

The identity of Aboriginal people in southern Australia and in other areas settled early by the British has the characteristics of a distinct subculture of contemporary Australian society, rather than existing as a completely separate entity. These people are no longer able to speak a predominantly Aboriginal language, cannot hunt and gather, are unable to practise Aboriginal religion and do not possess detailed knowledge of the Dreamings of the pre-European landscape. And yet through their family histories and historical records, they are directly connected with past Aboriginal cultures. Many of them also possess a distinctive Aboriginal lifestyle, an Aboriginal form of speaking English, beliefs in spirits and sorcerers, a continuation of certain forms of pre-European Aboriginal kinship connections, and some knowledge of pre-European Aboriginal beliefs and practices. The growing awareness of this has produced a new sense of their identity through cultural revitalisation.

The sense of belonging that Aboriginal people feel with the past is constantly being explored through their participation in various cultural activities, including art, literature, family history research and museum displays. Apart from exploring their pre-European identity, many Indigenous people place social importance on their involvement as an Indigenous

Ngarrindjeri primary school children and teachers surround the Aboriginal flag in celebration of the National Aboriginal and Islander Day Observance Committee (NAIDOC). The black on the top of the flag represents the Aboriginal people, the red on the bottom the earth and the spiritual connections to the land, and yellow circle the sun, which gives life. PHOTO: P.A. CLARKE, TERINGIE SAND DUNES, LOWER MURRAY, SOUTH AUSTRALIA, 1989.

community in such things as sport and world music. Contemporary Aboriginal people possess a distinct culture, albeit a changing one that sits alongside Australian European culture.[40]

Indigenous people in Australia are often hampered in their aim of rebuilding a modern identity by non-Aboriginal people's expectations that they possess hunting and gathering knowledge, or knowledge of practices which may have ended over a hundred years ago. As stated to me by one Aboriginal man, 'I can't make a boomerang. Does that make me not Aboriginal?', or by historian Tom Griffiths, 'Although Kooris [Aboriginal people] mostly seek to emphasise the continuities of tradition and identity, they do not deny the loss—or the invention.'[41]

We must acknowledge that a vast amount of cultural change has taken place within virtually all the Aboriginal communities in Australia. In most cases Aboriginal societies have existed to a large extent as a function of their linkages and connections with European culture for the past hundred years. For example, geographically remote Aboriginal communities have retained much of their pre-European customs and traditions. What varies across

Australia is the extent to which Aboriginal people have been able to control this relationship. Many Aboriginal communities have 'home-made' models of continuity to balance profound change in other areas of their society. Aboriginal identity survives if the self-identifying group believes that continuity has taken place. While cultures change, the land also has been profoundly altered through the replacement of Aboriginal land management with that of the Europeans. The land and the people on it are locked in an endless cycle of change. The Australian landscape, as a human artefact, bears witness to the cultural changes upon it.

Notes

Preface

1 Anderson & Gale (1992), Baker (1999), Clarke (1994), David (1998, 2002) and Head (2000).
2 Strang (1997).
3 Clarke (2000).
4 Mühlhäusler (1991, 1996a, 1996d).

Chapter 1   First Human Colonisation

1 Lourandos (1997, pp. 80–111) and Mulvaney & Kamminga (1999, pp. 103–46).
2 Allen (1998a, 1998b). The age of Aboriginal settlement of Australia is still a matter of academic debate, with dates likely to be refined over the next few years.
3 Butlin (1993, Map 4).
4 Tindale & Lindsay (1954, pp. ix–xi, 122–6).
5 Golson (1971).
6 Allen (2000), Jones (1989), Lourandos (1997, pp. 247–54) and Mulvaney & Kamminga (1999, pp. 180–9).
7 Diamond (1997, pp. 35–52), and Thorne & Raymond (1989, pp. 11–27).
8 Abbie (1976, pp. 194–213), Birdsell (1949, 1967, 1993) and Thorne (1971, 1976).
9 Cleland (1966, p. 123).
10 Tindale (1972).
11 Chaloupka (1993, p. 96).

12 Roberts et al. (2001).
13 Flannery (1994) and Murray (1991).
14 Horton (2000, pp. 102–26).
15 Paddle (2000, pp. 20–2).
16 Moore (1979, p. 279).

Chapter 2   Religious Landscapes

1 Arthur (1996, pp. 27–8), Maddock (1982, pp. 105–20), Rose (1992, pp. 42–57), Spencer (1896, p. 51), Stanner (1953) and Sutton (1988a, pp. 14–9).
2 Berndt & Berndt (1989), Charlesworth (1998), Charlesworth et al (1984), Hiatt (1975), Kolig (1989) and Stanner (1953 [1979]).
3 Berndt & Berndt (1993, pp. 13–16, 229–33, 433–41), Clarke (1995) and Meyer (1846 [1879, pp. 205–6]).
4 Clarke (1995).
5 Berndt (1970, pp. 53–7), Elkin (1934, pp. 171–4) and Jones (1991, pp. 39–43).
6 Myers (1986, p. 53).
7 Isaacs (1980), Parker (1896), Reed (1980), Smith (1930) and Wilson (1950).
8 Mountford & Roberts (1965; 1969; 1971; 1973; 1975).
9 Strehlow (1970, p. 94).
10 Rose (1992, pp. 52–6).
11 Strehlow (1970, pp. 93–4).
12 Layton (1989, pp. 3–10).
13 Amery (2000, p. 196), Black (1920, p. 84), Gell (1841 [1904, pp. 97, 100]) and Teichelmann & Schürmann (1840, pt 2, pp. 44, 75).
14 Berndt & Berndt (1970, pp. 18, 51, 192) and Taylor (1996, pp. 183–9).
15 Holmes (1992, plates 52, 54, 121, 134–5, 139) and Taçon & Garde (1995, pp. 33–4).
16 Barrett (1946), Clarke (1999a, pp. 157–9), Holden (2001) and Mulvaney (1994).
17 Taplin Journals (2–3 July 1860).
18 Layton (1989, p. 14).
19 W.K. Mallyon in the *Observer* newspaper, Adelaide, 31 December 1910.
20 Johnston (1941, p. 33), Tindale (1978, p. 158) and Wilhelmi (1861, p. 177).
21 Howitt (1904, p. 433).
22 Clarke (1990; 1991, pp. 63–6), Johnson (1998), MacPherson (1882), Sims (1978), Stanbridge (1857) and Strehlow (1970, p. 95).
23 Teichelmann (1841, p. 8).
24 Eyre (1845, vol. 2, p. 367).
25 Harvey (1939).
26 Clarke (1997) and Elkin (1977).
27 Teichelmann & Schürmann (1840, vol. 2, pp. 13, 22).
28 Dawson (1881, pp. 57–8) and Smith (1880, p. 30).
29 Clarke (1997, pp. 127–8) and Johnson (1998, pp. 13–6).
30 Wyatt (1879, p. 166).
31 Johnston (1941, pp. 37–8).
32 Mountford (1958, p. 174).
33 Howitt (1904, pp. 427–8).

34   Howitt (1904, p. 432).
35   Beveridge (1883, pp. 60–1).
36   Adelaide *Register* newspaper, 5 October 1887.
37   Dawson (1881, pp. 98–9).

Chapter 3   Social Life

1   Berndt & Berndt (1985, pp. 91–106), Edwards (1988, pp. 42–64) and Jacob (1991, pp. 80–145).
2   Berndt (1940a, pp. 286–8) and Howitt (1904, pp. 773–7).
3   Berndt & Berndt (1970, p. 106).
4   Thomson (1983a, pp. 52–8; 1983b, pp. 53–5).
5   Keesing (1975, pp. 78–84) and Scheffler (1978).
6   Spencer & Gillen (1899, pp. 573–4).
7   Scheffler (1978, 1994).
8   Thomson (1983a, p. 54).
9   Tindale (1986, p. 242).
10   Tindale (1986, p. 243).
11   Elkin (1931, pp. 64, 69), Hamilton (1982, pp. 100–3) and Toyne & Vachon (1984, pp. 12–15).
12   Myers (1986, pp. 127–58).
13   Berndt & Berndt (1993, pp. 33, 41–57), Brown (1918, pp. 228–41) and Taplin (1879, pp. 156–64).
14   Berndt & Berndt (1985, pp. 44–5, 59–66), Blake (1981, pp. 36–40), Meggitt (1962, pp. 188–232), Scheffler (1978), D. Williams (1981, pp. 102–19) and N.M. Williams (1986, pp. 57–8, 79–80).
15   Berndt & Berndt (1985, pp. 46–59), Elkin (1940), Fry (1934), Meggitt (1962, pp. 61–2), Munn (1973, pp. 13–23) and Myers (1986, pp. 184–91).
16   Berndt & Berndt (1985, pp. 80–5), Maddock (1982, pp. 56–104) and Tonkinson (1978, pp. 47–8).
17   Collins (1804, p. 385).
18   Jacob (1991, pp. 121–5) and Maddock (1982, pp. 28–55).
19   Crawford (1982, p. 28) and Kaberry (1939, pp. 136–7).
20   R.M. Berndt (1976), Clark (1990, pp. 17–21), Hiatt (1996, pp. 13–35), Peterson (1976), Sutton (1995a) and Tindale (1940; 1974).
21   Henderson & Nash (2002) and Sutton (1995a, pp. 47, 50, 134–6).
22   Goddard (1992, pp. 118, 204).
23   Blake (1981) and Yallop (1982).
24   Blake (1981), McGregor (1994) and Yallop (1982).
25   Harris (1987) and Tindale (1926, pp. 128–9; 1978, p. 158).
26   Edwards (1998, pp. 86–7) and Kendon (1988).
27   Howitt (1904, p. 725).
28   Roth (1897, pp. 71–89).
29   Blake (1981, pp. 43–4) and Kendon (1988).
30   Wilhelmi (1860, pp. 174–5).
31   Magarey (1893).

32   Howitt (1904, pp. 721).
33   Gould (1969, p. 13).
34   Petrie (1932, p. 95).
35   Allen (1995c), Jacob (1991, pp. 96–100) and Malinowski (1913 [1963, pp. 234–57]).
36   Thomson (1983b, p. 7).
37   Berndt (1940b), Beveridge (1883, pp. 50–5), Bulmer (1887, pp. 28–9, 31–3), Haagen (1994), Petrie (1932, pp. 109–14), Roth (1902, pp. 7–19), Thomson (1983b) and Wallace & Wallace (1968).
38   Berndt (1952–54).
39   Beveridge (1883, p. 53–4) and Tunbridge (1985, p. 23).
40   Beveridge (1883, pp. 52–3), Bulmer (1887, p. 32), Howitt (1904, p. 770) and Petrie (1932, p. 109).
41   Wilhelmi (1860, p. 174).
42   Fison & Howitt (1880, pp. 192–200), Hiatt (1996, pp. 165–82), Jacob (1991, pp. 100–5), Keen (1994), Meggitt (1962, pp. 281–316) and Warner (1958, pp. 120–6).
43   Elkin (1964, pp. 195–9, 202, 204–5), Howitt (1904, pp. 743–6) and Worsnop (1897, pp. 2, 163–4).
44   Bonney (1884, pp. 126–8), Cameron (1885, p. 359), Howitt (1904, pp. 569, 574–6, 586–92), Petrie (1932, pp. 52–7) and Roth (1910, pp. 30–2).
45   Dousset (1997, p. 51).
46   Meggitt (1962, pp. 317–30).
47   Strehlow (1978, p. 35).
48   Berndt & Johnston (1942), Beveridge (1883, pp. 20–3), Blandowski (1858, pp. 136–7), Elkin (1937) and Meggitt (1962, pp. 317–30).
49   Maddock (1982, pp. 152–6) and Morphy (1984).
50   Berndt & Johnston (1942), Jacob (1991, pp. 106–17), Malinowski (1913 [1963], pp. 84–8, 271–2, 308) and Morphy (1984).
51   Teichelmann (1841, p. 7).
52   Bates (1947, p. 28).
53   Gale (1989), Hamilton (1981), Hiatt (1996, pp. 57–77), Jacobs (1989) and Payne (1989).
54   Brock (1989), Clarke (1998, pp. 29–30), Hamilton (1975) and Huffer (1980, pp. 144–6).
55   Berndt (1981, pp. 174–7; 1982, pp. 42–51).
56   Kaberry (1939, p. 15).
57   Tindale (1972, p. 245).
58   Clarke (1997, p. 128).
59   C.H. Berndt (1970, 1980, 1981, 1982, 1989), Jacobs (1989), Kaberry (1939) and Payne (1989).
60   Berndt & Berndt (1993, pp. 71, 285), Hercus (1989, pp. 105–6) and Tindale (1934–37, vol. 2, p. 223).
61   Angas (1847b, p. 94).
62   Jorgensen (1837 [1991, p. 67]).
63   Goddard (1992, p. 43).
64   Berndt (1940a, p. 291) and Howitt (1904, pp. 736–7).

Chapter 4   Hunting and Gathering

1   Dampier (1697 [1998, p. 218]).
2   Cook (1770 [1893, p. 320]).
3   Hiatt (1996, pp. 33–4) and Reynolds (1989, pp. 66–8).
4   Eyre (1845, vol. 2, p. 368).
5   Abbie (1976, p. 46), Butlin (1993), Couper Black (1966, p. 97), Lourandos (1997, pp. 35–8), Mulvaney & Kamminga (1999, p. 68) and Smith (1980, pp. 67–77).
6   Jones (1974, pp. 325–7) and Jorgenson (1837 [1991, p. 69]).
7   Lee & de Vore (1968, pp. 244–5) and Smith (1980, pp. 68–90).
8   Abbie (1976, pp. 77–80, 140–2).
9   Abbie (1976, pp. 27, 188), Berndt & Berndt (1985, pp. 453–4) and Berndt & Berndt (1993, pp. 138–40).
10 McCarthy (1957, p. 59).
11 Wilhelmi (1860, p. 177).
12 Irvine (1970, p. 278) and Gregory (1887, p. 131).
13 Tindale (1977, p. 349).
14 Batey (1909–10, cited in Frankel 1982). Recorded variations of *murnong* include *myrnong* and *myrrnong*.
15 Goddard & Kalotus (1988, pp. 14–5), Tindale (1978, pp. 160–2) and Wilhelmi (1860, p. 172).
16 Sutton (1995b, p. 154).
17 Brand Miller et al. (1993), Cherikoff & Isaacs (1989), Cribb & Cribb (1987), Low (1991) and Maiden (1889).
18 Baker (1999, pp. 45–50), Clarke (1986b, pp. 41–4), Davis (1989), Latz (1995, pp. 44–60), Lawrence (1968, pp. 48–60), Levitt (1981, pp. 32–47) and Rose (1987, pp. 50–1).
19 Dawson (1881, p. 21).
20 Maiden (1889, pp. 7–8, 377), Petrie (1932, pp. 11–7) and Smyth (1878, vol. 2, pp. 218–9).
21 Hayden (1975) and Lourandos (1997, p. 295).
22 Beveridge (1883, p. 58).
23 Tindale (1981, pp. 1882–3).
24 Thomson (1985, p. 170).
25 Bates (1901–14 [1985, p. 243]).
26 Wilhelmi (1860, p. 176).
27 Berndt (1947), Cawte (1974) and Elkin (1977).
28 Berndt & Berndt (1993, pp. 140–4), Goodale (1971, pp. 146–50) and Huffer (1980, pp. 48–9).
29 Barr et al. (1988), Cribb & Cribb (1981), Lassak & McCarthy (1983) and Maiden (1889).
30 Reid (1982, 1983).
31 Howitt (1904) and Sagona (1994, pp. 15–38).
32 Elkin (1934, pp. 184–90), Eyre (1845, vol. 2, p. 335), Horne & Aiston (1924, p. 40), Howitt (1904, p. 232) and Shaw (cited in Taplin 1879, p. 28).
33 Stone (1911, p. 440) and Thomas (1860, cited Smyth 1878, vol. 2, p. 264).
34 Hossfeld (1926, p. 295) and Newland (1895, p. 7).
35 Latz (1995), Smyth (1878, vol. 2, pp. 222–3) and Watson (1983).

36 Collected by J. B. Cleland from the Nukunu people about 1922. S.A. Museum item A48948.
37 Dampier (1688, cited Mulvaney 1989, p. 19).
38 Mulvaney & Kamminga (1999, pp. 34–5) and Newland (1889, pp. 23–4).
39 Hahn (1838–39 [1964, p. 133]).
40 Angas (1847b, p. 112) and Clarke (2002, pp. 154–7).
41 Worsnop (1897, p. 106).
42 Coutts et al. (1978), Flood (1983, pp. 205–8) and Worsnop (1897, pp. 104–6).
43 Hamlyn-Harris & Smith (1916) and Webb (1959).
44 Baker (1999, p. 47).
45 McCarthy (1957, p. 60).
46 Tonkinson (1978, p. 24).
47 Parker (1905, pp. 105, 108, 114) and Tindale (1977, p. 345).
48 Worsnop (1897, pp. 81–2).
49 Strehlow (1947, pp. 34–5).
50 Hiatt (1996, pp. 105–6, 168), Howitt (1904, pp. 399–400, 798) and Mulvaney et al. (1997, pp. 103, 191, 198, 343, 506).
51 Howitt (1904, pp. 399–400).
52 Baker (1999, p. 49).
53 Tonkinson (1978, pp. 20–1).
54 Newsome (1980).
55 Finlayson (1903, pp. 40–1).
56 *Adelaide Chronicle and South Australian Literary Record*, 22 December 1841.
57 *Observer* newspaper, 31 May 1851.
58 Tilbrook (1983, pp. 6–7).
59 Eyre (1845, vol. 1, p. 36).
60 Gould (1971), Hallam (1975), Hiatt (1967–68, pp. 212, 219), Jones (1974), Kimber (1976) and Latz (1995).
61 Baker (1999, p. 50).
62 Jackson (1968), Jones (1969) and Lourandos (1997, pp. 95–6).
63 Flannery (1994).
64 Jackson (1968), Latz (1995, p. 32), Lewis (1986, pp. 45–67) and Tindale (1972, p. 241).
65 Burbidge et al. (1988, pp. 20, 26) and Latz (1995, p. 32).
66 Jones (1969).
67 Gott (1982a, p. 65; 1983, pp. 11–12) and Hallam (1975, pp. 12–13, 72, 74). A recorded variation of *warran* is *warrine*.
68 Cribb et al. (1988) and Mulvaney & Kamminga (1999, pp. 280–1).
69 Flannery (1994), Hallam (1975), Low (2002) and Tindale (1959b).

Chapter 5 Aboriginal Artefacts

1 C.H. Berndt (1970), Goodale (1971, pp. 151–82), Lakic (1995a, pp. 1–10) and Rose (1987, pp. 89–97).
2 Bindon & Gough (1993, p. 12).
3 Thomson (1975, p. 99).

4   Dixon et al. (1992, p. 185) and Ramson (1988, p. 201).
5   Hahn (1838–9 [1964, p. 131]) and Tunbridge (1985, p. 33).
6   Davidson (1933), Hodgson (1988), McConnel (1953, pp. 13–4), Plomley (1993, pp. 51–2), Robson (1986), Roth (1901a) and Worsnop (1897, p. 88).
7   Brokensha (1975, pp. 46–51), Dixon et al. (1992, pp. 184, 186) and Ramson (1988, pp. 167–8, 483).
8   Plomley (1993, p. 54).
9   Davidson (1936).
10 Horne & Aiston (1924, pp. 71–80).
11 Plomley (1993, p. 48) and Roth (1897, p. 141).
12 Dixon et al. (1992, pp. 180–3) and Ramson (1988, pp. 440, 704, 740).
13 Davidson (1936), Jones (1996), Luebbers (1975) and McCarthy (1961).
14 Dixon et al. (1992, pp. 175–7) and Ramson (1988, pp. 80–1).
15 Tench (1788 [1996, p. 55]).
16 Davidson (1934) and Roth (1909, pp. 189–97).
17 Roth (1909, p. 197).
18 Mountford (1958, p. 98, plates 32a & b).
19 Dixon et al. (1992, p. 184) and Ramson (1988, p. 743).
20 Cundy (1980; 1989).
21 Levitt (1981, p. 20).
22 McCarthy (1974, pp. 14–8, 24, 26–7, 30–2, 51–2) and Roth (1897, pp. 149–50; 1909, pp. 203–6, plates LIX, LX).
23 Baker (1988), Davidson (1935), Edwards (1972) and Worsnop (1897, pp. 118–22).
24 Beveridge (1883, pp. 40–2), Edwards (1972) and Krefft (1862–65, pp. 362–4).
25 Plomley (1993, p. 55).
26 Baker (1988, Fig. 3, p. 176), Haddon (1913), Thomson (1949, p. 58) and Tindale (1926, pp. 103–12).
27 Lourandos (1997, pp. 282–95), McCarthy (1976), Mulvaney & Kamminga (1999, pp. 133–5, 213–56) and Wright (1977).
28 McBryde (1986; 1987).
29 Akerman (1979), Hayden (1998), McCarthy (1976), McCourt (1975) and Sutton (1994).
30 Allen (1995b), Angas (1847a, plate LVI), Crawford (1982, Figs. 16–9 & p. 62), Hodgson (1988), Levitt (1981, pp. 19–20), Plomley (1993, pp. 50–2), Robson (1986), Tindale (1926, pp. 115–6), West (1999) and Worsnop (1897, p. 92).
31 Buhmann et al. (1976) and Kamminga (1988).
32 Cleland (1966, pp. 120–2, 146–7), Latz (1995, pp. 66–7) and Roth (1904, pp. 11–14).
33 Lourandos (1997, chapters 8 & 9) and Mulvaney & Kamminga (1999, chapters 12 to 17).
34 Kuhn & Fowler (1886, p. 143).
35 Plomley (1993, p. 46).
36 Hahn (1838–39 [1964, pp. 129, 131]).
37 Berndt & Berndt (1954, p. 16) and McCourt (1975, pp. 38–41).
38 Memmott (1983; 2002) and Ross (1987).
39 Howitt (1904, pp. 773–7) and Sansom (1980, pp. 53–7, 176–91).
40 Dixon et al. (1992, pp. 199–202) and Ramson (1988, pp. 299, 319, 393, 751).
41 McCourt (1975, pp. 135–40) and Tindale (1977).

42 Dixon et al. (1992, p. 187) and Ramson (1988, p. 755).
43 McBryde (1987, pp. 271–3), Newland (1889, p. 22) and Worsnop (1897, p. 98).
44 Tindale (1977, p. 347).
45 Crawford (1982, Figs. 6, p. 11).
46 Levitt (1981, p. 49).
47 Beveridge (1883, pp. 67–8), Howitt (1904, pp. 770–3) and Petrie (1932, p. 95).
48 N.B. Tindale (no date) 'Strike-a-lights, Fire Flints'. Tindale collection, miscellaneous papers, Anthropology Archives, S.A. Museum.
49 Gould (1971, p. 16).
50 Mountford & Berndt (1941, pp. 343–4).
51 N.B. Tindale (no date) 'Strike-a-lights, Fire Flints'. Tindale collection, miscellaneous papers, Anthropology Archives, S.A. Museum.
52 Dawson (1881, p. 4).
53 Angas (1847b, pp. 58, 89–90), Bulmer (1887, p. 15), Eyre (1845, vol. 2, pp. 289–92) and Worsnop (1897, pp. 82–3).
54 Tindale (1981, p. 1869).
55 B. David, pers. comm.
56 Hackett (1937, p. 297), Palmer (1999, pp. 32–4) and Smyth (1878, vol. 2, p. 187).
57 Jorgensen (1837 [1991, p. 55]) and Wilhelmi (1861, p. 175).
58 Mowaljarlai & Malnic (1993, pp. 10–1).
59 Worsnop (1897, p. 82).
60 Beveridge (1883, pp. 38–40), Etheridge (1893), Meehan (1982), Mulvaney & Kamminga (1999, pp. 19–23, 276–7, 280–1, 286–7, 349–50) and Smyth (1878, vol. 2, pp. 238–44).
61 Worsnop (1897, p. 83).
62 Flood (1980, pp. 62, 66, 68).
63 Lakic (1995b) and Roth (1897, pp. 108–16; 1910).
64 Tindale (1925, p. 73) and Wilhelmi (1860, p. 168).
65 Angas (1847a, various plates), Tilbrook (1983, pp. 12–6) and Wilhelmi (1861, pp. 166–7).
66 J. Smithies (cited in Tilbrook 1983, p. 12).
67 Worsnop (1897, p. 51).
68 Howitt (1904, pp. 741–2), Smith (1930, p. 333) and Tindale (1935, p. 269).

Chapter 6   Art of the Dreaming

1 Tindale (1974, pp. 44–9).
2 Anderson & Dussart (1988, pp. 118–32), Morphy (1998, pp. 183–218), Smith (1992) and Warlukurlangu Artists (1992).
3 Anderson & Dussart (1988, pp. 93–5, 101–3, 105–6, 140).
4 Morphy (1998, pp. 149–59, 415–8).
5 Morphy (1998, pp. 185–92).
6 Jones & Meehan (1978).
7 Anderson & Dussart (1988, pp. 111–8).
8 Anderson & Dussart (1988, p. 116).

9   Sagona (1994, pp. 8–38).
10 Brandl (1988, pp. 105–6) and Edwards & Guerin (1969).
11 Brandl (1988, p. 105), Edwards & Guerin (1969) and McCourt (1975, pp. 129–30).
12 Chippindale & Taçon (1998) and Flood (1997, pp. ix, 24).
13 Chaloupka (1993) and Crawford (1968).
14 Chippindale & Taçon (1998).
15 Tindale (1978, p. 157). See also Tindale (1972, pp. 240–1).
16 Hale & Tindale (1929, pp. 30–1) and Mountford (1929).
17 Berndt (1987).
18 Flood (1997, pp. 300–20).
19 Etheridge (1918), Howitt (1904, fig. 31, p. 540; p. 594) and McCarthy (1940a).
20 Mountford (1958), Sculthorpe (1995, p. 33) and Smith (1990).
21 Berndt & Berndt (1999, pp. 84–102) and Morphy (1998, pp. 37–9, 239–2).
22 Morphy (1998, pp. 177–80) and Sutton (1988a, pp. 23–9).
23 Mountford (1957), Sutton (1988b, p. 216 & Fig. 53) and Taylor (1996, pp. 16–7).
24 Tindale (1926, p. 117).
25 Allen (1995a), Bardon (1979; 1991), Berndt & Berndt (1999, pp. 125–45), Cochrane (2001), Isaacs (1992), Morphy (1998, pp. 369–420), Stack (2002), Sutton (1988b) and Taylor (1996, pp. 15–48).
26 Dixon et al. (1992, pp. 152–3) and Ramson (1988, p. 172–3).
27 Angas (1847a, plate XV; 1847b, pp. 102–8), Clarke (1991, p. 56), Gell (1841 [1904, p. 93]), Teichelmann & Schürmann (1840, p. 14) and Williams (1839 [1926, p. 60]).
28 Hercus (1980).
29 Roth (1902, pp. 20–4).
30 Beveridge (1883, p. 66), Roth (1897, p. 120), Schürmann ('The Aborigines of South Australia' in the *South Australian Colonist* newspaper, vol. 1, no. 2, 10 March, pp. 23–4) and Worsnop (1897, p. 155).
31 Dixon et al. (1992, p. 188), Ramson (1988, p. 199) and Tindale (1925, pp. 90–2).
32 Moyle (1981).
33 Bradley (1995).

Chapter 7   Living in a Varied Land

1   Akerman (1980), McBryde (1986; 1987), McCarthy (1938–40) and Specht & White (1978).
2   McBryde (1987, pp. 261–2, 271–3), Moore (1978) and Tindale (1977, p. 347).
3   Berndt & Berndt (1981, pp. 122–34) and Tindale (1974, pp. 75–88).
4   Stone (1911, pp. 459–60).
5   Bates (1901–14 [1985, pp. 280–1]).
6   Akerman (1980; 1994, map 2) and Blundell & Layton (1978).
7   Peterson & Lampert (1985) and Sagona (1994).
8   Cooper (1948, p. 7), Jones (1984), McBryde (1987, pp. 259–62, 269–71) and Wilhelmi (1860, p. 168).
9   Berndt & Berndt (1993, pp. 118–21), Smith (1930, pp. 216–8), Taplin (1874 [1879, pp. 32–3]) and Tindale (1981, p. 1872).

10 Taplin (1874 [1879, p. 33]).
11 Taplin (1874 [1879, pp. 32–3]) and Taplin (1879, p. 41).
12 Presland (1994, pp. 137–41).
13 Howitt (1904, pp. 340–1), McBryde (1986, pp. 136–7) and Tindale (1981, p. 1879).
14 Tindale (1974, p. 60).
15 Jones et al. (1997) and Reid (1995).
16 Breeden & Wright (1989).
17 Clarke (1991, pp. 58–9) and Ellis (1976, pp. 116–17).
18 Johnston (1941).
19 Jones (1974, p. 332).
20 Jones (1993, vol. 1, pp. 142–50).
21 Bottoms (1999, pp. 12–13).
22 Stephens (1889, p. 477) and Sweetman (1928 [1988, p. 4]).
23 Stone (1911, p. 434).
24 Cockburn (1984, p. 245).
25 Tunbridge (1987, p. 3).
26 Crawford (1982, pp. 19–24).
27 Tindale (1974, p. 60).
28 Tindale (1938, p. 21; 1974, pp. 61–2).
29 Clarke (1991, pp. 58–60) and Tindale (1974, p. 61).
30 Jones (1974, p. 329).
31 Teichelmann & Schürmann (1840, vol. 2, p. 36).
32 Teichelmann & Schürmann (1840, vol. 2, p. 75).
33 Tunbridge (1988, p. 147).
34 Tindale (1974, pp. 42, 192).
35 Buku-larrnggay Mulka Centre (1999), Peterson & Rigsby (1998) and Smyth (1993).

Chapter 8 The South

1 Carter (1964, pp. 232–6), Fenner (1931, pp. 126–7) and Seddon (1972, pp. 20–6).
2 Morphett (1836, p. 6).
3 Clarke (1988), Gott (1983), Plomley & Cameron (1993, pp. 17, 21), Smyth (1878, vol. 2, pp. 209, 214–15), Stewart & Percival (1997, p. 48) and Zola & Gott (1992, pp. 6–9).
4 Eyre (1845, vol. 2, pp. 254, 269). See Gott (1982a pp. 59–62) and Zola & Gott (1992, p. 13).
5 Bates (1901–14 [1985, p. 261]).
6 Clarke (1988, pp. 67–8), Maiden (1889, p. 27) and Zola & Gott (1992, p. 30).
7 Clarke (1986b, pp. 43–5), Plomley & Cameron (1993, p. 8), Smyth (1878, vol. 2, p. 209), Stewart & Percival (1997, pp. 8, 12), Tindale (1977, p. 347) and Zola & Gott (1992, p. 63).
8 Bulmer (1887, pp. 15–43), Smyth (1878, vol. 2, pp. 209, 214–7), Stewart & Percival (1997, p. 38) and Zola & Gott (1992, pp. 27–8).
9 Clarke (1985b, p. 12; 1987, p. 5).

10   Clarke (1985b, p. 13), Gott (1982b), McBryde (1986, pp. 133, 136–8, 142, 148–9, 151), Smith (1880, p. 130), Tindale (1981, p. 1879) and Zola & Gott (1992, p. 21).

11   Bates (1901–14 [1985, p. 261]), Smyth (1878, vol. 2, p. 215) and Stewart & Percival (1997, p. 37).

12   Angas (1847b, p. 150), Clarke (1986a pp. 5–6), Stewart & Percival (1997, pp. 13, 49) and Zola & Gott (1992, p. 22).

13   Teichelmann & Schürmann (1840, vol. 2, p. 35) and Wyatt (1879, p. 174). Wyatt records this Kaurna term as 'paipola'.

14   Clarke (1987, p. 4), MacPherson (1925, pp. 593–4), Plomley & Cameron (1993, pp. 15, 24) and Zola & Gott (1992, p. 63).

15   Clarke (1986a, p. 10; 1987, p. 9).

16   Angas (1847b, pp. 54–5).

17   Bates (1901–14 [1985, p. 261]), Clarke (1986a, pp. 8–9), Plomley & Cameron (1993, pp. 3–4, 19, 23) and Zola & Gott (1992, p. 20).

18   Clarke (1985a, p. 5; 1986a, p. 12; 1988, p. 69) and Plomley & Cameron (1993, pp. 5–7, 15, 20, 23).

19   Smyth (1878, vol. 2, pp. 206–8) and Tindale (1966).

20   Eyre (1845, vol. 2, p. 274) and Wilhelmi (1861, p. 170–1).

21   Flood (1980), Mulvaney & Kamminga (1999, p. 34) and Worsnop (1897, p. 84).

22   Eyre (1845, vol. 2, pp. 273–4).

23   Taplin (1874 [1879, p. 31]).

24   Dixon et al. (1992, pp. 107–8) and Ramson (1988, p. 366).

25   Beveridge (1883, pp. 64–5).

26   Beveridge (1883, pp. 49–50) and Eyre (1845, vol. 2, p. 267).

27   Eyre (1845, vol. 2, pp. 267–8).

28   Angas (1847b, p. 90).

29   Eyre (1845, vol. 2, p. 267).

30   Angas (1847b, pp. 55, 92, 96, 98).

31   Angas (1847b, p. 134), Cann et al. (1991) and Luebbers (1978).

32   Taplin Journals (10 October 1861).

33   Eyre (1845, vol. 2, p. 266) and Clarke (2002, p. 154).

34   Taplin Journals (19 May 1860) and Clarke (2002, p. 154).

35   Clarke (2002), Curr (1883, p. 110), Davies (1881, p. 129), Eyre (1845, vol. 2, pp. 266–7), Massola (1956), Meyer (1846 [1879, p. 192]), Roth (1901b, pp. 20–1), Smyth (1878, vol. 2, pp. 202–3) and Worsnop (1897, pp. 95–6).

36   Gerritsen (2001) and Pretty (1977, pp. 321–2).

37   Mulvaney & Kamminga (1999, p. 292).

38   Worsnop (1897, pp. 90–1). See also Beveridge (1883, pp. 46–8).

39   Angas (1847b, p. 112).

40   Angas (1847b, pp. 54, 101, 107, 112) and Meyer (1846 [1879, p. 193]).

41   Meyer (1846 [1879, pp. 192–3]) and Smith (1930, pp. 230–1).

42   Unaipon (1924–25 [2001, pp. 19–24]).

43   Eyre (1845, vol. 2, p. 253), Smith (1930, p. 229) and Tindale (1974, pp. 61–2).

44   Coutts et al. (1978) and Mulvaney & Kamminga (1999, p. 34).

45   Dargin (1976, pp. 32–49).

46   Bates (1901–14 [1985, p. 251]).

47   Horton (2000, pp. 39–52) and Jones (1978).

48 Smith (1930, pp. 224–5), Smyth (1878, vol. 2, pp. 196–7) and Worsnop (1897, pp. 114–5).
49 Angas (1847b, pp. 90–1), Meyer (1846 [1879, p. 193]), Smith (1930, pp. 223–4) and Worsnop (1897, pp. 115–6).
50 Angas (1847b, p. 91).
51 Smith (1930, pp. 220–1) and Worsnop (1897, p. 116).
52 Smith (1930, pp. 221–2) and Museum Board (1887, p. 33).
53 Beveridge (1883, pp. 45–6), Eyre (1845, vol. 2, pp. 286–7), Krefft (1862–65, pp. 368–9), Smith (1930, p. 223) and Worsnop (1897, pp. 92–3).
54 Beveridge (1883, pp. 45–6).
55 Eyre (1845, vol. 2, p. 283).
56 Smith (1930, p. 227).
57 Angas (1847b, p. 55).
58 Angas (1847b, p. 91), Eyre (1845, vol. 2, pp. 267) and Smyth (1878, vol. 2, p. 197).
59 Eyre (1845, vol. 2, p. 268), Krefft (1862–65, p. 370), Smyth (1878, vol. 2, p. 199) and Worsnop (1897, p. 83).
60 'The Passing of the Australian Native. The Wanmaring Group (Head of the Great Australian Bight)', D.M. Bates manuscript collection at the Barr-Smith Library in Box 12/Section XIII/Part 6b.
61 Clarke (2001, pp. 20–2), Smith (1880, p. 139) and Tindale (1937, pp. 107, 112; 1974, pp. 18, 23, 80).
62 Tindale (1941b, p. 241).
63 Smith (1930, p. 225).
64 Worsnop (1897, p. 116).
65 Bates (1901–14 [1985, p. 244]), Beveridge (1883, pp. 44–5), Eyre (1845, vol. 2, p. 277, 280), Hahn (1838–39 [1964, p. 133]) and Smyth (1878, vol. 2, p. 185).
66 Eyre (1845, vol. 2, p. 283) and Smith (1930, pp. 226–7).
67 Bates (1901–14 [1985, p. 245]).
68 Eyre (1845, vol. 2, pp. 280–1), Meyer (1846 [1879, pp. 194–5]) and Smith (1930, pp. 226–7).
69 Plomley (1993, p. 50).
70 Eyre (1845, vol. 2, pp. 280–1).
71 Angas (1847b, pp. 68, 84, 132).
72 Eyre (1845, vol. 2, p. 268).
73 Angas (1847b, pp. 68, 84, 132) and Smith (1930, p. 227).
74 'Transactions of the Statistical Society. Report on the Aborigines of South Australia.' Published in the *Register* newspaper, 8 January 1842. Clarke (1988) and Wilhelmi (1861, p. 173).
75 Bates (1901–14 [1985, pp. 240–1]) and Bindon & Whalley (1992).
76 Beveridge (1883, pp. 62–3).
77 J. Lalor (cited Howitt, 1904, p. 432).
78 Clarke (1997, p. 137) and Johnson (1998, pp. 23–37).
79 Clarke (1991, pp. 58–9; 1997, p. 137), Ellis (1976, pp. 116–7), Gell (1841 [1904, p. 96]), Ross (1984, p. 5) and Tindale (1974, pp. 60–1).
80 Berndt & Berndt (1993, pp. 21, 76, 163, 240–2), Meyer (1843, p. 78) and Taplin (1879, p. 126).
81 Tindale (1930–52, p. 266).

82 Berndt & Berndt (1993, pp. 58, 75–6, 230, 261–2, 229–31) and Clarke (1999b, pp. 57–9).
83 Stanbridge (1857, p. 138).
84 Bulmer (1887, p.32) and Wilhelmi (1861, p. 178).
85 Dixon et al. (1992, pp. 139–40), Ramson (1988, pp. 383–4) and Thieberger & McGregor (1994, p. 32).
86 Tindale (1974, p. 62).
87 Tindale (1938, p. 21; 1974, pp. 61–2).

Chapter 9   The Central Deserts

1 Berndt (1941, p. 3; 1959, pp. 84–95), Douglas (1977; 1988), Elkin (1931, pp. 60–4) and Tindale (1959a, 1981).
2 Van Oosterzee (1995, p. 65).
3 Burbidge et al. (1988), Finlayson (1952), Tunbridge (1991) and Tyler (1979).
4 Latz (1995), Morton & Mulvaney (1996) and Spencer (1896).
5 Spencer & Gillen (1899; 1904). See Mulvaney et al. (1997; 2000).
6 Bates (1901–14; 1918; 1947) and Salter (1971).
7 Tindale (1981, p. 1855). See Birdsell (1953; 1976; 1993).
8 Tonkinson (1978, p. 22).
9 Berndt (1985).
10 Schürmann (1846 [1879, p. 217]).
11 Bates (1947), Berndt (1941, pp. 1–6), Mattingley & Hampton (1992, pp. 210–19, 235–46, 254–62) and Tindale (1953a, pp. 171–2).
12 Mattingley & Hampton (1992, pp. 84–95).
13 Kolig (1981, pp. 109–30) and Merlan (1998, pp. 42–4, 190).
14 Berndt (1972, p. 179).
15 Cleland (1966, p. 142), Dixon et al. (1992, pp. 193–4), Magarey (1895, pp. 12–13) and Ramson (1988, p. 275).
16 Gara (1985, p. 8).
17 Cleland (1966, p. 142).
18 Maurice (1905, cited in Gara, 1994, p. 46).
19 Maurice (1905, cited in Gara, 1994, p. 46).
20 Bates (1947), Bolam (1930, pp. 14–9), Johnston (1941, pp. 38–41) and Turner (1950).
21 Gara (1985, pp. 6–7) and Tonkinson (1978, p. 23).
22 Magarey (1895, p. 4) and Smyth (1878, vol. 2, pp. 220–2).
23 Magarey (1895, p. 7).
24 Cleland (1966, p. 142).
25 Elkin (1977, pp. 11, 22, 102, 118, 121, 127) and Howitt (1904, pp. 394–9).
26 Cleland (1936; 1966, pp. 138–50), Cleland & Johnston (1933), Goddard & Kalotus (1988), Johnston & Cleland (1943), Latz (1995), Lawrence (1968, pp. 55–70, 76–84), Meggitt (1962, pp. 5–9), Tindale (1972, pp. 248–54) and Wightman et al. (1994).
27 Dixon et al. (1992, p. 120).
28 Worsnop (1897, p. 81).

29 Tindale (1981, pp. 1859–60, 1873–4).
30 Tindale (1977, p. 345).
31 Gregory (1887, p. 131).
32 Tindale (1977, p. 346). See also Tindale (1981, pp. 1865–6).
33 Goddard & Kalotus (1988, pp. 102–5).
34 Lawrence (1968, p. 57) and Tindale (1977, p. 346).
35 Lourandos (1997, pp. 188–94).
36 Tindale (1966).
37 Dixon et al. (1992, pp. 108–9).
38 Hackett (1937, p. 297) and Turner (1974, pp. 29–33).
39 Turner (1994, p. 8).
40 Cleland (1966, p. 144).
41 Horne & Aiston (1924, pp. 62–4 & fig. 48), Lamond (1950) and Reuther artefact
    collection, South Australian Museum.
42 Tindale (1981, p. 1874).
43 Thomson (1975, p. 43).
44 Mountford (cited Tunbridge 1991, pp. 63–4).
45 Gosse cited Worsnop (1897, p. 117).
46 Tonkinson (1978, p. 22).
47 Tonkinson (1978, p. 23).
48 Turner (1994, p. 39).
49 Thomson (1975, p. 157).
50 Bindon & Gough (1993, p. 14).
51 Kalma & McAlpine (1983, pp. 49–57).
52 Henderson & Dobson (1994, pp. 92, 585, 613–14).
53 Goddard (1992, pp. 39, 97, 116, 247), Mutitjulu Community & Baker (1996,
    pp. 1–5, 51) and Tindale (1933; 1957; 1959a; 1972, pp. 228–38; 1978, pp. 158–9;
    1981, pp. 1867–8).
54 Mutitjulu Community & Baker (1996, p. 1).
55 Cleland (1966, pp. 146–8).
56 Tindale (1974, pp. 62–3).
57 Tindale (1974, p. 63).
58 Tindale (1981, p. 1864).
59 Tindale (1978, p. 159).

Chapter 10   Beyond Capricorn

1   Hale & Tindale (1933, pp. 113–15), Lands (1987), Lawrence (1968, pp. 205–9,
    212–14), Levitt (1981, pp. 32–47), McConnel (1953, p. 7), Roth (1901b, pp. 9–16),
    Smith & Wightman (1990), Smith et al. (1993), Thomson (1936, p. 72; 1939,
    pp. 215–6), Thozet (in Smyth [1878, vol. 2, pp. 227–34]), Wightman & Smith
    (1989, pp. 10–24), Wightman et al. (1991), Wightman et al. (1992a) and Wightman
    (1992b).
2   Smith (1990, p. 57).
3   Levitt (1981, p. 38) and Tindale (1925, p. 78).
4   Levitt (1981, p. 32).

5   Everist (1981, pp. 233–4), Mountford (1958, pp. 129, 130–43), Smith (1990, pp. 19, 37), Smith & Wightman (1990, p. 10) and Wightman & Smith (1989, pp. 2, 21).
6   Hart & Pilling (1960, pp. 34, 38).
7   Levitt (1981, pp. 38, 44, 48–51).
8   Levitt (1981, pp. 32–3).
9   Altman (1987, pp. 41–4, 62–3, 74–6, 176–7).
10 Hale & Tindale (1933, p. 111), Roth (1901b, pp. 21–2) and Thomson (1985, pp. 187–9).
11 Hamlyn-Harris & Smith (1916) and Roth (1901b, pp. 19–20).
12 Roth (1901b, p. 23).
13 Hale & Tindale (1933, p. 109) and Roth (1901b, pp. 24–5).
14 Browne (1895, p. 12). See Lewis (1988).
15 Roth (1901b, pp. 27–9).
16 Roth (1901b, p. 28).
17 Thomson (1934; 1985, pp. 156–62) and South Australian Museum specimens.
18 Tindale (1925, pp. 78–9).
19 Jardine cited in Worsnop (1897, p. 95).
20 Hale & Tindale (1933, pp. 107–8) and Roth (1901b, pp. 26–9).
21 Thomson (1949, p. 16).
22 Crawford (1982, pp. vii–viii, 17–9), Kaberry (1939, pp. 11, 409–10), Reid (1995, p. 4) and Smith & Kalotus (1985, p. 323).
23 Breeden & Wright (1991, p. 109), Davis (1989) and Hiatt & Jones (1988, pp. 8–9).
24 Reid (1995, p. 4).
25 Chase & Sutton (1981).
26 Smith & Kalotus (1985, pp. 322–4).
27 Crawford (1982, pp. vii–viii, 17–9, 26–8, 35–6).
28 Breeden & Wright (1991, p. 109).
29 Davis (1989).
30 Baker (1999, p. 47).
31 Aurukun School & Community Calendar (1985), McConnel (1930, pp. 6–10) and Reid (1995, p. 4). Chase & Sutton (1981, pp. 1835–8) and Sutton (1995b, pp. 151, 169, 179–80) record the Wik-Ngathan language terms for the seasons.
32 Chase & Sutton (1981, pp. 1830–4).

Chapter 11   Northern Contacts

1   Baker (1999, pp. 65–74), McCarthy (1938–40, 1940b), Turner (1974, p. 197) and Urry & Walsh (1981).
2   Macknight (1976, pp. 39–40, 49–50, 143) and Thomson (1949, pp. 82–94).
3   Hughes (1987, p. 47).
4   Berndt & Berndt (1954, pp. 40–122) and Macknight (1976, pp. 38–47).
5   Macknight (1976) and Tindale (1926, p. 132).
6   Baker (1999), Berndt & Berndt (1954, pp. 40–8), Hercus & Sutton (1986) and Tindale (1925, pp. 66–7).
7   Tindale (1974, p. 141).
8   Berndt & Berndt (1954, pp. 72–90), Macknight (1976, pp 48–82) and Tindale (1974, pp. 36, 141).

9   Bradley (1988, p. 73).
10 Flinders (1814, [in Flannery 2000, pp. 203–7]).
11 Baudin (1803, cited in Mulvaney 1989, p. 23).
12 Berndt & Berndt (1954, pp. 15–16), Macknight (1976, pp. 61–82) and Mulvaney (1989, pp. 22–8).
13 Berndt & Berndt (1954, pp. 40–8).
14 Baker (1982, p. 182), Berndt & Berndt (1954, p. 15) and Mulvaney (1989, p. 26).
15 Tindale (1974, pp. 36–7, 151–3, 262).
16 Berndt & Berndt (1954).
17 Berndt & Berndt (1954, pp. 44–6) and Urry & Walsh (1981, pp. 99–100).
18 Warner (1958, pp. 420–3, 458) and Williams (1986, pp. 28–9).
19 Thomson (1949, pp. 91–2).
20 Beckett (1987) and Sharp (1993).
21 Thomson (1933; 1934).
22 Akerman (1994, p. 1).
23 Haddon (1935, p. 300), McCarthy (1938–40) and McConnel (1953).
24 McConnel (1953, p. 3).
25 Berndt & Berndt (1954, pp. 66–8).

Chapter 12   Arrival of Europeans

1   Tench (1788 [1996, pp. 40–1]).
2   Tench (1788 [1996, p. 41]).
3   Blackburn (1979).
4   Meyer (1843, p. 60) and Taplin (1879, p. 37).
5   Buckley (recorded by Morgan, 1852, pp. 32–3).
6   Teichelmann [in *The South Australian Colonist* newspaper, vol. 1, no. 18, 7 July 1840].
7   Teichelmann & Schürmann (1840, pt 2, p. 39).
8   Taplin (1874 [1879, p. 3]).
9   Dawson (1881, p. 105).
10 Dawson (1881, p. 105).
11 Smith (1880, p. 25).
12 Kimber (1982).
13 Diamond (1997, pp. 77–8, 197–9, 210–3, 320, 357, 373–4).
14 Tench (1789, [1996, pp. 102–3]).
15 Berndt (1989, p. 64), Berndt & Berndt (1993, p. 292), Bulmer (1887, p. 31) and Stirling (1911).
16 Cleland (1966, pp. 155–6), Lawrence (1968, p. 227) and Lourandos (1997, pp. 35–8).
17 Clarke (1995, p. 156, footnote 1).
18 Howitt (1904, p. 427), Massola (1968, pp. 105–6), Morgan (1852 [1980, pp. 64–5]) and Willey (1985, pp. 54–5).
19 Willey (1985, p. 55).
20 Stirling (1911, p. 18).
21 Clarke (1997) and Tindale (1937, pp. 111–2; 1941b, pp. 233–4).
22 Tindale (1931–34, pp. 232, 251–2).

23   Jones (1974, p. 319), Plomley (1966, pp. 966, 1009) and Ryan (1996, pp. 67–9).
24   Jones (1990).
25   Rowley (1970), Smith (1980) and Tindale (1941a).
26   Eyre (1845, vol. 2, pp. 358–9).
27   Blackburn (1979, pp. 124–39).
28   Swain (1993).
29   Maddock (1982, pp. 178, 181) and Worms & Petri (1968, p. 218).
30   Kolig (1981; 1995) and Lommel (1950).

Chapter 13   Aboriginal Australia Transformed

1   Attwood (1989, p. x), Baker (1999, pp. 75–85) and Rowley (1972, part 2).
2   Flannery (2000, pp. xiv, xviii).
3   Sturt (1844–45 [1984, pp. 18, 23, 31–6, 40, 103, 105]).
4   Leichhardt (1847, p. 77).
5   Bull (1884, p. 292).
6   Grey (1841, p. 110).
7   Bonney (cited in Bull, 1884, p. 78).
8   Wills (1863, p. 212).
9   Smith (1880, p. 43).
10   *Public Service Review, S. Aust.*, May 1929. Cited Fenner (1931, pp. 169–70).
11   Jones (1974, p. 321) and Tindale (1974, p. 148).
12   Moorehead (1968, pp. 62–75).
13   Ramson (1988, p. 430).
14   Attwood (1989), Berndt & Berndt (1951) and Swain & Rose (1988).
15   Worsnop (1897, p. 51).
16   *Register* newspaper, 21 November 1840.
17   Hercus (1985) and Strehlow (1970, p. 97).
18   Hercus (1990, p. 149).
19   Blandowski (1858, p. 127) and Moyal (1986, p. 24).
20   Magarey (1899, pp. 120–1).
21   Cameron-Bonney (1990, p. 11).
22   Holmes (2000) and S.M. Jones (1990).
23   Williams (1986, p. 29).
24   Tindale (1934–37, vol. 2, p. 57; 1938, p. 20).
25   Hiatt (1996, p. 29).

Chapter 14   Changing Cultural Landscapes

1   Amery (2000), Berndt (1977), Clifford (1988) and Keen (1988).
2   Morgan (1987).
3   Clifford (1988).
4   Dixon et al. (1992, pp. 67–8) and Troy (1993).
5   Dixon et al. (1992, pp. 65–6, 87, 192, 119) and Ramson (1988, pp. 79, 203, 271, 355).

6   Dixon et al. (1992, pp. 102–3, 107–10) and Ramson (1988, pp. 109, 366, 753).
7   Amery & Mühlhäusler (1996), Clark et al. (1996), Crowley (1996), Harris (1993), Mühlhäusler (1974, 1991, 1996a-d) and Rhydwen (1993).
8   Harkins (1994) and Schmidt (1993).
9   Mühlhäuster (1974, 1991).
10   Cochrane (2001), Morphy (1998, Chapter 11) and Berndt & Berndt (1999, pp. 136–44).
11   Clifford (1988) and Hobsbawn & Ranger (1983).
12   Curr (1886–87), Taplin (1879) and Woods (1879).
13   Schürmann Diaries (6 June 1839).
14   Schürmann Diaries (19 June 1839).
15   Attwood (1989) and Rowley (1970; 1972).
16   Taplin Journals (25 June 1859; 22 September 1859).
17   Swain (1988).
18   Mackinolty & Wainburranga (1988, p. 356).
19   Maddock (1988) and Rose (1992, pp. 186–202).
20   Rowley (1972, p. 135) and Rowse (1993, pp. 13–6).
21   Clarke (1998), Darian-Smith (1993) and Schaffer (1993).
22   Clarke (1994, p. 58) and Taplin Journals (17–18 August 1859).
23   Strehlow (1970, p. 110) and Taplin Journals (6–9 August 1860; 23 April 1863).
24   Muecke (1992b).
25   Taplin Journals (11 February 1860 & 11 July 1864).
26   Burbidge et al. (1988, p. 36) and Strehlow (1970, p. 103).
27   Thomas (1983, pp. 17–25).
28   Clark (1987, pp. 19–20), Reynolds (1989, pp. 67–8, 94, 98) and Williams (1985).
29   Johnston et al. (1986, pp. 164, 527).
30   Clarke (1996, pp. 70–7) and Reynolds (1990, pp. 1–3).
31   Stanner (1938 [1979, pp. 207–17]).
32   Attwood (1989), Baker (1999), Bottoms (1999), Brock (1993), Hercus & Sutton (1986), Jenkin (1979), Mattingley & Hampton (1992), Reynolds (1972, 1982, 1989, 1990), Ryan (1996) and Simpson & Hercus (1998).
33   Brennan (1998), Butt & Eagleson (1998), McCorquodale (1987), Rowse (1993), Stephenson (1995), Toyne & Vachon (1984) and Williams (1986).
34   Berndt & Berndt (1951, pp. 95–100), Gale (1964, 1969, 1972), Gale & Wundersitz (1982, p. 37), Stanner (1938 [1979, pp. 17–8]) and Tindale (1941a). Refer to Australian Census Reports.
35   Attwood (1996), Gilbert (1977), Keen (1988), Muecke (1992a) and Nelson (1988).
36   McCorquodale (1987).
37   Baker (1999, pp. 88–90) and Foster (1989).
38   Ryan (1996).
39   Altman (1987).
40   Beckett (1988), Gelder & Jacobs (1998) and Reay (1988, p. x).
41   Griffiths (1996, p. 226).

References

Abbie, A.A. 1976. *The Original Australians*. Revised edition. Seal Books, Adelaide.

Akerman, K. 1979. Heat and lithic technology in the Kimberley, W.A. *Archaeology and Physical Anthropology on Oceania*. Vol. 14, pp. 144–51.

Akerman, K. 1980. Material culture and trade in the Kimberleys today, pp. 243–51 in R.M. & C.H. Berndt (eds) *Aborigines of the West. Their Past and Their Present*. University of Western Australia Press, Perth.

Akerman, K. with Stanton, J. 1994. *Riji and Jakoli: Kimberley Pearlshell in Aboriginal Australia*. Monograph Series 4. Northern Territory Museum of Arts & Sciences, Darwin.

Allen, J. 1998a. Antiquity, pp. 9–12 in T. Murray (ed.) *Archaeology of Aboriginal Australia*. Allen & Unwin, Sydney.

Allen, J. 1998b. When did humans first colonise Australia? pp. 50–60 in T. Murray (ed.) *Archaeology of Aboriginal Australia*. Allen & Unwin, Sydney.

Allen, J. 2000. A matter of time. *Nature Australia*. Vol. 26, no. 10, pp. 60–9.

Allen, L. (ed.) 1995a. *Women's Work. Aboriginal Women's Artefacts in the Museum of Victoria*. Museum of Victoria, Melbourne.

Allen, L. 1995b. Fibrecraft, pp. 11–8 in L. Allen (ed.) *Women's Work. Aboriginal Women's Artefacts in the Museum of Victoria*. Museum of Victoria, Melbourne.

Allen, L. 1995c. Children's Lives, pp. 53–8 in L. Allen (ed.) *Women's Work. Aboriginal Women's Artefacts in the Museum of Victoria*. Museum of Victoria, Melbourne.

Altman, J.C. 1987. *Hunter-gatherers Today. An Aboriginal Economy in North Australia*. Australian Institute of Aboriginal Studies, Canberra.

Amery, R. 2000. *Warrabarna Kaurna! Reclaiming an Australian Language*. Multilingualism and Linguistic Diversity 1. Swets & Zeitlinger Publishers, Leiden, The Netherlands.

Amery, R. & Mühlhäusler, P. 1996. Pidgin English in New South Wales. Map 6

& pp. 33–52 in S.A. Wurm, P. Mühlhäusler & D.T. Tryon (eds), *Atlas of Languages of Intercultural Communication in the Pacific, Asia, and the Americas*. 3 vols. Mouton de Gruyter, Berlin.

Anderson, C. & Dussart, F. 1988. Dreamings in acrylic: Western Desert art, pp. 89–142 in P. Sutton (ed.). *Dreamings: The Art of Aboriginal Australia*. Penguin Books, Melbourne.

Anderson, K.J. & Gale, F. (eds) 1992. *Inventing Places. Studies in Cultural Geography*. Longman Cheshire, Melbourne.

Angas, G. French. 1847a. *South Australia Illustrated*. T. McLean, London.

Angas, G. French. 1847b. *Savage Life and Scenes in Australia*. Smith, Elder & Co., London.

Arthur, J.M. 1996. *Aboriginal English. A Cultural Study*. Oxford University Press, Melbourne.

Attwood, B. 1989. *The Making of the Aborigines*. Allen & Unwin, Sydney.

Attwood, B. (ed.) 1996. *In the Age of Mabo. History, Aborigines and Australia*. Allen & Unwin, Sydney.

Aurukun School & Community Calendar. 1985. Seasons and Event Calendar. Aurukun Community, Northern Queensland.

Baker, R.M. 1988. Yanyuwa Canoe Making. *Records of the South Australian Museum*. Vol. 22, pt 2, pp. 173–88.

Baker, R.M. 1999. *Land is Life. From Bush to Town. The Story of the Yanyuwa People*. Allen & Unwin, Sydney.

Bardon, G. 1979. *Aboriginal Art of the Western Desert*. Rigby, Adelaide.

Bardon, G. 1991. *Papunya Tula. Art of the Western Desert*. McPhee Gribble, Melbourne.

Barr, A., Chapman, J., Smith, N. & Beveridge, M. 1988. *Traditional Bush Medicines: An Aboriginal Pharmacopoeia*. Greenhouse Publications, Melbourne.

Barrett, C. 1946. *The Bunyip*. Reed & Harris, Melbourne.

Bates, D.M. 1901–14. *The Native Tribes of Western Australia*. Edited by I. White, 1985. National Library of Australia, Canberra.

Bates, D.M. 1918. Aborigines of the west coast of South Australia. Vocabularies and ethnographical notes. *Transactions and Proceedings of the Royal Society of South Australia*. Vol. 42, pp. 152–67.

Bates, D.M. 1947. *The Passing of the Aborigines*. Australian edition. John Murray, London.

Bauer, F.H. 1969. Climate and man in north-western Queensland, pp. 51–63 in F. Gale & G.H. Lawton (eds) *Settlement and Encounter: Geographical Studies Presented to Sir Grenfell Price*. Oxford University Press, Melbourne.

Beckett, J.R. 1987. *Torres Strait Islanders: Custom and Colonialism*. Cambridge University Press, Cambridge.

Beckett, J.R. (ed.) 1988. *Past and Present. The Construction of Aboriginality*. Aboriginal Studies Press, Canberra.

Berndt, C.H. 1970. Digging sticks and spears, or, the two-sex model, pp. 39–48 in F. Gale (ed.) *Woman's Role in Aboriginal Society*. Australian Aboriginal Studies No. 36. Social Anthropology Series No. 6. Australian Institute of Aboriginal Studies, Canberra.

Berndt, C.H. 1980. Aboriginal women and the notion of 'The Marginal Man', pp. 28–38 in R.M. Berndt & C.H. Berndt (eds) *Aborigines of the West. Their Past and Their Present*. University of Western Australia Press, Perth.

Berndt, C.H. 1981. Interpretations and 'facts' in Aboriginal Australia, pp. 153–203 in F. Dahlberg (ed.) *Woman the Gatherer*. Yale University Press, New Haven.

Berndt, C.H. 1982. Aboriginal women, resources and family life, pp. 39–52 in R.M. Berndt (ed.). *Aboriginal Sites, Rights and Resource Development.* Academy of the Social Sciences in Australia. Fifth Academy Symposium, 11 November 1981, Proceedings. University of Western Australia Press, Perth.

Berndt, C.H. 1989. Retrospect and prospect: Looking back after 50 years, pp. 1–20 in P. Brock (ed.) *Women, Rites and Sites: Aboriginal Women's Cultural Knowledge.* Allen & Unwin, Sydney.

Berndt, R.M. 1940a. Aboriginal sleeping customs and dreams, Ooldea, South Australia. *Oceania.* Vol. 10, no. 3, pp. 286–94.

Berndt, R.M. 1940b. Some Aboriginal children's games. *Mankind.* Vol. 2, no. 9, pp. 289–95.

Berndt, R.M. 1941. Tribal migrations and myths centring on Ooldea, South Australia. *Oceania.* Vol. 12, pt 1, pp. 1–20.

Berndt, R.M. 1947. Wuradjeri magic and 'clever men'. *Oceania.* Vol. 17, pt 4, pp. 327–65; vol. 18, no. 1, pp. 60–86.

Berndt, R.M. 1952–54. A selection of children's songs from Ooldea, western South Australia. *Mankind.* Vol. 4, no. 9, pp. 364–76; vol. 4, no. 10, pp. 423–34 & vol. 4, no. 12, pp. 501–8.

Berndt, R.M. 1959. The concept of 'the Tribe' in the Western Desert of Australia. *Oceania.* Vol. 30, pt 2, pp. 82–107.

Berndt, R.M. 1970. The sacred site: The western Arnhem Land example. Australian Aboriginal Studies No. 29. Social Anthropology Series No. 4. Australian Institute of Aboriginal Studies, Canberra.

Berndt, R.M. 1972. The Walmadjeri and Gugadja, pp. 177–216 in M.G. Bicchieri (ed.) *Hunters and Gatherers Today. A Socioeconomic Study of Eleven Such Cultures in the Twentieth Century.* Holt, Rinehart & Winston, New York.

Berndt, R.M. 1976. Territoriality and the problem of demarcating sociocultural space, pp. 133–61 in N. Peterson (ed.) *Tribes and Boundaries in Australia.* Australian Institute of Aboriginal Studies, Canberra.

Berndt, R.M. (ed.) 1977. *Aborigines and Change: Australia in the '70s.* Social Anthropology Series No. 11. Australian Institute of Aboriginal Studies, Canberra.

Berndt, R.M. 1985. Traditional Aborigines, pp. 127–38 in C.R. Twidale, M.J. Tyler & M. Davies (eds) *Natural History of Eyre Peninsula.* Royal Society of South Australia, Adelaide.

Berndt, R.M. 1987. Panaramittee magic. *Records of the South Australian Museum.* Vol. 22, pt 2, pp. 15–28.

Berndt, R.M. 1989. Aboriginal fieldwork in South Australia in the 1940s and implications for the present. *Records of the South Australian Museum.* Vol. 23, pt. 1, pp. 59–68.

Berndt, R.M. & Berndt, C.H. 1951. *From Black to White in South Australia.* Cheshire, Melbourne.

Berndt, R.M. & Berndt, C.H. 1954. *Arnhem Land. Its History and Its People.* Cheshire, Melbourne.

Berndt, R.M. & Berndt, C.H. 1970. *Man, Land and Myth in North Australia. The Gunwinggu People.* Ure Smith, Sydney.

Berndt, R.M. & Berndt, C.H. 1985. *The World of the First Australians.* Rigby, Adelaide.

Berndt, R.M. & Berndt, C.H. 1989. *The Speaking Land. Myth and Story in Aboriginal Australia.* Penguin Books, Melbourne.

Berndt, R.M., Berndt, C.H., with Stanton, J.E. 1993. *A World That Was. The Yaraldi of the*

Murray River and the Lakes, South Australia. Melbourne University Press at the Miegunyah Press, Melbourne.

Berndt, R.M., Berndt, C.H., with Stanton, J.E. 1999. *Aboriginal Art. A Visual Perspective.* Revised edition. Methuen Australia, Sydney.

Berndt, R.M. & Johnston, T.H. 1942. Death, burial and associated ritual at Ooldea, South Australia. *Oceania.* Vol. 12, no. 3, pp. 189–208.

Beveridge, P. 1883. Of the Aborigines inhabiting the Great Lacustrine and Riverine Depression of the Lower Murray, Lower Murrumbidgee, Lower Lachlan, and Lower Darling. *Journal & Proceedings of the Royal Society of New South Wales.* Vol. 17, pp. 19–74.

Bindon, P. & Gough, D. 1993. Digging sticks and desert dwellers. *Landscope.* Spring, pp. 11–16.

Bindon, P. & Whalley, T. 1992. Hunters and Gatherers. *Landscope.* Spring, pp. 28–35.

Birdsell, J.B. 1949. The racial origins of the extinct Tasmanians. *Records of the Queen Victoria Museum.* Vol. 2, pt 3, pp. 105–22.

Birdsell, J.B. 1953. Some environmental and cultural factors influencing the structuring of Australian aboriginal populations. *American Naturalist.* Vol. 87, pp. 171–207.

Birdsell, J.B. 1967. Preliminary data on the trihybrid origin of the Australian Aborigines. *Archeology and Physical Anthropology in Oceania.* Vol. 2, pt 2, pp. 100–55.

Birdsell, J.B. 1976. Realities and transformations: the tribes of the Western Desert of Australia, pp. 95–120 in N. Peterson (ed.) *Tribes and Boundaries in Australia.* Australian Institute of Aboriginal Studies, Canberra.

Birdsell, J.B. 1993. *Microevolutionary Patterns in Aboriginal Australia. A Gradient Analysis of Clines.* Oxford University Press, New York.

Black, J.M. 1920. Vocabularies of four South Australian languages, Adelaide, Narrunga, Kukata, and Narrinyeri, with special references to speech sounds. *Transactions of the Royal Society of South Australia.* Vol. 44, pp. 76–93.

Blackburn, J. 1979. *The White Men.* Times, London.

Blake, B.J. 1981. *Australian Aboriginal Languages. A General Introduction.* Angus & Robertson, Sydney.

Blandowski, W. 1858. Recent discoveries in Natural History on the Lower Murray. *Transactions of the Philosophical Institute of Victoria.* Vol. 2, pp. 124–37.

Blundell, V. & Layton, R. 1978. Marriage, myth and models of exchange in the West Kimberleys. *Mankind.* Vol. 11, pp. 231–45.

Bolam, A.G. 1930. *The Trans-Australian Wonderland.* Seventh edition. Barker & Company. Melbourne.

Bonney, F. 1884. On some customs of the Aborigines of the River Darling, New South Wales. *Journal of the Anthropological Institute of Great Britain & Ireland.* Vol. 13, pp. 122–37.

Bottoms, T. 1999. *Djabugay Country. An Aboriginal History of Tropical North Queensland.* Allen & Unwin, Sydney.

Bradley, K. 1995. Leaf music in Australia. *Australian Aboriginal Studies.* No. 2, pp. 2–14.

Bradley, R. 1988, *Yanyuwa Country,* Richmond, Greenhouse Publications.

Brand Miller, J., James, K.W. & Maggiore, P.M.A. 1993. *Tables of composition of Australian Aboriginal Foods.* Aboriginal Studies Press, Canberra.

Brandl, E.J. 1988. *Australian Aboriginal Paintings in Western and Central Arnhem Land. Temporal Sequences and Elements of Style in Cadell River and Death Adder Creek Art.* Aboriginal Studies Press, Canberra.

Breeden, S. & Wright, B. 1991. *Kakadu: Looking After Country—the Gagudju Way*. Simon & Schuster, Sydney.

Brennan, F. 1998. *The Wik Debate: Its Impact on Aborigines, Pastoralists and Miners*. University of New South Wales Press, Sydney.

Brock, P. (ed.) 1989. *Women, Rites and Sites: Aboriginal Women's Cultural Knowledge*. Allen & Unwin, Sydney.

Brock, P. 1993. *Outback Ghettos. A History of Aboriginal Institutionalisation and Survival*. Cambridge University Press, Cambridge.

Brokensha, P. 1975. *The Pitjantjatjara and Their Crafts*. Aboriginal Arts Board, Australia Council, Sydney.

Brown, A.R. (= Radcliffe Brown) 1918. Notes on the social organisation of Australian tribes. *Journal of the Anthropological Institute of Great Britain*. Vol. 48, pp. 222–53.

Browne, H.Y.L. 1895. Government Geologist's report on explorations in the Northern Territory. *South Australian Parliamentary Papers*. No. 82, pp. 3–13.

Buhmann, J., Robins, R. & Cause, M. 1976. Wood identification of spearthrowers in the Queensland Museum. *Australian Institute of Aboriginal Studies Newsletter. New Series*. Vol. 5, pp. 43–4.

Buku-larrnggay Mulka Centre. 1999. *Saltwater. Yirrkala Bark Paintings of Sea Country. Recognising Indigenous Sea Rights*. Jennifer Isaacs Publishing, New South Wales, in association with Buku-larrnggay Mulka Centre.

Bull, J.W. 1884. *Early Experiences of Life in South Australia and an Extended Colonial History*. E.S. Wigg & Son, Adelaide.

Bulmer, J. 1887. Some account of the Aborigines of the Lower Murray, Wimmera, Gippsland and Maneroo. *Transactions & Proceedings of the Royal Geographical Society of Australasia. Victorian Branch*. Vol. 5, pt 1, pp. 15–43.

Burbidge, A.A., Johnson, K.A., Fuller, P.J. & Southgate, R.I. 1988. Aboriginal knowledge of the mammals of the Central Deserts of Australia. *Australian Wildlife Research*. Vol. 15, pp. 9–39.

Butlin, N.G. 1993. *Economics and the Dreamtime. A Hypothetical History*. Cambridge University Press, Cambridge.

Butt, P.J. & Eagleson, R. 1998. *Mabo, Wik and Native Title*. Third edition. Federation Press, Sydney.

Cameron, A.L.P. 1885. Notes on some tribes of New South Wales. *The Journal of the Anthropological Institute of Great Britain & Ireland*. Vol. 14, pp. 344–70.

Cameron-Bonney, L. 1990. *Out of the Dreaming*. South East Kingston Leader, Kingston.

Cann, J.H., De Deckker, P. & Murray-Wallace, C.V. 1991. Coastal Aboriginal shell middens and their palaeoenvironmental significance, Robe Range, South Australia. *Transactions of the Royal Society of South Australia*. Vol. 115, pt 4, pp. 161–75.

Carter, G.F. 1964. *Man and the Land. A Cultural Geography*. Holt, Rinehart & Winston, New York.

Cawte, J. 1974. *Medicine is the Law*. University Press of Hawaii, Honolulu.

Chaloupka, G. 1993. *Journey in Time. The World's Longest Continuing Art Tradition. The 50,000-year Story of the Australian Aboriginal Rock Art of Arnhem Land*. Reed, Sydney.

Charlesworth, M. (ed.) 1998. *Religious Business. Essays on Australian Aboriginal Spirituality*. Cambridge University Press, Cambridge.

Charlesworth, M., Morphy, H., Bell, D. & Maddock, K. (eds) 1984. *Religion in Aboriginal Australia. An Anthology*. University of Queensland Press, St Lucia.

Chase, A. & Sutton, P. 1981. 'Hunter-gatherers in a rich environment: Aboriginal coastal exploitation in Cape York Peninsula', pp. 1819–52 in A. Keast (ed.) *Ecological Biogeography of Australia*. Junk, The Hague.

Cherikoff, V. & Isaacs, J. 1989. *The Bush Food Handbook. How to Gather, Grow, Process and Cook Australian Wild Foods*. Ti Tree Press, Sydney.

Chippindale, C. & Taçon, P.S.C. (eds) 1998. *The Archaeology of Rock-art*. Cambridge University Press, Cambridge.

Clark, I.D. 1990. *Aboriginal Languages and Clans: An Historical Atlas of Western and Central Victoria, 1800–1900*. Monash Publications in Geography no. 37. Monash University, Melbourne.

Clark, I.D., Mühlhäusler, P. & Amery, R. 1996. Language contacts and Pidgin English in Victoria. Map 6 & pp. 53–68 in S.A. Wurm, P. Mühlhäusler & D.T. Tryon (eds), *Atlas of Languages of Intercultural Communication in the Pacific, Asia, and the Americas*. 3 vols. Mouton de Gruyter, Berlin.

Clark, M. 1987. *A Short History of Australia*. Third edition. NAL Penguin, New York.

Clarke, P.A. 1985a. The importance of roots and tubers as a food source for southern South Australian Aborigines. *Journal of the Anthropological Society of South Australia*. Vol. 23, pt 6, pp. 2–12.

Clarke, P.A. 1985b. Fruits and seeds as food for southern South Australian Aborigines. *Journal of the Anthropological Society of South Australia*. Vol. 23, pt 9, pp. 9–22.

Clarke, P.A. 1986a. Aboriginal use of plant exudates, foliage and fungi as food and water sources in southern South Australia. *Journal of the Anthropological Society of South Australia*. Vol. 24, pt 3, pp. 3–18.

Clarke, P.A. 1986b. The study of ethnobotany in southern South Australia. *Australian Aboriginal Studies*. Pt 2, pp. 40–7.

Clarke, P.A. 1987. Aboriginal uses of plants as medicines, narcotics and poisons in southern South Australia. *Journal of the Anthropological Society of South Australia*. Vol. 25, pt 5, pp. 3–23.

Clarke, P.A. 1988. Aboriginal use of subterranean plant parts in southern South Australia. *Records of the South Australian Museum*. Vol. 22, pt 1, pp. 63–76.

Clarke, P.A. 1990. Adelaide Aboriginal cosmology. *Journal of the Anthropological Society of South Australia*. Vol. 28, pt 1, pp. 1–10.

Clarke, P.A. 1991. Adelaide as an Aboriginal Landscape. *Aboriginal History*. Vol. 15, pt 1, pp. 54–72.

Clarke, P.A. 1994. Contact, Conflict and Regeneration. Aboriginal Cultural Geography of the Lower Murray, South Australia. Postgraduate thesis. University of Adelaide, Adelaide.

Clarke, P.A. 1995. Myth as history: The Ngurunderi mythology of the Lower Murray, South Australia. *Records of the South Australian Museum*. Vol. 28, pt 2, pp. 143–57.

Clarke, P.A. 1996. Early European interaction with Aboriginal hunters and gatherers on Kangaroo Island, South Australia. *Aboriginal History*. Vol. 20, pt 1, pp. 51–81.

Clarke, P.A. 1997. The Aboriginal cosmic landscape of southern South Australia. *Records of the South Australian Museum*. Vol. 29, pt 2, pp. 125–45.

Clarke, P.A. 1998. The Aboriginal presence on Kangaroo Island, South Australia, pp. 14–48 in J. Simpson & L. Hercus (eds) *Aboriginal Portraits of Nineteenth-century South Australia*. Australian National University, Canberra.

Clarke, P.A. 1999a. Spirit beings of the Lower Murray, South Australia. *Records of the South Australian Museum*. Vol. 31, pt 2, pp. 149–63.

Clarke, P.A. 1999b. Waiyungari and his role in the mythology of the Lower Murray, South Australia. *Records of the South Australian Museum.* Vol. 32, pt 1, pp. 51–67.

Clarke, P.A. 2000. *The Australian Aboriginal Cultures Gallery.* South Australian Museum, Adelaide.

Clarke, P.A. 2001. The significance of whales to the Aboriginal people of southern South Australia. *Records of the South Australian Museum.* Vol. 34, pt 1, pp. 19–35.

Clarke, P.A. 2002. Early Aboriginal Fishing Technology in the Lower Murray, South Australia. *Records of the South Australian Museum.* Vol. 35, pt 2, pp. 147–67.

Cleland, J.B. 1936. Ethno-botany in relation to the Central Australian Aboriginal. *Mankind.* Vol. 2, no. 1, pp. 6–9.

Cleland, J.B. 1966. The ecology of the Aboriginal in South and Central Australia, pp. 111–58 in B.C. Cotton (ed.) *Aboriginal Man in South and Central Australia. Pt 1.* South Australian Government Printer, Adelaide.

Cleland, J.B. & Johnston, T.H. 1933. The ecology of the Aborigines of Central Australia; botanical notes. *Transactions of the Royal Society of South Australia.* Vol. 57, pp. 113–24.

Clifford, J. 1988. *The Predicament of Culture. Twentieth-century Ethnography, Literature, and Art.* Harvard University Press, Massachusetts.

Cochrane, S. (ed.) 2001. *Aboriginal Art Collections. Highlights from Australia's Public Museums and Galleries.* Craftsman House, Sydney.

Cockburn, R. 1984. *What's in a Name? Nomenclature of South Australia.* Revised edition. Ferguson, Adelaide.

Collins, D. 1804. *An Account of the English Colony in New South Wales from its First Settlement in January 1788 to August 1801.* T. Cadell & W. Davies, London.

Cook, J. 1893. *Captain Cook's Journal During His First Voyage Round the World Made in H.M. Bark 'Endeavour' 1768–71.* Elliot Stock, London.

Cooper, H.M. 1948. Examples of native material culture from South Australia. *The South Australian Naturalist.* Vol. 25, no. 1, pp. 1–8.

Couper Black, E. 1966. Population and tribal distribution, pp. 97–109 in B.C. Cotton (ed.) *Aboriginal Man in South and Central Australia.* South Australian Government Printer, Adelaide.

Coutts, P.J.F., Frank, R.K. & Hughes, P. 1978. Aboriginal engineers of the Western District, Victoria. *Records of the Victorian Archaeological Survey.* No. 7.

Crawford, I.M. 1968. *The Art of the Wandjina: Aboriginal Cave Painting in Kimberley, Western Australia.* Oxford University Press, Melbourne.

Crawford, I.M. 1982. Traditional Aboriginal plant resources in the Kalumburu area: aspects in ethno-economics. *Records of the Western Australian Museum Supplement.* No. 15. Western Australian Museum, Perth.

Cribb, A.B. & Cribb, J.W. 1981. *Wild Medicine in Australia.* Fontana/Collins, Sydney.

Cribb, A.B. & Cribb, J.W. 1987. *Wild Food in Australia.* Fontana/Collins, Sydney.

Cribb, R., Walmbeng, R., Wolmby, R. & Taisman, C. 1988. Landscape as cultural artefact: Shell mounds and plants in Aurukun, Cape York Peninsula. *Australian Aboriginal Studies.* No. 2, pp. 60–73.

Crowley, T. 1996. Early language contact in Tasmania. Map 27 & pp. 25–32 in S.A. Wurm, P. Mühlhäusler & D.T. Tryon (eds), *Atlas of Languages of Intercultural Communication in the Pacific, Asia, and the Americas.* 3 vols. Mouton de Gruyter, Berlin.

Cundy, B.J. 1980. *Australian Spear and Spear-thrower Technology. An Analysis of Structural Variation.* Postgraduate thesis. Australian National University, Canberra.

Cundy, B.J. 1989. *Formal Variation in Australian Spear and Spearthrower Technology.* BAR International, Oxford.

Curr, E.M. 1883. *Recollections of Squatting in Victoria.* Melbourne University Press, Melbourne.

Curr, E.M. 1886–87. *The Australian Race.* Trubner, London.

Dampier, W. 1697. *A New Voyage Round the World. The Journal of an English Buccaneer.* Edited & revised 1998. Hummingbird Press, London.

Dargin, P. 1976. *Aboriginal Fisheries of the Darling–Barwon Rivers.* Brewarrina Historical Society, Brewarrina.

Darian-Smith, K. 1993. The white woman of Gippsland: A frontier myth, pp. 14–34 in K. Darian-Smith, R. Poignant & K. Schaffer (eds), *Captured Lives. Australian Captivity Narratives.* Sir Robert Menzies Centre for Australian Studies, Institute of Commonwealth Studies, University of London, London.

David, B. 1998. Introduction, pp. 1–26 in B. David (ed.) *Ngarrabullgan: Geographical Investigations in Djungan Country, Cape York Peninsula.* Monash Publications in Geography and Environmental Science No. 51. Monash University, Clayton, Victoria.

David, B. 2002. *Landscapes, Rock-art and the Dreaming: An Archaeology of Preunderstanding.* Continuum, London.

Davidson, D.S. 1933. Australian netting and basketry techniques. *Journal of the Polynesian Society.* Vol. 42, pp. 257–99.

Davidson, D.S. 1934. Australian spear-traits and their derivations. *Journal of the Polynesian Society.* Vol. 43, pp. 41–72, 143–62.

Davidson, D.S. 1935. The chronology of Australian watercraft. *Journal of the Polynesian Society.* Vol. 44, pp. 1–16, 69–84, 137–52, 193–207.

Davidson, D.S. 1936. Australian throwing-sticks, throwing clubs, and boomerangs. *American Anthropologist.* Vol. 38, pp. 76–100.

Davies, E. 1881. *The Story of an Earnest Life. A Woman's Adventures in Australia, and in Two Voyages Around the World.* Central Book Concern, Cincinnati.

Davis, S. 1989. *Man of all Seasons. An Aboriginal Perspective of the Natural Environment.* Angus & Robertson, Sydney.

Dawson, J. 1881. *Australian Aborigines.* Robertson, Melbourne.

Diamond, J. 1997. *Guns, Germs and Steel: A Short History of Everybody for the Last 13,000 Years.* Jonathon Cape, London.

Dixon, R.M.W., Ramson, W.S. & Thomas, M. 1992. *Australian Aboriginal Words in English. Their Origin and Meaning.* Oxford University Press Australia, Melbourne.

Douglas, W.H. 1977. *Illustrated Topical Dictionary of the Western Desert Language.* Revised edition. Australian Institute of Aboriginal Studies, Canberra.

Douglas, W.H. 1988. *An Introductory Dictionary of the Western Desert Language.* Institute of Applied Language Studies, Perth.

Dousset, L. 1997. Naming and personal names of Ngaatjatjarra-speaking people, Western Desert: Some questions related to research. *Australian Aboriginal Studies.* No. 2, pp. 50–4.

Edwards, R. 1972. *Aboriginal Bark Canoes of the Murray Valley.* Rigby, Adelaide.

Edwards, R. & Guerin, B. 1969. *Aboriginal Bark Paintings.* Rigby, Adelaide.

Edwards, W.H. 1988. *An Introduction to Aboriginal Societies.* Social Science Press, Wentworth Falls, NSW.

Elkin, A.P. 1931. The social organisation of South Australian tribes. *Oceania.* Vol. 2, no. 1, pp. 44–73.

Elkin, A.P. 1934. Cult-totemism and mythology in northern South Australia. *Oceania.* Vol. 5, no. 2, pp. 171–92.

Elkin, A.P. 1937. Beliefs and practices connected with death in north-eastern and western South Australia. *Oceania.* Vol. 7, pt 3, pp. 275–99.

Elkin, A.P. 1940. Kinship in South Australia. *Oceania.* Vol. 10, pt 3, pp. 295–349; pt 4, pp. 369–88.

Elkin, A.P. 1964. *The Australian Aborigines. How to Understand Them.* Fourth edition. Angus & Robertson, Sydney.

Elkin, A.P. 1977. *Aboriginal Men of High Degree.* Second edition. University of Queensland Press, St Lucia.

Ellis, R.W. 1976. The Aboriginal inhabitants and their environment, pp. 113–20 in C.R. Twidale, M.J. Tyler & B.P. Webb (eds) *Natural History of the Adelaide Region.* Royal Society of South Australia, Adelaide.

Etheridge, R. 1893. The 'mirrn-yong' heaps at the northwest bend of the River Murray. *Transactions & Proceedings & Report of the Royal Society of South Australia.* Vol. 17, pp. 21–4.

Etheridge, R. 1918. *The Dendroglyths, or 'Carved Trees' of New South Wales.* Government Printer, Sydney.

Everist, S.L. 1981. *Poisonous Plants of Australia.* Revised edition. Angus & Robertson, Sydney.

Eyre, E.J. 1845. *Journals of Expeditions of Discovery.* 2 vols. Boone, London.

Fenner, C.A.E. 1931. *South Australia: A Geographical Study.* Whitcombe & Tombs, Melbourne.

Finlayson, H. 1952. *The Red Centre: Man and Beast in the Heart of Central Australia.* Angus & Robertson, Sydney.

Finlayson, W. 1903. Reminiscences of Pastor Finlayson. *Proceedings of the Royal Geographical Society of Australasia, South Australian Branch.* Vol. 6, pp. 39–55.

Fison, L. & Howitt, A.W. 1880. *Kamilaroi and Kurnai. Group-Marriage and Relationship, and Marriage by Elopement. Drawn Chiefly from the Usage of the Australian Aborigines. Also the Kurnai Tribe. Their Customs in Peace and War.* George Robertson, Melbourne.

Flannery, T.F. 1994. *The Future Eaters. An Ecological History of the Australasian Lands and People.* Reed Books, Sydney.

Flannery, T.F. 2000. The Indefatigable Matthew Flinders, pp. vii–xxiv *Terra Australis. Matthew Flinders' Great Adventures in the Circumnavigation of Australia.* Originally published by M. Flinders, 1814. Edited and introduced by T.F. Flannery. Text Publishing, Melbourne.

Flood, J. 1980. *The Moth Hunters: Aboriginal Prehistory of the Australian Alps.* Australian Institute of Aboriginal Studies, Canberra.

Flood, J. 1983. *Archaeology of the Dreamtime.* Collins, Sydney.

Flood, J. 1997. *Rock Art of the Dreamtime: Images of Ancient Australia.* Angus & Robertson, Sydney.

Foster, R. 1989. Feasts of the full-moon: The distribution of rations to Aborigines in South Australia: 1836–1861. *Aboriginal History.* Vol. 13, pt 1, pp. 63–78.

Frankel, D. 1982. An account of Aboriginal use of the yam-daisy. *The Artefact.* Vol. 7, pp. 43–5.

Fry, H.K. 1934. Kinship in western Central Australia. *Oceania.* Vol. 4, pt 4, pp. 472–8.

Gale, F. 1964. *A Study of Assimilation: Part-Aborigines in South Australia.* Libraries Board of South Australia, Adelaide.

Gale, F. 1969. A changing Aboriginal population, pp. 65–88 in F. Gale & G.H. Lawton (eds) *Settlement and Encounter: Geographical Studies Presented to Sir Grenfell Price*. Oxford University Press, Melbourne.

Gale, F. 1972. *Urban Aborigines*. Australian National University Press, Canberra.

Gale, F. 1989. Roles revisited. The women of southern South Australia, pp. 120–35 in P. Brock (ed.) *Women Rites and Sites. Aboriginal Women's Cultural Knowledge*. Allen & Unwin, Sydney.

Gale, F. & Wundersitz, J. 1982. *Adelaide Aborigines. A Case Study of Urban Life 1966–1981*. The Aboriginal Component in the Australian Economy. Vol. 4. Australian National University, Canberra.

Gara, T. 1985. Aboriginal techniques for obtaining water in South Australia. *Journal of the Anthropological Society of South Australia*. Vol. 23, pt 2, pp. 6–11.

Gara, T. 1994. 'Tackling the back country': Richard Maurice's expeditions in the great Victoria Desert, 1897–1903. *South Australian Geographical Journal*. Vol. 93, pp. 42–60.

Gelder, K. & Jacobs, J.M. 1998. *Uncanny Australia. Sacredness and Identity in a Postcolonial Nation*. Melbourne University Press, Melbourne.

Gell, J.P. 1841. The vocabulary of the Adelaide tribe. Published in the *Proceedings of the Royal Geographical Society of Australasia, South Australian Branch*. 1904, vol. 7, pp. 92–100.

Gerritsen, R. 2001. Aboriginal fish hooks in southern Australia: Evidence, arguments and implications. *Australian Archaeology*. Vol. 52, pp. 18–28.

Gilbert, K. 1977. *Living Black. Blacks Talk to Kevin Gilbert*. Allen Lane, Melbourne.

Goddard, C. 1992. *Pitjantjatjara/Yankunytjatjara to English Dictionary*. Second edition. Institute of Aboriginal Development, Alice Springs.

Goddard, C. & Kalotus, A. (eds) 1988. *Punu. Yankunytjatjara Plant Use*. Angus & Robertson, Sydney.

Golson, J. 1971. Australian Aboriginal food plants: some ecological and culture-historical implications, pp. 196–238 in D.J. Mulvaney & J. Golson (eds) *Aboriginal Man and Environment in Australia*. Australian National University Press, Canberra.

Goodale, J.C. 1971. *Tiwi Wives. A Study of the Women of Melville Island, North Australia*. University of Washington Press, Seattle.

Gott, B. 1982a. Ecology of root use by the Aborigines of Southern Australia. *Archaeology in Oceania*. Vol. 17, pp. 59–67.

Gott, B. 1982b. '*Kunzea pomifera*—Dawson's "Nurt"'. *The Artefact*. Vol. 7, pts 1–2, pp. 3–17.

Gott, B. 1983. Murnong—*Microseris scapigera*. A study of a staple food of Victorian Aborigines. *Australian Aboriginal Studies*. Pt 2, pp. 2–17.

Gould, R.A. 1969. *Yiwara: Foragers of the Australian Desert*. Collins, London.

Gould, R.A. 1971. Uses and effects of fire among the Western Desert aborigines of Australia. *Mankind*. Vol. 8, no. 1, pp. 14–24.

Gregory, A.C. 1887. Memoranda on the Aborigines of Australia. *Journal of the Anthropological Institute*. Vol. 16, pp. 131–3.

Grey, G. 1841. *Journals of Two Expeditions of Discovery in northwest and Western Australia, During the Years 1837, 38, and 39, Under the Authority of Her Majesty's Government*. T. & W. Boone, London.

Griffin, T. & McCaskill, M. (eds). 1986. *Atlas of South Australia*. South Australian Government Printer, Adelaide.

Griffiths, T. 1996. *Hunters and Collectors. The Antiquarian Imagination in Australia*. Cambridge University Press, Melbourne.

Haagen, C. 1994. *Bush Toys. Aboriginal Children at Play.* Aboriginal Studies Press, Canberra.

Hackett, C. 1937. Man and Nature in Central Australia. Reprinted from *The Geographical Magazine.* Vol. 4, no. 4.

Haddon, A.C. 1913. The outrigger canoes of Torres Strait and North Queensland, pp. 609–34 in E.C. Quiggen (ed.) *Essays and Studies Presented to Wm. Ridgeway.* Cambridge University, Cambridge.

Haddon, A.C. 1935. *Reports of the Anthropological Expeditions to Torres Strait.* Vol. 1. Cambridge University, Cambridge.

Hahn, D.M. 1838–39. Extracts from the 'Reminiscences of Captain Dirk Meinertz Hahn, 1838–39.' Translated by F.J.H. Blaess & L.A. Triebel, 1964. *South Australiana.* Vol. 3, no. 2, pp. 97–134.

Hale, H.M. & Tindale, N.B. 1929. Further notes on Aboriginal rock carvings in South Australia. *South Australian Naturalist.* Vol. 10, pt 2, pp. 30–4.

Hale, H.M. & Tindale, N.B. 1933. Aborigines of Princess Charlotte Bay, North Queensland. *Records of the South Australian Museum.* Vol. 5, pt 1, pp. 63–116.

Hallam, S.J. 1975. *Fire and Hearth: A Study of Aboriginal Usage and European Usurpation in South-western Australia.* Australian Institute of Aboriginal Studies, Canberra.

Hamilton, A. 1975. Aboriginal women: The means of production, pp. 167–79 in J. Mercer (ed.) *The Other Half. Women in Australian Society.* Penguin, Melbourne.

Hamilton, A. 1981. A complex strategical situation: Gender and power in Aboriginal Australia, pp. 69–85 in N. Grieve & P. Grimshaw (eds) *Australian Women: Feminist Perspectives.* Oxford University Press, Melbourne.

Hamilton, A. 1982. Descended from father, belonging to country: Rights to land in the Australian Western Desert, pp. 85–108 in E.B. Leacock & R.B. Lee (eds) *Politics and History in Band Societies.* Cambridge University Press, Cambridge.

Hamlyn-Harris, R. & Smith, F. 1916. On fish poisoning and poisons employed among the Aborigines of Queensland. *Memoirs of the Queensland Museum.* Vol. 5, pp. 1–9.

Harkins, J. 1994. *Bridging Two Worlds: Aboriginal English and Crosscultural Understanding.* University of Queensland Press, St Lucia.

Harris, J. 1987. Australian Aboriginal and Islander mathematics. *Australian Aboriginal Studies.* No. 2, pp. 29–37.

Harris, J. 1993. Losing and gaining a language: the story of Kriol in the Northern Territory, pp. 145–54 in M. Walsh & C. Yallop (eds) *Language and Culture in Aboriginal Australia.* Aboriginal Studies Press, Canberra.

Hart, C.W.M. & Pilling, A.R. 1960. *The Tiwi of North Australia.* Holt, Rinehart & Winston, New York.

Harvey, A. 1939. Field Notebook. Fry Collection, South Australian Museum Archives, Adelaide.

Hayden, B. 1975. Dingoes: Pets or producers? *Mankind.* Vol. 10, pp. 11–5.

Hayden, B. 1998. Stone tool functions in the Western Desert, pp. 266–84 in T. Murray (ed.) *Archaeology of Aboriginal Australia. A Reader.* Allen & Unwin, Sydney.

Head, L. 2000. *Second Nature. The History and Implications of Australia as Aboriginal Landscape.* Syracuse University Press, New York.

Henderson, J. & Dobson, V. 1994. *Eastern and Central Arrernte to English Dictionary.* Arandic Languages Dictionaries Program, Language Centre, Institute for Aboriginal Development, Alice Springs.

Henderson, J. & Nash, D. (eds) 2002. *Language and Native Title.* Aboriginal Studies Press, Canberra.

Hercus, L.A. 1980. 'How we danced the Mudlungga': Memories of 1901 and 1902. *Aboriginal History*. Vol. 4, pt 1, pp. 4–31.

Hercus, L.A. 1985. Leaving the Simpson Desert. *Aboriginal History*. Vol. 9, pt 1, pp. 22–43.

Hercus, L.A. 1989. The status of women's cultural knowledge. Aboriginal society in northeast South Australia, pp. 99–119 in P. Brock (ed.) *Women, Rites and Sites: Aboriginal Women's Cultural Knowledge*. Allen & Unwin, Sydney.

Hercus, L.A. 1990. Aboriginal people, pp. 149–60 in M.J. Tyler, C.R. Twidale, M. Davies & C.B. Wells (eds) *Natural History of the North East Deserts*. Royal Society of South Australia, Adelaide.

Hercus, L.A. & Sutton, P. (eds) 1986. *This Is What Happened*. Australian Institute of Aboriginal Studies, Canberra.

Hess, F. 1968. The aerodynamics of boomerangs. *Scientific American*. Vol. 219, No. 5, pp. 124–36.

Hiatt (Meehan), B. 1967–68. The food quest and economy of the Tasmanian Aborigines. *Oceania*. Vol. 38, pt 2, pp. 99–133 & pt 3, pp. 190–219.

Hiatt, L.R. (ed.) 1975. *Australian Aboriginal Mythology. Essays in Honour of W.E.H. Stanner*. Australian Institute of Aboriginal Studies, Canberra.

Hiatt, L.R. 1996. *Arguments about Aborigines. Australia and the Evolution of Social Anthropology*. Cambridge University Press, Cambridge.

Hiatt, L.R. & Jones, R. 1988. Aboriginal conceptions of the workings of nature, pp. 1–22 in R.W. Howe (ed.) *Australian Science in the Making*. Cambridge University Press, Melbourne.

Hobsbawm, E. & Ranger, T. 1983. *The Invention of Tradition*. Cambridge University Press, Cambridge.

Hodgson, R. 1988. *Peppimenarti Basketmakers*. Self-published, Darwin.

Holden, R. 2001. *Bunyips. Australia's Folklore of Fear*. National Library of Australia, Canberra.

Holmes, R. 2000. *Lost and Found. The Life of Jimmy James Black Tracker*. The Printing Press, Port Lincoln.

Holmes, S. 1992. *Yirawala, Painter of the Dreaming*. Hodder & Stoughton, Sydney.

Horne, G. & Aiston, G. 1924. *Savage Life in Central Australia*. Macmillan, London.

Horton, D. 2000. *The Pure State of Nature. Sacred Cows, Destructive Myths and the Environment*. Allen & Unwin, Sydney.

Hossfeld, P. S. 1926. Aborigines of South Australia: Native occupation of the Eden Valley and Angaston districts. *Transactions of the Royal Society of South Australia*. Vol. 50, pp. 287–97.

Howitt, A.W. 1904. *Native Tribes of South-east Australia*. Macmillan, London.

Huffer, V. 1980. *The Sweetness of the Fig. Aboriginal Women in Transition*. New South Wales University Press, Sydney.

Hughes, R. 1987. *The Fatal Shore. A History of the Transportation of Convicts to Australia, 1787–1868*. Harvill Press, London.

Irvine, F.R. 1970. Evidence of change in the vegetable diet of Australian Aborigines, pp. 278–84 in A.R. Pilling & R.A. Waterman (eds) *Diprotodon to Detribalisation*. Michigan State University Press, East Lansing.

Isaacs, J. 1980. *Australian Dreaming: 40,000 Years of Aboriginal History*. Lansdowne Press, Sydney.

Isaacs, J. 1992. *Aboriginality. Contemporary Aboriginal Paintings and Prints*. University of Queensland Press, St Lucia.

Jackson, W.D. 1968. Fire, air, water and earth—an elemental ecology of Tasmania. *Proceedings of the Ecological Society of Australia*. Vol. 3, pp. 9–16.

Jacob, T.K. 1991. *In the Beginning: A Perspective on Traditional Aboriginal Societies*. Ministry of Education, Western Australia, Perth.

Jacobs, J.M. 1989. 'Women talking up big'. Aboriginal women as cultural custodians, a South Australian example, pp. 76–98 in P. Brock (ed.) *Women, Rites and Sites: Aboriginal Women's Cultural Knowledge*. Allen & Unwin, Sydney.

Jenkin, G. 1979. *Conquest of the Ngarrindjeri: the Story of the Lower Lakes Tribes*. Rigby, Adelaide.

Johnson, D. 1998. *Night Skies of Aboriginal Australia. A Noctuary*. Oceania Monograph no. 47. University of Sydney, Sydney.

Johnston, R.J., Gregory, D. & Smith, D.M. (eds). 1986. *The Dictionary of Human Geography*. Second edition. Basil Blackwell, Oxford.

Johnston, T. Harvey 1941. Some Aboriginal routes in the western portion of South Australia. *Proceedings of the Royal Geographical Society, South Australian Branch*. Vol. 42, Pp. 33–65.

Johnston, T. Harvey & Cleland, J.B. 1943. Native names and uses of plants in the northeastern corner of South Australia. *Transactions of the Royal Society of South Australia*. Vol. 67, pt 1, pp. 149–73.

Jones, D.S. 1993. Traces in the Country of the White Cockatoo (Chinna Junnak Cha Knaek Grugidj): A Quest for Landscape Meaning in the Western District, Victoria, Australia. A Dissertation in Landscape Architecture. Postgraduate thesis. University of Pennsylvania, Philadelphia.

Jones, D.S., Mackay, S. & Pisani, A.M. 1997. Patterns in the valley of the Christmas Bush. *Victorian Naturalist*. Vol. 114, no. 5, pp. 246–9.

Jones, P.G. 1984. Red ochre expeditions. *Journal of the Anthropological Society of South Australia*. Vol. 22, pt 7, pp. 3–10; vol. 22, pt 8, pp. 10–19.

Jones, P.G. 1990. Ngapamanha: A case study in the population history of north-eastern South Australia, pp. 157–73 in P. Austin, R.M.W. Dixon, T. Dutton & I. White (eds) *Language and History: Essays in Honour of Luise Hercus*. Pacific Linguistics, C-116. Australian National University, Canberra.

Jones, P.G. 1996. *Boomerang. Behind an Australian Icon*. Wakefield Press, Adelaide.

Jones, R.M. 1969. Firestick farming. *Australian Natural History*. Vol. 16, pp. 224–8.

Jones, R.M. 1974. Appendix on Tasmanian Tribes, pp. 317–54 in N.B. Tindale (1974) *Aboriginal Tribes of Australia: Their Terrain, Environmental Controls, Distribution, Limits, and Proper Names*. Australian National University Press, Canberra.

Jones, R.M. 1978. Why did the Tasmanians stop eating fish? pp. 11–47 in R.A. Gould (ed.) *Explorations in Ethnoarchaeology*. School of American Research Advanced Seminar Series. University of New Mexico Press, Albuquerque.

Jones, R.M. 1989. East of Wallace's line: Issues and problems in the colonisation of the Australian continent, pp. 743–82 in P. Mellars & C. Stringer (eds) *The Human Revolution: Behavioural and Biological Perspectives on the Origin of Modern Humans*. Princeton University Press, Princeton.

Jones, R.M. 1991. Landscapes of the mind: Aboriginal perceptions of the natural world, pp. 21–48 in D.J. Mulvaney (ed.) *Humanities and the Australian Environment*. Occasional paper no. 11. Australian Academy of the Humanities, Canberra.

Jones, R.M. & Meehan, B. 1978. Anbarra concept of colour, pp. 20–39 in L.R. Hiatt (ed.) *Australian Aboriginal Concepts*. Australian Institute of Aboriginal Studies, Canberra.

Jones, S.M. 1990. *Tracks*. Self-published, Renmark, South Australia.

Jorgenson, J. 1837. 'Manners and Customs of the Aborigines.' Published & edited by N.J.B. Plomley (1991), *Jorgen Jorgenson and the Van Diemen's Land*. Blubber Head Press, Hobart.

Kaberry, P.M. 1939. *Aboriginal Woman: Sacred and Profane*. Routledge, London.

Kalma, J.D. & McAlpine, J.R. 1983. Climate and man in the centre, pp. 46–69 in G. Crook (ed.) *Man in the Centre*. CSIRO Division of Groundwater Research, Perth.

Kamminga, J. 1988. Wood artefacts: A checklist of plant species utilised by Australian Aborigines. *Australian Aboriginal Studies*. Vol. 2, pp. 26–55.

Keen, I. (ed.) 1988. *Being Black: Aboriginal Cultures in 'Settled' Australia*. Aboriginal Studies Press, Canberra.

Keen, I. 1994. *Knowledge and Secrecy in an Aboriginal Religion. Yolngu of northeast Arnhem Land*. Oxford University Press, Melbourne.

Keesing, R.M. 1975. *Kin Groups and Social Structure*. Holt, Rinehart & Winston, New York.

Kendon, A. 1988. *Sign Languages of Aboriginal Australia: Cultural, Semiotic and Communicative Perspectives*. Cambridge University Press, Cambridge.

Kimber, R.G. 1976. Beginnings of farming? Some man–plant–animal relationships in Central Australia. *Mankind*. Vol. 10, no. 3, pp. 142–50.

Kimber, R.G. 1982. Walawurru, the giant eaglehawk: Aboriginal reminiscences of aircraft in Central Australia, 1921–1931. *Aboriginal History*. Vol. 6, pp. 49–60.

Kolig, E. 1981. *The Silent Revolution. The Effects of Modernization on Australian Aboriginal Religion*. Institute for the Study of Human Issues, Philadelphia.

Kolig, E. 1989. *Dreamtime Politics: Religion, World View and Utopian Thought in Australian Aboriginal Society*. Reimer, Berlin.

Kolig, E. 1995. Darrugu—secret objects in a changing world, pp. 27–42 in C. Anderson (ed.) *Politics of the Secret*. Oceania Monograph No. 45. University of Sydney, Sydney.

Krefft, G. 1862–65. On the manners and customs of the Aborigines of the River Murray and Darling. *Transactions of the Philosophical Society of New South Wales*, pp. 357–74.

Kuhn, W. & Fowler, W. 1886. Yorke's Peninsula, South Australia. In E.M. Curr (ed.) 1886–87. *The Australian Race*. Trubner, London.

Lakic, M. 1995a. Domestic technology, pp. 1–10 in L. Allen (ed.) *Women's Work. Aboriginal Women's Artefacts in the Museum of Victoria*. Museum of Victoria, Melbourne.

Lakic, M. 1995b. Dress and ornamentation, pp. 19–30 in L. Allen (ed.) *Women's Work. Aboriginal Women's Artefacts in the Museum of Victoria*. Museum of Victoria, Melbourne.

Lamond, H.G. 1950. Aboriginal net making. *Mankind*. Vol. 4, no. 4, pp. 168–9.

Lands, M. (ed.) 1987. *Mayi. Some Bush Fruits of Dampierland*. Magabala Books, Kimberley Aboriginal Law & Culture Centre, Broome.

Lassak, E.V. & McCarthy, T. 1983. *Australian Medicinal Plants*. Methuen, Melbourne.

Latz, P. 1995. *Bushfires and Bushtucker. Aboriginal Plant Use in Central Australia*. Institute of Aboriginal Development, Alice Springs.

Lawrence, R. 1968. *Aboriginal Habitat and Economy*. Geography Occasional Paper No. 6. Australian National University, Canberra.

Layton, R. 1989. *Uluru. An Aboriginal History of Ayers Rock*. Aboriginal Studies Press, Canberra.

Lee, R.B. & de Vore, I. 1968. *Man the Hunter*. Aldine Publishing, Chicago.

Leichhardt, L. 1847. *Journal of an Overland Expedition in Australia, from Moreton Bay to Port*

Essington, a Distance of Upward of 3000 Miles, During the Years 1844–1845. T. & W. Boone, London.

Levitt, D. 1981. *Plants and People: Aboriginal Uses of Plants on Groote Eylandt.* Aboriginal Studies Press, Canberra.

Lewis, D. 1988. Hawk hunting hides in the Victoria River district. *Australian Aboriginal Studies.* No. 2, pp. 74–8.

Lewis, H.T. 1986. Fire technology and resource management in Aboriginal North America and Australia, pp. 45–67 in N.M. Williams, & E.S. Huhn (eds) *Resource Managers: North American and Australian Hunter-gatherers.* Australian Institute of Aboriginal Studies, Canberra.

Lommel, A. 1950. Modern culture influences on the Aborigines. *Oceania.* Vol. 11, no. 1, pp. 14–24.

Lourandos, H. 1997. *Continent of Hunter-gatherers. New Perspectives in Australian Prehistory.* Cambridge University Press, Cambridge.

Low, T. 1991. *Wild Food Plants of Australia.* Angus & Robertson, Sydney.

Low, T. 2002. *The New Nature. Winners and Losers in Wild Australia.* Viking, Melbourne.

Luebbers, R. 1975. Ancient boomerangs discovered in South Australia. *Nature.* Vol. 253, p. 39.

Luebbers, R. 1978. Meals and Menus: A Study of Change in Prehistoric Coastal Settlements in South Australia. Postgraduate thesis. Australian National University, Canberra.

McBryde, I. 1986. Exchange in south-eastern Australia: An ethnohistorical perspective. *Aboriginal History.* Vol. 8, pt 2, pp. 132–53.

McBryde, I. 1987. Goods from another country: exchange networks and then people of the Lake Eyre Basin, pp. 253–459 in D.J. Mulvaney & J.P. White (eds) *Australians to 1788.* Fairfax, Syme & Weldon Associates, Sydney.

McCarthy, F.D. 1938–40. 'Trade' in Aboriginal Australia and 'trade' relationships with Torres Strait, New Guinea and Malaya. *Oceania.* Vol. 9, pp. 405–38; vol. 10, pp. 80–104, 171–95.

McCarthy, F.D. 1940a. The carved trees of New South Wales. *Australian Museum Magazine.* 1 June 1940, pp. 160–7.

McCarthy, F.D. 1940b. Aboriginal Australian material culture: Causative factors in its composition. *Mankind.* Vol. 2, pp. 241–69, 294–320.

McCarthy, F.D. 1957. *Australia's Aborigines. Their Life and Culture.* Colorgravure Publications, Melbourne.

McCarthy, F.D. 1961. The boomerang. *Australian Museum Magazine.* 15 September 1961, pp. 343–9.

McCarthy, F.D. 1974. *Australian Aboriginal Decorative Art.* Eighth edition. Australian Museum, Sydney.

McCarthy, F.D. 1976. *Australian Aboriginal Stone Implements. Including Bone, Shell and Tooth Implements.* Second edition. Australian Museum Trust, Sydney.

McConnel, U.H. 1930. The Wik-Munkan tribe of Cape York Peninsula. *Oceania* reprint (originally *Oceania.* Vol. 1, pt 1, pp. 97–104, 181–205).

McConnel, U.H. 1953. Native arts and industries on the Archer, Kendall and Holroyd Rivers, Cape York Peninsula, north Queensland. *Records of the South Australian Museum.* Vol. 11, no. 1, pp. 1–42.

McCorquodale, J. 1987. *Aborigines and the Law: A Digest.* Aboriginal Studies Press, Canberra.

McCourt, T. 1975. *Aboriginal Artefacts.* Rigby, Adelaide.

McGregor, W. 1994. Introduction, pp. xi–iii in Thieberger & McGregor (eds) *Macquarie*

Aboriginal Words: A Dictionary of Words from Australian Aboriginal and Torres Strait Islander Languages. The Macquarie Library, Sydney.

Mackinolty, C. & Wainburranga, P. 1988. Too many Captain Cooks, pp. 355–60 in T. Swain & D. Bird Rose (eds) *Aboriginal Australians and Christian Missions. Ethnographic and Historical Studies.* The Australian Association for the Study of Religions, Adelaide.

Macknight, C.C. 1976. *The Voyage to Marege: Macassan Trepangers in Northern Australia,* Melbourne University Press, Melbourne.

MacPherson, J. 1925. The gum-tree and wattle in Australian Aboriginal medical practice. *Australian Nurses Journal.* December 15. Vol. 23, pt 12, pp. 588–96.

MacPherson, P. 1882. Astronomy of the Australian Aborigines. *Journal & Proceedings of the Royal Society of New South Wales.* Vol. 15, pp. 71–9.

Maddock, K. 1982. *The Australian Aborigines. A Portrait of their Society.* Second edition. Penguin Books, Melbourne.

Maddock, K. 1988. Myth, history and a sense of oneself, pp. 11–30 in J.R. Beckett (ed.) *Past and Present. The Construction of Aboriginality.* Aboriginal Studies Press, Canberra.

Magarey, A.T. 1893. Smoke signals of Australian Aborigines. *Australian & New Zealand Association for the Advancement of Science Report.* Vol. 5, pp. 498–513.

Magarey, A.T. 1895. Aboriginal water quest. *Proceedings of the Royal Geographical Society of Australasia. South Australia Branch.* Printed as a booklet, pp. 1–15.

Magarey, A.T. 1899. Tracking by the Australian Aborigines. *Proceedings of the Royal Geographical Society of Australasia. South Australian Branch.* Vol. 3, pp. 119–26.

Maiden, J.H. 1889. *The Useful Native Plants of Australia.* Trubner, London.

Malinowski, B. 1913. *The Family Among the Australian Aborigines. A Sociological Study.* Reprinted in 1963. Schocken Books, New York.

Massola, A. 1956. Australian Fish Hooks and Their Distribution. *National Museum of Victoria Memoirs,* No. 22, pp. 1–16.

Massola, A. 1968. *Bunjil's Cave. Myths, Legends and Superstitions of the Aborigines of Southeast Australia.* Lansdowne Press, Melbourne.

Mattingley, C. & Hampton, K. (eds). 1992. *Survival in Our Own Land: Aboriginal Experiences in South Australia Since 1836, Told by Nungas and Others.* Revised edition. Wakefield Press, Adelaide.

Meehan (Hiatt), B. 1982. *Shell Bed to Shell Midden.* Australian Institute of Aboriginal Studies, Canberra.

Meggitt, M.J. 1962. *Desert People. A Study of the Walbiri Aborigines of Central Australia.* Angus & Robertson, Sydney.

Memmott, P. 1983. Social structure and use of space amongst the Lardil, pp. 33–65 in N. Peterson & M. Langton (eds) *Aborigines, Land and Land Rights.* Australian Institute of Aboriginal Studies, Canberra.

Memmott, P. 2002. Sociospatial structures of Australian Aboriginal settlements. *Australian Aboriginal Studies.* Pt 1, pp. 67–86.

Merlan, F. 1998. *Caging the Rainbow. Places, Politics and Aborigines in a North Australian Town.* University of Hawaii Press, Honolulu.

Meyer, H.A.E. 1843. *Vocabulary of the Language Spoken by the Aborigines of South Australia.* Allen, Adelaide.

Meyer, H.A.E. 1846. Manners and Customs of the Aborigines of the Encounter Bay Tribe, South Australia. Reprinted on pp. 183–206 in J.D. Woods (ed.) 1879. *The Native Tribes of South Australia.* E.S. Wigg & Son, Adelaide.

Moore, D.R. 1978. Cape York Aborigines: Fringe participants in the Torres Strait trading system. *Mankind*. Vol. 11, pp. 319–25.

Moore, D.R. 1979. *Islanders and Aborigines at Cape York*. Australian Institute of Aboriginal Studies, Canberra.

Moorehead, A. 1968. *The Fatal Impact*. Penguin Books, Melbourne.

Morgan, J. 1852. *The Life and Adventures of William Buckley: Thirty-two Years a Wanderer Amongst the Aborigines of the Unexplored Country Round Port Phillip*. Republished in 1980 by Australian National University Press, Canberra.

Morgan, S. 1987. *My Place*. Fremantle Arts Centre Press, Fremantle.

Morphett, J. 1836. *Latest Information from the Colony*. John Gliddon, London.

Morphy, H. 1984. *Journey to the Crocodile's Nest. An Accompanying Monograph to the Film Madarrpa Funeral at Gurka'wuy*. Australian Institute of Aboriginal Studies, Canberra.

Morphy, H. 1998. *Aboriginal Art*. Phaidon Press, London.

Morton, S.R. & Mulvaney, D.J. (eds) 1996. *Exploring Central Australia. Society, the Environment and the 1894 Horn Expedition*. Surrey Beatty & Sons, Sydney.

Mountford, C.P. 1929. A unique example of Aboriginal rock engraving at Panaramittee north. *Transactions of the Royal Society of South Australia*. Vol. 53, pp. 243–8.

Mountford, C.P. 1957. Aboriginal bark paintings from Field Island, Northern Territory. *Records of the South Australian Museum*. Vol. 13, pp. 87–9.

Mountford, C.P. 1958. *The Tiwi. Their Art, Myth and Ceremony*. Phoenix House, London.

Mountford, C.P. & Berndt, R.M. 1941. Making fire by percussion in Australia. *Oceania*. Vol. 11, no. 4, pp. 342–4.

Mountford, C. P. & Roberts, A. 1965. *The Dreamtime*. Rigby, Adelaide.

Mountford, C. P. & Roberts, A. 1969. *The Dawn of Time*. Rigby, Adelaide.

Mountford, C. P. & Roberts, A. 1971. *The First Sunrise*. Rigby, Adelaide.

Mountford, C. P. & Roberts, A. 1973. *The Dreamtime Book*. Rigby, Adelaide.

Mountford, C. P. & Roberts, A. 1975. *Dreamtime Heritage*. Rigby, Adelaide.

Mowaljarlai, D. & Malnic, J. 1993. *Yorro Yorro. Aboriginal Creation and the Renewal of Nature. Rock Paintings and Stories from the Australian Kimberley*. Inner Traditions, Rochester, Vermont.

Moyal, A. 1986. *'A Bright & Savage land'. Scientists in Colonial Australia*. Collins, Sydney.

Moyle, A.M. 1981. The Australian didjeridu: A late musical introduction. *World Archaeology*. Vol. 3, no. 3, pp. 321–31.

Muecke, S. 1992a. *Textual Spaces. Aboriginality and Cultural Studies*. New South Wales University Press, Sydney.

Muecke, S. 1992b. History as texts: Pigeon the 'bushranger', pp. 60–75 in S. Muecke (ed.) *Textual Spaces. Aboriginality and Cultural Studies*. New South Wales University Press, Sydney.

Mühlhäusler, P. 1974. *Pidginization and Simplification of Language*. Department of Linguistics, Research School of Pacific Studies, Australian National University. Pacific linguistics, series B, no. 26.

Mühlhäusler, P. 1991. Overview of the pidgin and creole languages of Australia, pp. 159–73 in S. Romaine (ed.), 1991, *Language in Australia*. Cambridge University Press, Cambridge.

Mühlhäusler, P. 1996a. Post-contact languages in mainland Australia, pp. 11–6 in S.A. Wurm, P. Mühlhäusler & D.T. Tryon (eds). *Atlas of Languages of Intercultural Communication in the Pacific, Asia, and the Americas*. 3 vols. Mouton de Gruyter, Berlin.

Mühlhäusler, P. 1996b. Pidgins and creoles of Queensland. Map 8 & pp. 69–82 in S.A. Wurm, P. Mühlhäusler & D.T. Tryon (eds). *Atlas of Languages of Intercultural Communication in the Pacific, Asia, and the Americas*. 3 vols. Mouton de Gruyter, Berlin.

Mühlhäusler, P. 1996c. Post-contact Aboriginal languages in the Northern Territory. Map 12 & pp. 123–32 in S.A. Wurm, P. Mühlhäusler & D.T. Tryon (eds). *Atlas of Languages of Intercultural Communication in the Pacific, Asia, and the Americas*. 3 vols. Mouton de Gruyter, Berlin.

Mühlhäusler, P. 1996d. The diffusion of Pidgin English in Australia. Map 15 & pp. 144–6 in S.A. Wurm, P. Mühlhäusler & D.T. Tryon (eds). *Atlas of Languages of Intercultural Communication in the Pacific, Asia, and the Americas*. 3 vols. Mouton de Gruyter, Berlin.

Mulvaney, D.J. 1989. *Encounters in Place. Outsiders and Aboriginal Australians 1606–1985*. University of Queensland Press, St Lucia.

Mulvaney, D.J. 1994. The Namoi bunyip. *Australian Aboriginal Studies*. No. 1, pp. 36–8.

Mulvaney, D.J. & Kamminga, J. 1999. *Prehistory of Australia*. Allen & Unwin, Sydney.

Mulvaney, D.J., Morphy, H. & Petch, A. (eds) 1997. *My Dear Spencer. The Letters of F.J. Gillen to Baldwin Spencer*. Hyland House, Melbourne.

Mulvaney, D.J, with Petch, A. & Morphy, H. (eds) 2000. *From the Frontier. Outback Letters to Baldwin Spencer*. Allen & Unwin, Sydney.

Munn, N.D. 1973. *Walbiri Iconography. Graphic Representation and Cultural Symbolism in a Central Australia Society*. Cornell University Press, Ithaca.

Murray, P. 1991. The Pleistocene megafauna of Australia, pp. 1071–164 in P. Vickers-Rich, J.M. Monaghan, R.F. Baird & T.H. Rich (eds) *Vertebrate Palaeontology of Australia*. Melbourne University Press, Melbourne.

Museum Board 1887. *Notes Upon Additions to the Museum of the South Australian Public Library, Museum, and Art Gallery by 'An Amateur Naturalist'*. Reprinted from *The South Australian Register* & *Adelaide Observer*. W.K. Thomas & Co. Printers, Adelaide.

Mutitjulu Community & Baker, L. 1996. *Mingkiri. A Natural History of Uluru by the Mutitjulu Community*. Institute of Aboriginal Development Press, Alice Springs.

Myers, F.R. 1986. *Pintupi Country, Pintupi Self*. Australian Institute of Aboriginal Studies, Canberra.

Nelson, E.S. 1988. *Essays on Black Literatures. Connections*. Aboriginal Studies Press, Canberra.

Nelson, R.C. 2000. Why flutes on boomerangs and throwing sticks? *Records of the South Australian Museum*. Vol. 33, pt 1, pp. 21–7.

Newland, S. 1889. Parkengees or Aboriginal tribes on the Darling River. *Proceedings of the Royal Geographical Society of Australasia. South Australian Branch*, pp. 20–32. Also booklet, pp. 1–16.

Newland, S. 1895. Some aboriginals I have known. *Proceedings of the Royal Geographical Society of Australasia. South Australian Branch*. Vol. 8, pp. 37–54.

Newsome, A.E. 1980. The eco-mythology of the red kangaroo in Central Australia. *Mankind*. Vol. 12, no. 4, pp. 327–33.

Paddle, R. 2000. *The Last Tasmanian Tiger. The History and Extinction of the Thylacine*. Cambridge University Press, Cambridge.

Palmer, K. 1999. *Swinging the Billy. Indigenous and Other Styles of Australian Bush Cooking*. Aboriginal Studies Press, Canberra.

Parker, K. Langloh 1896. *Australian Legendary Tales*. Republished in 1953 in a selection edited by H. Drake-Brockman. Angus & Robertson, Sydney.

Parker, K. Langloh 1905. *Euahlayi Tribe. A study of Aboriginal life in Australia*. Archibald Constable, London.

Payne, H. 1989. Rites for sites or sites for rites? The dynamics of women's cultural life in the Musgraves, pp. 41–59 in P. Brock (ed.) *Women, Rites and Sites: Aboriginal Women's Cultural Knowledge*. Allen & Unwin, Sydney.

Peterson, N. (ed.) 1976. *Tribes and Boundaries in Australia*. Social Anthropology Series No.10. Australian Institute of Aboriginal Studies, Canberra.

Peterson, N. & Lampert, R. 1985. A Central Australian ochre mine. *Records of the Australian Museum*. Vol. 37, no. 1, pp. 1–9.

Peterson, N. & Rigsby, B. (eds) 1998. *Customary Marine Tenure in Australia*. Oceania Monograph No. 48. University of Sydney, Sydney.

Petrie, T. 1932. *Tom Petrie's Reminiscences of Early Queensland*. Second edition. Angus & Robertson, Sydney.

Plomley, N.J.B. 1966. *Friendly Mission. The Tasmanian Journals and Papers of George Augustus Robinson. 1829–1834*. Tasmanian Historical Research Association, Hobart.

Plomley, N.J.B. 1993. *The Tasmanian Aborigines*. The Plomley Foundation, Launceston.

Plomley, N.J.B. & Cameron, M. 1993. Plant foods of the Tasmanian Aborigines. *Records of the Queen Victoria Museum*. No. 101, pp. 1–27.

Presland, G. 1994. *Aboriginal Melbourne. The Lost Land of the Kulin People*. Revised edition. McPhee Gribble, Melbourne.

Pretty, G.L. 1977. The cultural chronology of the Roonka Flat, pp. 288–331 in R.V.S. Wright (ed.) *Stone Tools as Cultural Markers: Change, Evolution and Complexity*. Australian Institute of Aboriginal Studies, Canberra, & Humanities Press, Atlantic Highlands, N.J.

Ramson, W.S. (ed.) 1988. *The Australian National Dictionary: A Dictionary of Australianisms on Historical Principles*. Oxford University Press, Oxford.

Reay, M. 1988. Foreword, pp. ix–xi in I. Keen (ed.) *Being Black: Aboriginal Cultures in 'Settled' Australia*. Aboriginal Studies Press, Canberra.

Reed, A.W. 1980. *Aboriginal Stories of Australia*. Reed Books, Sydney.

Reid, A. 1995a. *Banksias and Bilbies: Seasons of Australia*. Gould League, Melbourne.

Reid, A. 1995b. A plan for all seasons. *Habitat Australia*. Vol. 23, no. 2.

Reid, J. (ed.) 1982. *Body, Land and Spirit. Health and Healing in Aboriginal Society*. University of Queensland Press, St Lucia.

Reid, J. 1983. *Sorcerers and Healing Spirits. Continuity and Change in an Aboriginal Medical System*. Australian National University Press, Canberra.

Reynolds, H. 1972. *Aborigines and Settlers. The Australian Experience 1788–1939*. Cassell Australia, Melbourne.

Reynolds, H. 1982. *The Other Side of the Frontier: An Interpretation of the Aboriginal Response to the Invasion and Settlement of Australia*. Penguin, Melbourne.

Reynolds, H. 1989. *Dispossession: Black Australians and White Invaders*. Allen & Unwin, Sydney.

Reynolds, H. 1990. *With the White People*. Penguin, Melbourne.

Rhydwen, M. 1993. Kriol: The creation of a written language and a tool of colonisation, pp. 155–68 in M. Walsh & C. Yallop (eds) *Language and Culture in Aboriginal Australia*. Aboriginal Studies Press, Canberra.

Roberts, R.G., Flannery, T.F., Ayliffe, L.K., Yoshida, H., Olley, J.M., Prideaux, G.J.,

Laslett, G.M., Baynes, A., Smith, M.A., Jones, R. & Smith, B.L. 2001. New ages for the last of the Australian megafauna: Continent-wide extinction about 46,000 years ago. *Science*. Vol. 292, pp. 1888–92.

Robson, M.K. 1986. *Keeping the Culture Alive*. Aboriginal Keeping Place, Hamilton and Western District Museum, Victoria.

Rose, D. Bird 1992. *Dingo Makes Us Human: Life and Land in an Aboriginal Australian Culture*. Cambridge University Press, Cambridge.

Rose, D. Bird 1996. *Nourishing Terrains: Australian Aboriginal Views of Landscape and Wilderness*. Australian Heritage Commission, Canberra.

Rose, F.G.G. 1987. *The Traditional Mode of Production of the Australian Aborigines*. Angus & Robertson, Sydney.

Ross, B. (ed.) 1984. *Aboriginal and Historic Places around Metropolitan Adelaide and the South Coast*. Anthropological Society of South Australia, Adelaide.

Ross, H. 1987. *Just for Living. Aboriginal Perceptions of Housing in Northwest Australia*. Aboriginal Studies Press, Canberra.

Roth, W.E. 1897. *Ethnological Studies Among the northwest-central Queensland Aborigines*. Government Printer, Brisbane.

Roth, W.E. 1901a. *North Queensland Ethnography. String, and Other Forms of Strand: Basketry, Woven Bag, and Net-work*. Bulletin 1. Government Printer, Brisbane.

Roth, W.E. 1901b. *North Queensland Ethnography. Food: Its Search, Capture, and Preparation*. Bulletin 3. Government Printer, Brisbane.

Roth, W.E. 1902. *North Queensland Ethnography. Games, Sports and Amusements*. Bulletin 4. Government Printer, Brisbane.

Roth, W.E. 1904. *North Queensland Ethnography. Domestic Implements, Arts, and Manufactures*. Bulletin 7. Government Printer, Brisbane.

Roth, W.E. 1909. *North Queensland Ethnography. Fighting Weapons*. Bulletin 13. Government Printer, Brisbane.

Roth, W.E. 1910. *North Queensland Ethnography. Decoration, Deformation, and Clothing*. Bulletin 15. Government Printer, Brisbane.

Rowley, C.D. 1970. *Outcasts in White Australia*. Pelican, Melbourne.

Rowley, C.D. 1972. *The Destruction of Aboriginal Society*. Pelican, Melbourne.

Rowse, T. 1993. *After Mabo. Interpreting Indigenous Traditions*. Melbourne University Press, Melbourne.

Ryan, L. 1996. *The Aboriginal Tasmanians*. Second edition. Allen & Unwin, Sydney.

Sagona, A. (ed.) 1994. *Bruising the Red Earth. Ochre Mining and Ritual in Aboriginal Tasmania*. Melbourne University Press, Melbourne.

Salter, E. 1971. *Daisy Bates. The Great White Queen of the Never Never*. Angus & Robertson, Sydney.

Sansom, B. 1980. *The Camp at Wallaby Cross. Aboriginal Fringe Dwellers in Darwin*. Australian Institute of Aboriginal Studies, Canberra.

Schaffer, K. 1993. Captivity narratives and the idea of 'nation', pp. 1–13 in K. Darian-Smith, R. Poignant & K. Schaffer (eds) *Captured Lives. Australian Captivity Narratives*. Sir Robert Menzies Centre for Australian Studies, Institute of Commonwealth Studies, University of London, London.

Scheffler, H.W. 1978. *Australian Kin Classification*. Cambridge University Press, Cambridge.

Scheffler, H.W. 1994. Kinship, pp. 551–3 in D. Horton (ed.) *The Encyclopaedia of Aboriginal Australia*. 2 vols. Aboriginal Studies Press, Canberra.

Schmidt, A. 1993. *The Loss of Australia's Aboriginal Language Heritage*. Aboriginal Studies Press, Canberra.

Schürmann, C.W. 1839–40. Diaries. Copy held in the Mortlock Library, Adelaide.

Schürmann, C.W. 1846. The Aboriginal Tribes of Port Lincoln in South Australia, Their Mode of Life, Manners, Customs . . . Reprinted in J.D. Woods (ed.) 1879. *The Native Tribes of South Australia*. E.S. Wigg & Son, Adelaide.

Sculthorpe, G. 1995. Carving, pp. 31–8 in L. Allen (ed.) *Women's Work. Aboriginal Women's Artefacts in the Museum of Victoria*. Museum of Victoria, Melbourne.

Seddon, G. 1972, *Sense of Place. A Response to an Environment: The Swan Coastal Plain, Western Australia*. University of Western Australia Press, Perth.

Sharp, N. 1993. *Stars of Tagai: The Torres Strait Islanders*. Aboriginal Studies Press, Canberra.

Silberbauer, G.B. 1981. *Hunter and Habitat in the Central Kalahari Desert*. Cambridge University Press, Cambridge.

Simpson, J. & Hercus, L. (eds) 1998. *History on Portraits. Biographies of Nineteenth-century South Australian Aboriginal People*. Australian National University, Canberra.

Sims, M. 1978. Tiwi cosmology, pp. 164–67 in L. Hiatt (ed.) *Australian Aboriginal Concepts*. Australian Institute of Aboriginal Studies, Canberra.

Smith, C. 1880. *The Booandik Tribe of South Australian Aborigines*. South Australian Government Printer, Adelaide.

Smith, C. 1992. The articulation of style and social structure in Australian Aboriginal art. *Australian Aboriginal Studies*. No. 1, pp. 28–34.

Smith, H. 1990. *Tiwi. The Life and Art of Australia's Tiwi People*. Angus & Robertson, Sydney.

Smith, L.R. 1980. *The Aboriginal Population of Australia*. Aborigines in Australia Society, No. 14. Academy of the Social Sciences. Australian National University Press, Canberra.

Smith, N.M., Wididburu, B., Harrington, R.N. & Wightman, G.M. 1993. *Ngarinyman Ethnobotany. Aboriginal Plant Use from the Victoria River Area, Northern Australia*. Northern Territory Botanical Bulletin No. 16. Conservation Commission of the Northern Territory, Darwin.

Smith, N.M. & Wightman, G.M. 1990. *Ethnobotanical Notes from Belyuen, Northern Territory, Australia*. Northern Territory Botanical Bulletin No. 10. Conservation Commission of the Northern Territory, Darwin.

Smith, P. Adam 1975. *Moonbird People*. Seal Books, Rigby Ltd, Adelaide.

Smith, W. Ramsay 1930. *Myths and Legends of the Australian Aboriginals*. Harrap, Sydney.

Smyth, D. 1993. *A Voice in all Places. Aboriginal and Torres Strait Islander Interests in Australia's Coastal Zone*. Revised edition. Resource Assessment Commission, Canberra.

Smyth, R.B. 1878. *The Aborigines of Victoria*. 2 vols. Victorian Government Printer, Melbourne.

Specht, J. & White, J.P. 1978. Trade and Exchange in Oceania and Australia. *Mankind*. Vol. 11, pt 3, pp. 161–435.

Spencer, W.B. 1896. *Report on the Work of the Horn Scientific Expedition to Central Australia*. Part 1. Melville, Mullin & Slade, Melbourne.

Spencer, W.B. & Gillen, F.J. 1899. *The Native Tribes of Central Australia*. Macmillan, London.

Spencer, W.B. & Gillen, F.J. 1904. *The Northern Tribes of Central Australia*. Macmillan, London.

Stack, R. 2002. The bark painting collection, pp. 37–51 in S.M. Davies (main author) & S. Mack (supervising ed.) *Collected: 150 Years of Aboriginal Art and Artifacts at the Macleay Museum*. Macleay Museum, University of Sydney, Sydney.

Stanbridge, W.E. 1857. On the astronomy and mythology of the Aborigines of Victoria. *Transactions of the Philosophical Institute of Victoria*. Vol. 2, pp. 137–40.

Stanner, W.E.H. 1938 (1979). The Aborigines, pp. 1–22 in *White Man Got No Dreaming*. Australian National University Press, Canberra.

Stanner, W.E.H. 1953 (1979). The Dreaming, pp. 23–40 in *White Man Got No Dreaming*. Australian National University Press, Canberra.

Stephens, 1889. Aborigines of Australia. *Journal and Proceedings of the Royal Society of New South Wales*. Vol. 23, pp. 476–503.

Stephenson, M.A. (ed.) 1995. *Mabo: The Native Title Legislation. A Legislative Response to the High Court's Decision*. University of Queensland Press, St Lucia.

Stewart, K. & Percival, B. 1997. *Bush Foods of New South Wales. A Botanical Record and an Aboriginal Oral History*. Royal Botanic Gardens, Sydney.

Stirling, E.C. 1911. Preliminary report on the discovery of native remains at Swanport, River Murray, with an enquiry into the alleged occurrence of a pandemic among the Australian Aborigines. *Transactions of the Royal Society of South Australia*. Vol. 35, pp. 4–46.

Stone, A.C. 1911. Aborigines of Lake Boga. *Proceedings of the Royal Society of Victoria*. Vol. 23, pp. 433–68.

Strang, V. 1997. *Uncommon Ground: Cultural Landscapes and Environmental Values*. Berg, Oxford.

Strehlow, T.G.H. 1947. *Aranda Traditions*. Melbourne University Press, Melbourne.

Strehlow, T.G.H. 1970. Geography and the totemic landscape in Central Australia: A functional study, pp. 92–140 in R.M. Berndt (ed.) *Australian Aboriginal Anthropology*. Australian Institute of Aboriginal Studies & University of Western Australia, Perth.

Strehlow, T.G.H. 1978. *Central Australian Religion. Personal Monototemism in a Polytotemic Community*. The Australian Association for the Study of Religions, Sturt College of Advanced Education, Adelaide.

Sturt, C. 1844–45. *Journal of the Central Australian Expedition 1844–45*. Published in 1984 by Caliban Books, London.

Sutton, P. 1988a. Dreamings, pp. 13–32 in P. Sutton (ed.) 1988. *Dreamings: The Art of Aboriginal Australia*. Penguin Books, Melbourne.

Sutton, P. (ed.) 1988b. *Dreamings: The Art of Aboriginal Australia*. Penguin Books, Melbourne.

Sutton, P. 1994. Material culture traditions of the Wik people, Cape York Peninsula. *Records of the South Australian Museum*. Vol. 27, pt 1, pp. 31–52.

Sutton, P. (ed.) 1995a. *Country. Aboriginal Boundaries and Land Ownership in Australia*. Aboriginal History Monograph Series No. 3, Australian National University, Canberra.

Sutton, P. 1995b. *Wik-Ngathan Dictionary*. Caitlin Press, Adelaide.

Swain, T. 1988. The ghosts of space: Reflections of Warlpiri Christian iconography and ritual, pp. 452–69 in T. Swain & D.B. Rose (eds) *Aboriginal Australians and Christian Missions. Ethnographic and historical studies*. Australian Association for the Study of Religion, Adelaide.

Swain, T. 1993. *A Place for Strangers. Towards a History of Australian Aboriginal Being*. Cambridge University Press, Cambridge.

Swain, T. & Rose, D. Bird (eds) 1988. *Aboriginal Australians and Christian Missions. Ethnographic and Historical Studies.* The Australian Association for the Study of Religions, Sturt College of Advanced Education, Adelaide.

Sweetman, R.T. 1928. Reminiscences of R.T. Sweetman. Originally published in *The Register*, Adelaide. Extracts published in 1988 in *Journal of the Anthropological Society South Australia.* Vol. 26, pt 7, pp. 3–5.

Taçon, P. S.C. & Garde, M. 1995. Kun-wardde Bim, rock art from western and central Arnhem Land, pp. 30–6 in M. West (ed.) *Rainbow, Sugarbag and Moon. Two Artists of the Stone Country: Bardayal Nadjamerrek and Mick Kubarkku.* Museum & Art Gallery of the Northern Territory, Darwin.

Taplin, G. 1859–79. Journals. Mortlock Library, Adelaide.

Taplin, G. 1874 [1879]. The Narrinyeri, pp. 1–156 in J.D. Woods (ed.) *The Native Tribes of South Australia.* E.S. Wigg & Son, Adelaide.

Taplin, G. 1879. *Folklore, Manners, Customs and Languages of the South Australian Aborigines.* South Australian Government Printer, Adelaide.

Taylor, L. 1996. *Seeing the Inside. Bark Painting in Western Arnhem Land.* Oxford University Press, Oxford.

Teichelmann, C.G. 1841. *Aborigines of South Australia . . .* Committee of the South Australian Wesleyan Methodist Auxiliary Missionary Society, Adelaide.

Teichelmann, C.G. 1857. Dictionary of the Adelaide tribe. Manuscript. South African Public Library.

Teichelmann, C.G. & Schürmann, C.W. 1840. *Outlines of a Grammar . . . of the Aboriginal Language of South Australia.* 2 vols. Thomas & Co., Adelaide.

Tench, W. 1788. *A Narrative of the Expedition to Botany Bay* and *A Complete Account of the Settlement at Port Jackson.* Edited by T. Flannery, 1966. Text Publishing, Melbourne.

Thieberger, N. & McGregor, W. (eds) 1994. *Macquarie Aboriginal Words: A Dictionary of Words from Australian Aboriginal and Torres Strait Islander Languages.* Macquarie Library, New South Wales.

Thomas, K. 1983. *Man and the Natural World: Changing Attitudes in England 1500–1800.* Allen Lane, London.

Thomson, D.F. 1934. The dugong hunters of Cape York. *Journal of the Royal Anthropological Institute.* Vol. 64, pp. 237–62.

Thomson, D.F. 1936. Notes on some bone and stone implements from North Queensland. *Journal of the Royal Anthropological Institute.* Vol. 66, pp. 71–4.

Thomson, D.F. 1939. The seasonal factor in human culture. *Prehistorical Society Proceedings.* No. 5, pt 2, pp. 209–21.

Thomson, D.F. 1949. *Economic Structure and the Ceremonial Exchange Cycle in Arnhem Land.* Macmillan, Melbourne.

Thomson, D.F. 1975. *Bindibu Country.* Nelson, Melbourne.

Thomson, D.F. 1983a. *Donald Thomson in Arnhem Land.* Compiled & introduced by N. Peterson. Currey O'Neil Ross, Melbourne.

Thomson, D.F. 1983b. *Children of the Wilderness.* Currey O'Neil Ross, Melbourne.

Thomson, D.F. 1985. *Donald Thomson's Mammals and Fishes of Northern Australia.* Edited & annotated by J.M. Dixon & L. Huxley. Thomas Nelson Australia, Melbourne.

Thorne, A.G. 1971. Mungo and Kow Swamp: Morphological variations in Pleistocene Australians. *Mankind.* Vol. 8, pt 2, pp. 85–9.

Thorne, A.G. 1976. Morphological contrasts in Pleistocene Australians, pp. 95–112 in

R.L. Kirk & A.G. Thorne (eds) *The Origin of the Australians*. Human Biology Series No. 6, Australian Institute of Aboriginal Studies. Humanities Press, New Jersey.

Thorne, A. & Raymond, R. 1989. *Man on the Rim. The Peopling of the Pacific*. Angus & Robertson, Sydney.

Tilbrook, L. 1983. *Nyungar Tradition. Glimpses of Aborigines of South-western Australia 1829–1914*. University of Western Australia Press, Perth.

Tindale, N.B. 1925. Natives of Groote Eylandt and of the West Coast of the Gulf of Carpentaria. Part 2. *Records of the South Australian Museum*. Vol. 3, no. 1, pp. 103–34.

Tindale, N.B. 1926. Natives of Groote Eylandt and of the West Coast of the Gulf of Carpentaria. Part 2. *Records of the South Australian Museum*. Vol. 3, no. 2, pp. 103–34.

Tindale, N.B. 1930–52. *Murray River Notes*. Museum Archives, South Australian Museum.

Tindale, N.B. 1931–34. *Journal of Researches in the South East of South Australia*. Vol. 1. Museum Archives, South Australian Museum.

Tindale, N.B. 1933. *Journal of an Anthropological Expedition to the Mann and Musgrave Ranges, North West of South Australia, May–July 1933, and a Personal Record of the Anthropological expedition to Ernabella, Aug. 1933*. Museum Archives, South Australian Museum, Adelaide.

Tindale, N.B. 1934–37. *Journal of Researches in the South East of South Australia*. Vol. 2. Museum Archives, South Australian Museum.

Tindale, N.B. 1935. Legend of Waijungari, Jaralde tribe, Lake Alexandrina, South Australia, and the phonetic system employed in its transcription. *Records of the South Australia Museum*. Vol. 5, pt 3, pp. 261–74.

Tindale, N.B. 1937. Native songs of the south east of South Australia. *Transactions of the Royal Society of South Australia*. Vol. 61, pp. 107–20.

Tindale, N.B. 1938. Prupe and Koromarange: A legend of the Tanganekald, Coorong, South Australia. *Transactions of the Royal Society of South Australia*. Vol. 62, pp. 18–23.

Tindale, N.B. 1940. Distribution of Australian Aboriginal tribes: A field survey. *Transactions of the Royal Society of South Australia*. Vol. 64, pt 1, pp. 140–231.

Tindale, N.B. 1941a. Survey of the half-caste problem in South Australia. *Proceedings of the Royal Geographical Society of Australasia. South Australia Branch*, pp. 66–161.

Tindale, N.B. 1941b. Native songs of the south east of South Australia. Part 2. *Transactions of the Royal Society of South Australia*. Vol. 65, pt 2, pp. 233–43.

Tindale, N.B. 1953a. Tribal and intertribal marriage among the Australian Aborigines. *Human Biology*. Baltimore. Vol. 25, pt 3, pp. 169–90.

Tindale, N.B. 1953b. Growth of a people. *Records of the Queen Victoria Museum*. Vol. 2, pp. 1–64.

Tindale, N.B. 1957. *Journal of Visit to the North West of South Australia and Adjacent Parts of Western Australia*. Museum Archives, South Australian Museum, Adelaide.

Tindale, N.B. 1959a. Totemic beliefs in the Western Desert of Australia—Part 1: Women who became the Pleiades. *Records of the South Australia Museum*. Vol. 13, pt 3, pp. 305–32.

Tindale, N.B. 1959b. Ecology of primitive man in Australia. Biogeography and ecology in Australia. *Monographiae Biologicae*. Vol. 8, pp. 36–51.

Tindale, N.B. 1966. Insects as food for the Australian Aborigines. *Australian Natural History*. Vol. 15, pp. 179–83.

Tindale, N.B. 1972. The Pitjandjara, pp. 217–68 in M.G. Bicchieri (ed.) *Hunters and*

Gatherers Today. A Socioeconomic Study of Eleven Such Cultures in the Twentieth Century. Holt, Rinehart & Winston, New York.

Tindale, N.B. 1974. *Aboriginal Tribes of Australia: Their Terrain, Environmental Controls, Distribution, Limits, and Proper Names.* Australian National University Press, Canberra.

Tindale, N.B. 1977. Adaptive significance of the Panara or grass seed culture of Australia, pp. 345–9 in R.V.S. Wright (ed.) *Stone Tools as Cultural Markers Change Evolution and Complexity.* Australian Institute of Aboriginal Studies, Canberra, & Humanities Press, Atlantic Highlands NJ.

Tindale, N.B. 1978. Notes on a few Australian Aboriginal concepts, pp. 156–63 in L.R. Hiatt (ed.) *Australian Aboriginal Concepts.* Australian Institute of Aboriginal Studies, Canberra.

Tindale, N.B. 1981. Desert Aborigines and the southern coastal peoples: some comparisons, pp. 1855–84 in A. Keast (ed.) *Ecological Biogeography of Australia.* Junk, The Hague.

Tindale, N.B. 1986. Anthropology, pp. 235–49 in C.R. Twidale, M.J. Tyler & M. Davies (eds) *Ideas and Endeavours—the Natural Sciences in South Australia.* Royal Society of South Australia, Adelaide.

Tindale, N.B. & Lindsay, H.A. 1954. *The First Walkabout.* Longmans, Green & Co., Melbourne.

Tonkinson, R. 1978. *The Mardudjara Aborigines. Living the Dream in Australia's Desert.* Holt, Rinehart & Winston, New York.

Toyne, P. & Vachon, D. 1984. *Growing Up the Country. The Pitjantjatjara Struggle for Their Land.* McPhee Gribble/Penguin Books, Melbourne.

Troy, S. 1993. Language contact in early colonial New South Wales 1788 to 1791, pp. 33–50 in M. Walsh & C. Yallop (eds) *Language and Culture in Aboriginal Australia.* Aboriginal Studies Press, Canberra.

Tunbridge, D. 1985. *Artefacts of the Flinders Ranges.* Pipa Wangka, Port Augusta.

Tunbridge, D. 1987. Aboriginal place names. *Australian Aboriginal Studies.* Vol. 2, pp. 2–13.

Tunbridge, D. 1988. *Flinders Ranges Dreaming.* Aboriginal Studies Press, Canberra.

Tunbridge, D. 1991. *The Story of the Flinders Ranges Mammals.* Kangaroo Press, Sydney.

Turner, D.H. 1974. Tradition and Transformation: A Study of Aborigines in the Groote Eylandt Area, northern Australia. *Australian Aboriginal Studies* No. 53. Social Anthropology Series no. 8. Australian Institute of Aboriginal Studies, Canberra.

Turner, M. 1994. *Arrente Foods. Foods from Central Australia.* Institute for Aboriginal Development, Alice Springs.

Turner, V.E. 1950. *Ooldea.* S. John Bacon, Melbourne.

Tyler, M.J. (ed.) 1979. *The Status of Endangered Australasian Wildlife.* Royal Zoological Society of South Australia, Adelaide.

Unaipon, D. 1924–25. *Legendary Tales of the Australian Aborigines.* Edited & introduced by S. Muecke & A. Shoemaker, 2001. Melbourne University Press at the Miegunyah Press, Melbourne.

Urry, J. & Walsh, M. 1981. The lost 'Macassar language' of Northern Australia. *Aboriginal History.* Vol. 5, pt 2, pp. 90–108.

Van Oosterzee, P. 1995. *A Field Guide to Central Australia. A Natural History Companion for the Traveller.* Reed Books, Sydney.

Wallace, P. & Wallace, N. 1968. *Children of the Desert.* Thomas Nelson, Melbourne.

Warlukurlangu Artists 1992. *Kuruwarri Yuendumu Doors.* Aboriginal Studies Press, Canberra.

Warner, W.L. 1958. *A Black Civilization: A Study of an Australian Tribe.* Revised edition. Harper & Row, New York.

Watson, P. 1983. This Precious Foliage. A Study of the Aboriginal Psycho-active Drug Pituri. *Oceania Monograph.* No. 26. University of Sydney, Sydney.

Webb, L.J. 1959. The use of plant medicines and poisons by Australian Aborigines. *Mankind.* Vol. 7, pp. 137–46.

West, A. 1999. *Aboriginal String Bags, Nets and Cordage.* Occasional Papers, Anthropology & History No. 2. Museum Victoria, Melbourne.

Wightman, G.M., Dixon, D., Williams, L.L.V & Injimadi Dalywaters. 1992a. *Mudburra Ethnobotany: Aboriginal Plant Use from Kulumindini (Elliot), Northern Australia.* Northern Territory Botanical Bulletin No. 14. Conservation Commission of the Northern Territory, Darwin.

Wightman, G.M., Gurindji elders, Frith, R.N.D. & Holt, S. 1994. *Gurindji Ethnobotany: Aboriginal Plant Use from Daguragu, Northern Australia.* Northern Territory Botanical Bulletin No. 18. Conservation Commission of the Northern Territory, Darwin.

Wightman, G.M., Jackson, D.M. & Williams, L.L.V. 1991. *Alawa Ethnobotany: Aboriginal Plant Use from Minyerri, Northern Australia.* Northern Territory Botanical Bulletin No. 11. Conservation Commission of the Northern Territory, Darwin.

Wightman, G.M., Roberts, J.G. & Williams, L.L.V. 1992b. *Mangarrayi Ethnobotany: Aboriginal Plant Use from the Elsey Area, Northern Australia.* Northern Territory Botanical Bulletin No. 15. Conservation Commission of the Northern Territory, Darwin.

Wightman, G.M. & Smith, N.M. 1989. *Ethnobotany, Vegetation and Floristics of Milingimbi, Northern Australia.* Northern Territory Botanical Bulletin No. 6. Conservation Commission of the Northern Territory, Darwin.

Wilhelmi, C. 1861. Manners and customs of the Australian Natives in particular of the Port Lincoln district. *Transactions of the Royal Society of Victoria.* Vol. 5, pp. 164–203.

Willey, K. 1985. *When the Sky Fell Down. The Destruction of the Tribes of the Sydney Region 1788–1850s.* Second edition. William Collins, Sydney.

Williams, D. 1981. *The Aboriginal Australian in North Eastern Arnhem Land. Exploring Aboriginal Kinship.* Curriculum Development Centre, Canberra.

Williams, G. 1985. Reactions to Cook's voyage, pp. 35–50 in I. & T. Donaldson (ed.) *Seeing the First Australians.* George Allen & Unwin, Sydney.

Williams, N.M. 1986. *The Yolngu and Their Land.* Australian Institute of Aboriginal Studies, Canberra.

Williams, W. 1839. A vocabulary of the language of the Aborigines of the Adelaide district. MacDougall, Adelaide. Reprinted in the *South Australian Colonist* newspaper, 7 July 1840. Also reprinted in T.A. Parkhouse (ed.) 1926, *Reprints and Papers Relating to the Autochthones of Australia.* Parkhouse, Woodville, pp. 57–70.

Wills, W.J. 1863. *A Successful Exploration through the Interior of Australia, from Melbourne to the Gulf of Carpentaria: From the Journals and Letters of William John Wills.* Edited by W. Wills. Richard Bentley, London.

Wilson, E. 1950. *Churinga Tales. Stories of Alchuringa—The Dreamtime of the Australian Aborigines.* The Australasian Publishing Co., Sydney.

Woods, J.D. (ed.) 1879. *The Native Tribes of South Australia.* E.S. Wigg & Son, Adelaide.

Worms, E.A. & Petri, H. 1968. *Australian Aboriginal Religions.* English translation, 1998.

Nelen Yubu Missiological Series No. 5. Nelen Yubu Missiological Unit, Kensington, New South Wales.

Worsnop, T. 1897. *The Prehistoric Arts, Manufactures, Works, Weapons, etc., of the Aborigines of Australia.* South Australian Government Printer, Adelaide.

Wright, R.V.S. (ed.) 1977. *Stone Tools as Cultural Markers: Change, Evolution and Complexity.* Australian Institute of Aboriginal Studies, Canberra, & Humanities Press, Atlantic Highlands, N.J.

Wyatt, W. 1879. Some account of manners and superstitions of the Adelaide and Encounter Bay Aboriginal tribes with a vocabulary of their languages, names of persons and places, &c, pp. 157–81 in J.D. Woods (ed.) *The Native Tribes of South Australia.* E.S. Wigg & Son, Adelaide.

Yallop, C. 1982. *Australian Aboriginal Languages.* Andre Deutsch, London.

Zola, N. & Gott, B. 1992. *Koorie Plants. Koorie People. Traditional Aboriginal Food, Fibre and Healing Plants of Victoria.* Koorie Heritage Trust, Melbourne.

Index